THE IVAN MOFFAT FILE

THE IVAN MOFFAT FILE

*Life Among the Beautiful and Damned in
London, Paris, New York, and Hollywood*

EDITED AND WITH A FOREWORD AND AFTERWORD
BY GAVIN LAMBERT

Pantheon Books ▥ NEW YORK

Copyright © 2004 by Gavin Lambert

All rights reserved under International and Pan-American Copyright Conventions. Published in the United States by Pantheon Books, a division of Random House, Inc., New York, and simultaneously in Canada by Random House of Canada Limited, Toronto.

Pantheon Books and colophon are registered trademarks of Random House, Inc.

Owing to limitations of space, all acknowledgments for permission to reprint previously unpublished and published material may be found following the index.

Library of Congress Cataloging-in-Publication Data
Moffat, Ivan.
The Ivan Moffat file : life among the beautiful and damned in London, Paris, New York, and Hollywood / edited and with a foreword and afterword by Gavin Lambert.
p.   cm.
Includes bibliographical references and index.
ISBN 0-375-42247-1
1. Moffat, Ivan. 2. Screenwriters—United States—Biography.   3. London (England)—Social life and customs—20th century.   4. Hollywood (Los Angeles, Calif.)—Social life and customs.   5. New York (N.Y.)—Social life and customs—20th century.   6. Paris (France)—Social life and customs—20th century.   7. Moffat, Ivan—Homes and haunts—England.
I. Lambert, Gavin.   II. Title.

PS3563.O276Z75 2004
812'.54—dc22
[B]   2004043431

www.pantheonbooks.com

Book design by Iris Weinstein

Printed in the United States of America

First Edition

9 8 7 6 5 4 3 2 1

In my beginning is my end. As the acorn contains the oak, so each human being possesses a form appropriate to him which time will educate and ripen. We are born with certain shapes ahead of us, certain ideas to fulfill; to seek unity or bring out diversity; to discover certain places, to love and lose certain faces.

— CYRIL CONNOLLY, *The Unquiet Grave*

Contents

THE IVAN MOFFAT FILE

INTRODUCTION
A MAN OF DIVERSE PARTS

10 July 2002. The living room of a small rundown apartment on a quiet, rundown Beverly Hills street, various cardboard boxes full of typescripts, exercise books, and paperbacks on the floor, several bulging, office-size manila envelopes piled on a worn leather armchair. At first glance, a stranger might have taken it for the kind of apartment where any hopeful but ultimately disappointed Los Angeles immigrant from Warsaw, Poland, or Warsaw, Illinois, ended up living alone on a modest pension and memories of better times.

At second glance a row of books on a wall shelf would have changed the stranger's mind. They included a biography of Sir Herbert Beerbohm Tree, famous actor and central figure in the London theatre from 1890 to 1916; a memoir of his remarkable daughter Iris Tree, poet, occasional actor, and frequent international adventurer; another memoir, privately printed, of Raimund von Hoffmannstal, whose father, Hugo, wrote the librettos for Richard Strauss's *Der Rosenkavalier* and *Elektra;* and a history of Dartington Hall, the experimental school founded in England during the 1920s, that became a kind of utopian compound of education, the arts, and agriculture.

The apartment on 249 S. Spalding Drive in fact belonged to a friend of mine, Ivan Moffat, who had died on July 4, and whose life was another kind of compound: son of an American father and English mother who grew up in an atmosphere of privilege and aristocracy during the 1920s; precocious and witty familiar of the Gargoyle, the London club where actors, writers, painters, well-heeled dilettantes, Bright and Foolish Young People met, ate, and drank from 1925 to 1950; mem-

ber of the U.S. Army film unit that recorded World War II from D-Day
to the fall of Berlin; Hollywood screenwriter and constant guest at A-list
parties in the final decades of a Golden Age that, as S. N. Behrman
wrote, had never happened before and would never happen again.

Several years before Ivan died, he started writing an autobiography
in longhand. The first section, covering his life until 1932, supposedly
existed in typescript, and its seventy-eight pages were found in one of
the cardboard boxes. A search of the other boxes and envelopes eventually yielded two large notebooks filled with densely handwritten pages.
Notebooks #1 and #2 formed a continuous narrative, ending with Ivan's
arrival in Los Angeles in October 1945. But Notebook #1 began in mid-
sentence in September 1940; and although a further search yielded
autobiographical fragments that Ivan obviously planned to insert in the
text already written, or to reserve for a future section, there was no trace
of a third notebook that might have accounted for the missing years.

Fortunately the additional fragments covered some important
events in Ivan's life during those years, and vivid reminiscences by
friends and relatives filled in some remaining gaps. About his professional life in Hollywood, and his impressions of people he met there,
transcripts of numerous taped interviews, and Ivan's work notes in the
George Stevens Collection at the Library of the Academy of Motion
Picture Arts and Sciences, provided detailed firsthand information.
About his personal life, Ivan was always discreet and sometimes secretive, but not long before he died, he talked on tape about the most loving, challenging, and painful relationship of his life, with Caroline
Blackwood, the novelist so well described by Ned Rorem as "savagely
original."

Lovers, friends, and relatives once again filled in some vital gaps
concerning his other important personal relationships. For the rest I
have relied on Ivan's surviving letters, on background information
gleaned from books, including some from his wall shelf, and a few private papers discovered in boxes and envelopes. Apart from this foreword, a few explanatory linking passages, and an afterword, *The Ivan
Moffat File* assembles a life in the voice, written and spoken, of the person who lived it.

• • •

It was once said of George Stevens, the movie director with whom Ivan worked so compatibly (on *A Place in the Sun, Shane,* and *Giant*), that "he was a man of diverse parts that only came together on a strip of film." Ivan was a man of equally diverse parts, and it could be said that they only started to come together when he began his autobiography.

The many stories he told and wrote were not simply entertaining anecdotes. His written comments, like his verbal snapshots, focused on something essential about a person, Aldous Huxley or Billy Wilder, Charles Chaplin or Diana Barrymore, Dylan Thomas or Ernst Lubitsch, Marion Davies or a fourteen-year-old boy who survived Dachau concentration camp, and they reflect an unusually wide range of experience.

Although Ivan never considered himself an artist, he explored the world like an artist, reacting with all his senses to what he saw and enjoyed and endured. The "Dark Ages" of childhood at his first boarding school. The suspended nocturnal calm of a dinner party on board a barge as it drifted across an Austrian lake in 1938, only a few months before the Nazi invasion. The first German air raid on London in 1940. George Stevens completely transforming a key scene in *A Place in the Sun* in the editing room. Ivan's mother, Iris Tree, during her final illness.

The man of diverse parts, one of Ivan's lovers noted, "liked to compartmentalize his life." The degree and variety of his sexual energy verged on the epic. Sometimes he expended it on one-night or one-afternoon stands, more often on romantic but brief affairs that evolved into friendship, or that alternated over the years between liaison and friendship; and on a couple of occasions he fell deeply in love.

Ivan was also capable of conducting two affairs simultaneously, and keeping each partner unaware of the other. In the same way he maintained separate circles of friends, who revolved around him like planets around the sun. A couple of friends and/or lovers, in fact, met for the first time when the sun was slipping over the horizon as Ivan lay on his deathbed.

All this suggests that the most appropriate way to introduce Ivan is to compartmentalize him, from prenatal beginnings (the genes he inherited from two extraordinary families) to the son who became a father, the husband who was always more in his element as a lover, the World War II soldier who witnessed unimaginable horrors that "turned my oversimplified world inside-out," the screenwriter and social figure who reached his peak as Hollywood neared the end of an era that would never happen again, and who took the aftermath in stride when the party was unmistakably over. Long ago, he once said, he had learned that what looked like reality today could turn into illusion overnight.

The Genes

Family Tree. Ivan's maternal grandfather, Sir Herbert Beerbohm Tree, founded the Royal Academy of Dramatic Art; and among the more than ninety plays he produced and starred in were *Julius Caesar* (as Marc Antony), *The Tempest* (as Caliban), *Richard II,* Ibsen's *An Enemy of the People,* an adaptation of *Oliver Twist* (as Fagin), *Trilby* (as Svengali), and Shaw's *Pygmalion* (with Mrs. Patrick Campbell as Eliza). He also acquired a wide range of admirers, including D.W. Griffith, Ellen Terry, Kaiser Wilhelm II (who issued a royal command that Tree's company give a performance in Berlin), and Oscar Wilde.

The first recorded members of the Beerbohm family are four brothers, born in the late seventeenth century in Pomerania, a province of the Kingdom of Prussia. Three of them became prosperous merchants, like many of their sons, grandsons, and great-grandsons. Beerbohms were also great breeders. Ernst Joachim fathered six children, his eldest son Ernst Heinrich produced eleven, and the youngest, Julius, sired nine.

Business and breeding were not the only family traditions. Beerbohms tended to live multiple lives, as company directors, art connoisseurs, country gentlemen, and polyglot hosts to kings and aristocrats from various countries. Julius, who spoke six languages and immigrated to England in 1830, quickly established himself as a corn merchant and high-profile dandy. He married an English wife, bought a house in fashionable Bayswater and rented Thurnham Court, an Elizabethan manor in the Kentish countryside, where Lord Byron had once lived.

In their different ways, three of Julius's sons were originals. The eldest, Ernest Frederick, became a cattle farmer in South Africa and married an illiterate Zulu. The second, baptized Herbert Draper in 1852, became Sir Herbert Beerbohm Tree. His half-brother Henry Maximilian, born twenty years later to Julius's second wife, became a famous writer under the name Max Beerbohm, and was dubbed Sir Max in 1930.

Max had no children, but Herbert continued one family tradition and founded another when he produced three daughters by his wife, actress Maud Holt; five sons and a daughter by his longtime mistress, May Pinney; and (at age sixty-four) another son by thirty-two-year-old Muriel Ridley, an English actress living in New York, whom he met while starring in *The Merchant of Venice* at the New Amsterdam Theatre.

Herbert installed May Pinney in a large Victorian house on Putney Hill, where she lived a discreetly fertile life, and changed her name by deed poll to Reed. Her fourth son by Herbert became the movie director Carol Reed, who always refused to discuss his parentage with journalists; and Herbert chose his professional name after Julius warned that an actor's life could be very precarious unless he reached the top of the tree. "But that's where I'm going," Herbert assured him; and in 1898 he built his own theatre, Her Majesty's in the Haymarket, still the most handsome and acoustically satisfactory in London.

Unfaithful to his faithful mistress as well as to his wife, Herbert also had affairs with actress Constance Collier and Olivia Truman, a young admirer who later published a memoir coyly entitled *Beerbohm Tree's Olivia*. (Like Maud and May Reed she attended his funeral.) Although Maud was bitterly humiliated when she first learned about May, the marriage settled into affectionate companionship. A talented comedy actress and sometimes devastating mimic, she enjoyed her position as the wife of a celebrated actor even more after Herbert was knighted in 1909, and she could call herself Lady Tree. As for his infidelities, she was soon shrugging them off with a wry wit. "Herbert's affairs," she once remarked, "begin with a compliment and end with a confinement," and when her husband invited the conspicuously gay actor Esme Percy to an after-theatre supper, she left them to enjoy their port together, then turned back for a moment with a smile. "Just remember," she cautioned Herbert, "it's adultery all the same."

During the 1914–18 World War, Iris Tree, Lady Diana Manners, and Nancy Cunard "formed an inseparable trio of beauties," Janet Flanner wrote in *The New Yorker,* "a kind of Mayfair troika of friendship, elegance, intelligence and daring as leaders of the new generation of debu-

*"Mameena," Lady Tree,
c. 1900*

tantes, who in evening clothes watched the Zeppelins from the roofs of great town mansions and voted Labour in the opening peace."

This was written in 1956, on the occasion of Nancy Cunard's death, and is not entirely accurate in the case of Iris, who was never a debutante and lived in America from late 1915 until the end of World War II. But the three privileged and unconventional beauties, friends from childhood, certainly formed a high-profile, high-bohemian troika during the 1920s. They had pedigrees of varying importance, with Diana, daughter of the Duke of Rutland, winning hands down over the others, whose fathers had not inherited their titles. Nancy Cunard's father was the shipping magnate Sir Bache Cunard, and Iris was the youngest of Sir Herbert's three (legitimate) daughters.

Iris had grown up in her parents' seventeenth-century Walpole House on Chiswick Mall. In spite of a two-acre formal garden and, supposedly, a royal ghost (the Duchess of Cleveland, mistress of Charles II, who had built the house for her), it was not quite as imperial as Sir Bache's Holt Castle, with its Tower Room, Breakfast Room, and Great Hall, its Cloisters where afternoon tea was served, its orchards, croquet and tennis lawns; or as the eighth Duke of Rutland's five-storied Georgian town house in Mayfair, where Diana grew up and nine servants were quartered in the basement. An archway led to a cobblestone courtyard, the front door opened to a hallway with marble pillars, and a series of stone stairways led to a Morning Room, a Dining Room, two Drawing Rooms (one with a skylight, the other with gold-leaf wall moldings), and a Grand Ballroom occupying most of the third floor. Diana's mother, the Duchess of Rutland, was a portrait artist who used the ballroom as a studio, and among those who sat for her were Queen Victoria, Ignace Paderewski, George Meredith, and Cecil Rhodes.

Like her sisters, Iris was educated by a series of governesses, but unlike them she established herself as the rebel in the family. At sixteen she insisted on studying at the Slade School of Fine Art, where she became friends with twenty-year-old Dora Carrington, already a talented artist who had sold several drawings and bobbed her dark golden hair before the style became fashionable. Her example prompted Iris to give her own flaxen hair the same treatment, and to add a personal touch by painting her eyelids to match the blue of her eyes.

Equality of the sexes was taken for granted at the Slade; and Iris reflected its atmosphere of personal freedom in the sophisticated, occasionally Haiku-like poetry that she began to write:

I have had 28
lovers, some more
some less -
I have Greek feet.

Through Carrington, who had recently met Lytton Strachey for the first time, Iris was introduced to several members of the Bloomsbury set. She made a strong impression on the art critic Clive Bell, and they began exchanging letters. "Were ever lust and languor, passivity and passion so admirably mingled as in me?" she once wrote him, and in reply he admired "your tow-colored hair and your white skin and your flighty impertinent brain."

In August 1914, six months after Iris enrolled at the Slade, World War I broke out. Although Carrington thought that Iris the poet should find it a source of inspiration, for a while Iris was absorbed in a flirtatious correspondence with Clive Bell, and her meetings with Augustus John, who did several portraits of her. Then the loss of several young friends who died on the Western Front made her abandon Haiku for A. E. Housman ("Strange eyes drop water that have never wept / Men rush to slaughter that have never slain").

After eighteen months at the Slade, Iris concluded that her talent was for poetry rather than art, and was delighted when Sir Herbert contracted to make a film of *Macbeth* for D. W. Griffith's Triangle Company, and decided to take her with him to Hollywood. They arrived in New York in late November 1915, and were met at the dock by one of Sir Herbert's illegitimate sons, Claude Reed, who had immigrated to America. Sir Herbert introduced him to Iris as "your cousin."

A month later they were in Los Angeles, where Constance Collier, who played Lady Macbeth, was then living. She introduced them to Chaplin, a great admirer of Sir Herbert, who also found his eighteen-year-old daughter original and attractive, even though she introduced herself as probably "the only person in the world who hasn't seen you on

Iris Tree, age seventeen, with the painter Augustus John

the screen." Later, when Iris visited the studio, she met D. W. Griffith as well as Lillian Gish, who often came to watch Sir Herbert at work.

After he finished the movie and went back to New York to appear in a season of Shakespeare, Iris stayed on for several months at Constance Collier's country bungalow, where she went horseback riding, wrote poetry, and delighted Collier by always being "full of humor" and "in a good temper." In June she returned to New York for the opening of *The Merchant of Venice*. A week later, Sir Herbert met Muriel Ridley for the first time, and Iris met a young painter at a party.

Opposites immediately attracted, Iris drawn to Curtis Moffat's dark melancholy eyes and quiet, rather enigmatic charm, Curtis to her vivid theatrical presence, adventurous clothes (hat with brim but no crown, bright gypsy-like embroidered blouse, harlequin stockings), and the "strange allure" that had fired Augustus John to paint her and Jacob Epstein to sculpt her head.

In July, having impregnated Muriel Ridley, Sir Herbert returned for a brief visit to his family in London, undeterred by warnings that a German submarine might torpedo his ship. Iris and Curtis spent a few weeks together at a beach house on Long Island; and when her father came back to New York for a week before starting a tour of three Shakespeare plays, she told him that she wanted to marry Curtis. He strongly opposed the idea, saying she was too young, but in December, while Sir Herbert played Chicago, they got married anyway.

Sir Herbert's displeasure at the news turned to approval after his tour ended, and he was favorably impressed by Curtis when they met for a long talk in New York. Back in England, he assured his wife that the marriage would be a success, made plans to produce and star in a play aptly titled *The Great Lover,* then ruptured a kneecap after a fall. It was decided to operate; the wound healed, but a blood clot formed, and on July 2, 1917, while Iris and Curtis were on a prolonged honeymoon in the Caribbean, Sir Herbert suddenly died.

Family Moffat/Tree. Curtis Moffat, ten years older than Iris, was born in 1887 to wealth that was made and lost on both sides of the family. His mother's brother, Robert Graves, was a Wall Street financier whose millions were largely wiped out by the stock market crash of 1929. His father, Edwin Moffat, was a banker who invested the greater part of his fortune in a Canadian gold-mining company that went bankrupt around 1915; and Curtis lived most of his life, in Ivan's words, "on the fringe of precarious luxury, which was the cause of wonder to his friends and the source of quiet anxiety to himself." At the same time, he had the outward self-possession of someone brought up in Old New York's "good" society.

Curtis had studied painting at the École des Beaux Arts in Paris, and returned to New York in 1916 to prepare his first one-man show: accomplished but subdued portraits, unlike his later still lifes with their bold dramatic Fauvist colors. After marrying Iris in December, he suggested they escape to a long summer in Nassau, where they rented a beachfront bungalow. While Curtis painted, Iris added to her adventurous wardrobe by making clothes out of local fabrics with colors as boldly dramatic as her husband's still lifes. In late November they decided to go to Havana, where Ivan Moffat was born on February 18, 1918, nine months before the end of World War I.

RIGHT: *Nancy Cunard, photographed by Curtis Moffat*
BELOW: *Iris, photographed by Curtis Moffat in 1923 and for his first London show in 1925*

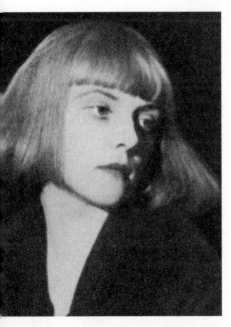

A few weeks later Curtis exhibited several paintings at a gallery in Havana, and in the spring he took wife and son to the house of a wealthy friend on Long Island. A letter from Iris to Lady Tree identifies her as "Mrs. McCullington" and describes her as "an angel" who bought one of Curtis's paintings for $600. In the same letter she wrote that "the baby has now two teeth, and is very happy though somewhat serious."

Soon after the November 11 armistice ended World War I, the Moffats left for England, where Lady Tree had found them a flat in Mayfair and engaged a nurse for Ivan. "Charming" was Lady Diana Manners's first impression of Curtis when Iris introduced them, and he soon charmed others in Iris's circle: Aldous Huxley, Augustus John, John Maynard Keynes, Osbert Sitwell, Lytton Strachey. The charm evidently created a lasting impression as well. In 2003, Ivan's cousin Virginia recalled Curtis as "very charming . . . adored women, and loved good food and wine," then agreed that she could equally well have been talking about Ivan.

Curtis himself was most impressed by Nancy Cunard, a more engaged rebel than Iris, who would soon spend years researching material for *Negro,* a massive pioneering anthology of black culture in Africa and the Americas, then live openly with a black lover, and travel to Spain during the civil war to write pro-Republican reports for the *Manchester Guardian.*

But in the London art scene, Curtis was an outsider. Competition from established British and French modernists was too strong, and after two years no gallery had offered to give him a show. Then, in the spring of 1923, he saw some reproductions of Man Ray's photograms and multiple-exposure portraits, and decided that the American photographer in Paris held the key to his creative future.

When Man Ray agreed to let Curtis work and learn as an apprentice, Iris joined her husband in Paris, but soon developed early-warning signs of the restlessness that would dominate her life. There was no definitive separation, just an agreement to take occasional breaks from each other, and Curtis made no objection when Iris rented an attic studio on the Île St. Louis, next door to Nancy Cunard's more luxurious ground-floor apartment. Meanwhile he continued to stay in a hotel near Man Ray's studio in Montparnasse, and began an affair with Nancy Cunard, who wrote him a series of love poems.

For Ivan, this meant a childhood with very infrequent visits from both parents. He was sent to live mainly in the country with Lady Tree; and, as he wrote in his autobiography, he was alone with his grandmother and his governess, except when Iris or Curtis "sometimes" came to see him, or his cousin Virginia came to stay. Kindly but remote, Curtis was an even more rare visitor than Iris, who at least tried to make up for her lack of maternal instinct in the loving letters she wrote, full of promises (often broken) to visit her son very soon, and of hopes that he was "growing up strong and wise" and "would have lots of things to tell me and talk about when I come back."

"Much that I did alone had become secret," Ivan noted about his childhood, and his favorite occupation was to peer into the depths of a pond, where newts and water beetles would suddenly and mysteriously appear, then vanish. Perhaps, without realizing it, he was in search of a clue to the world of human beings.

Curtis and Iris, holding a four-year-old Ivan in the garden at Mameena's country house

When not in Paris, Iris often stayed with Augustus John and his wife, Dorelia, at their country house in Dorset, or visited Diana (now married to Duff Cooper, and known as Lady Diana Cooper) in London. On one of her London visits she met Denys Finch Hatton, safari guide, pilot of his own Gypsy Moth plane, and collector of vintage port. A romance developed until he went back to Africa and the house of his lover, Baroness Blixen (Isak Dinesen), future author of *Out of Africa*. In January 1925 Curtis returned to England, where he bought and furnished a large eighteenth-century house at 4 Fitzroy Square in Bloomsbury. Nobody knew how or where he found the money, and Augustus John commented that his "fine eyes seemed to smolder with unaccountable amusement. Could it be his consciousness of the unknown, the unimaginable source of all this luxury, which so tickled him in secret?"

The top floor of the house became a private apartment, with one room converted to a photographic studio. Iris rejoined Curtis there for a few months while he made a series of dramatic head shots of celebrated friends and acquaintances, including Mrs. Patrick Campbell, Nancy Cunard, Diana Cooper, Augustus John, Bertrand Russell, Osbert Sitwell, and of course his wife. Hugely enlarged and mounted on colored papers, the portraits were much admired at his first one-man show at a Bond Street gallery in June. Cecil Beaton was so impressed that he tried to imitate them, but found that he lacked "the inimitable Curtis Moffat touch."

Soon after the show opened, Iris left Fitzroy Square and joined Diana Cooper at the Salzburg Festival, where her friend was due to appear as the Madonna in a revival of Max Reinhardt's production of *The Miracle*. A few years earlier, when the Coopers found themselves short of money, Diana had starred in a couple of silent movies; and when *The Miracle* was due to open on Broadway in 1924, Reinhardt's assistant suggested that the play's commercial appeal would be enhanced if he cast the famously beautiful daughter of an English Duke as the Madonna. He was proved right. The Madonna became her signature role; she would eventually play it in several European cities, and in 1925 she agreed to join a second American tour of *The Miracle* after the Salzburg revival.

*Ivan with Nancy Cunard at
4 Fitzroy Square, photographed
by Curtis Moffat*

As the actress who originally played the Nun was unavailable for the tour, Diana suggested that Iris replace her. Having never acted professionally before, she was understandably nervous before the audition at Reinhardt's baroque lakeside castle. But when he asked her to recite the Lord's Prayer, the Tree family instinct for theatre convinced the most famous director in Europe that she'd make a highly effective Nun.

Before sailing with Diana on the *Olympic* to New York, Iris promised to arrange for Ivan to stay with her in Philadelphia, where the tour was due to start. This was a promise that she kept, and the virtual end of her marriage to Curtis marked the beginning of seven-year-old Ivan's love affair with America.

The Son

By this time Ivan's interest in newts and water beetles had extended to the whole insect world. When he arrived (with his governess) in Philadelphia, he told Iris that after reading a description of its habits by the French entomologist Jean-Henri Fabre, he'd become especially fascinated by the praying mantis. A more conventional mother might have been seriously alarmed by her young son's fixation on this voracious predator, but Iris reacted by presenting him with a fine specimen she managed to capture in Fairmount Park. Curtis, also in Philadelphia for Iris's opening (in his role of friend), witnessed Ivan's delight and gave an approving nod.

In his autobiography, Ivan describes an experiment he conducted back at his hotel. In the washbasin of his room he found a small cockroach lurking, introduced the mantis to the defenseless creature, and watched how quickly and ruthlessly the predator devoured it. No comment, as in his account of pond life, but it seems clear that he'd found another clue to the world of adult human beings.

Before Ivan went back to England, his father took him to visit the estate of his wealthy uncle, Robert Graves, at Huntington Bay on Long Island. One day a guest mocked the boy's precocious use of long words, then imitated his upper-class English accent. When his father "smiled wanly" but said nothing, Ivan considered it an act of treachery. But all was forgiven because Curtis had just ordered, "especially for me, a live baby alligator brought to our suite at the Ambassador Hotel."

As a result of this bizarre offering, Ivan felt close to his father for the first time. But he didn't see him again for several years.

From Philadelphia, the special *Miracle* train, with its cast of three hundred, steamed west to Los Angeles, stopping at Chicago, Cincinnati, Kansas City, and San Francisco; and meanwhile Ivan, in the company of his governess, sailed back to England, another Christmas with Lady Tree, and then boarding school. At night in its ice-cold dormitory, he heard an unhappy boy crying and dreamed alternately of America and his adored cousin Virginia. He never told either parent how much he loathed the sadistic French teacher, the horrible food, and the way older boys bullied younger ones, because pride forbade it. To complain, he felt, would be a confession of failure.

In any case, Curtis became an even more remote presence than usual after his return to England. Photography preoccupied him more than his son when Nancy Cunard moved on to a new lover, the French poet Louis Aragon. And at a party in Los Angeles, where Iris shared a three-bedroom bungalow with Diana at the Garden of Allah, she'd met a handsome but impoverished Austrian count. It was love at first sight, and for the moment she intended to stay with Friedrich Ledebur in America. As the moment stretched to a year, Ivan divided his time between the hated boarding school and being alone again in the country with his grandmother and governess. But there was one consolation. When his cousin Virginia Parsons came to stay, a romantic friendship developed. "I was a year older than Ivan," Virginia recalled, "and my mother [Viola Tree, Iris's sister] was an actress, so we were thrown together as children, and were very attuned to each other. Lovely, happy times." The happy times included a few tentative erotic games, in Ivan's case not totally innocent. They were accompanied by precociously emphatic stirrings of puberty.

The "eternal winter" of boarding school ended in the summer of 1931, when Ivan paid a visit to his father at Fitzroy Square before traveling (with his governess) to Austria. Since *The Miracle* tour, Iris had become friendly with Max Reinhardt, and stayed with him twice at his Salzburg palace. There she had met and become close friends with Eleonora von Mendelssohn, actress daughter of one of Germany's leading bankers, and godchild of Eleonora Duse.

Eleonora owned a castle that overlooked Lake Attersee, near Salzburg. It was built around a courtyard at the end of a promontory, and reached by a causeway. Although Ivan was due to join his mother there, he had no idea that Iris and Count Ledebur had been staying at Schloss Kammer for over a year, with their three-year-old son Christian, to whom Curtis had gallantly agreed to give his name. When Ivan met Christian for the first time, he was introduced to "your little cousin," and when he met Friedrich for the first time, the count was introduced as a "friend" of Eleonora and his mother. As other guests were staying at the castle that summer, including two more counts and a baron, Friedrich had moved for discretion's sake to a nearby inn; and to complete the masquerade, Curtis arrived at Schloss Kammer a few days later to join his "family."

At summer's end Ivan was still ignorant of the real situation. Apparently Curtis never discussed it with him, but a few months later Iris confided, in a moment of casual intimacy, that she was in love with Friedrich, and Christian (whom she always referred to as Boon, "because he came as a blessing") was their son. But her love and admiration for Curtis, she added, would never change.

His mother had a way, Ivan recalled many years later, of revealing vitally important secrets as if they weren't all that important, and such things could be taken for granted. By the time he was thirteen, his exposure to adult manners made Iris's revelations seem no more unusual than his experiment with a praying mantis and a cockroach.

They were also taken for granted at Schloss Kammer, where "jealous intrigue and romantic complications flourished," according to Cecil Beaton. He was not the only visitor to find its atmosphere unsettling, due partly to the intrigues and partly to the surrounding mountains that cast a perpetual shadow over the place. Mercedes de Acosta, like Ivan, stayed there several times during the 1930s, and recalled that Eleonora, although generous and thoughtful, had sudden, extreme changes of mood as well as "violent fixations on men and women." One year she was in love with Toscanini, who admired a Guardi painting in the hallway. When Eleonora immediately laid it at his feet as a gift, he thanked her, carried it off, and locked it in his car. She was famous for changing her mind, he explained later, and he decided not to chance it. As it turned out, there was no need, but Eleonora's love, like so many others, remained unrequited.

At the end of that first summer Ivan also had no way of knowing that he would never see his father and mother together again. Over the next few years, Iris and Friedrich led nomadic lives, moving from England to

France to America. They subsisted on the dwindling remains of her trust fund, the occasional money he earned as a horse trainer, and the hospitality of friends. As Friedrich had hopes of becoming a movie actor, they settled in California for a while, living mainly in a trailer, but he had to wait fifteen years before a couple of small parts in Italian movies launched his modest career. By that time, he and Iris had separated.

Meanwhile Curtis continued to live at 4 Fitzroy Square, where he established Curtis Moffat Ltd in 1929, financed by the American millionaire Jock Whitney. Its showrooms displayed the latest in modernist furniture and lighting, some of it designed by Curtis himself, as well as ancient and modern artifacts: an antique globe positioned next to a metal cocktail set, Eskimo sculpture beside a leopard-skin cigarette box, African tribal masks and jewelry (Nancy Cunard bought her signature ebony bracelets there) alongside a steel and walnut dining-room set.

Later he added an art gallery, but although the Depression obliged Whitney to withdraw his support in 1933, and the company went out of business, Curtis continued to live in mysterious luxury. As well as hosting epicurean lunches for artists and writers, he exhibited a one-man show of striking color prints. As the catalogue explained, he created these abstracts and still lifes by superimposing a photographic image on a series of color separation plates. A beautiful but costly method of Curtis's own invention, it ensured that even though the show sold well, he lost money on it.

Iris and Curtis had originally agreed that Ivan should continue his education at Stowe, a school with a mildly progressive reputation, then changed their minds and opted for Dartington Hall. The first part of Ivan's autobiography ends immediately before the start of his time there, but from a fragment that he later began to write about the school, and the brief account he gave during a taped interview, it's clear that his parents did Ivan an enormous favor by sending him there.

The school, which opened in 1926, was the creation of a remarkable couple, Leonard Elmhirst and his American wife, Dorothy. Born into the Whitney family, Dorothy was an heiress with ideals, and Elmhirst had headed a school in India founded by the writer, social reformer, and Nobel laureate, Rabindranath Tagore. Dartington Hall's first brochure proclaimed that education should provide "freedom for growth, experi-

LEFT: *Curtis Moffat, c. 1920*
ABOVE: *Table setting for a Curtis Moffat luncheon at Fitzroy Square*
BELOW: *Diana Cooper, photographed by Curtis Moffat*

ment, enterprise and adventure," and encourage "Imagination, that function of the mind on which all true progress depends." When Dorothy's money enabled the couple to acquire and renovate a fifteenth-century manor house in Devon, they converted its three main farm buildings into a library, theatre, and school offices, its stables into dormitories, built cottages for the staff, schoolrooms in neo-Georgian style, and were soon growing produce on the manor's estate.

Coeducation, of course, was a given, and Dorothy's children by her first marriage, Whitney, Beatrice, and Michael Straight, were all enrolled at the school. During Ivan's time there, painter Mark Tobey and philosopher Gerald Heard taught special classes; Edith Wharton's niece, landscape artist Beatrix Farrand, came over from America to design the school gardens; and Uday Shankar (brother of musician Ravi Shankar) arrived to teach Indian dance.

Shankar's arrival cued the kind of episode that Ivan (like his parents and the cosmopolitan elite at Schloss Kammer) had begun to take for granted, and that caused only a minor ripple at the school. Eighteen-year-old Beatrice Straight, one of Shankar's students, fell in love with him, and they went off to India together in 1934. Another unexpected episode, which Ivan found equally unsurprising, was cued by Michael Chekhov's arrival to head a theatre studio. Nephew of the playwright, star and director of the Second Moscow Art Theatre, Chekhov had left Soviet Russia for New York, where he established a drama school, then an acting company. The company was partly financed by Beatrice Straight, who had broken off her affair with Shankar in 1935, returned to America, and was on the threshold of a successful career in the theatre. After seeing Chekhov in a production of *The Government Inspector* that also made a deep impression on members of the Group Theatre, she advised Dorothy to invite him to Dartington's theatre department.

Just before Ivan left the school in December 1935, his mother and Friedrich arrived to join the first group of Chekhov's students. By then Iris had divorced Curtis Moffat and married Count Ledebur, and the couple had left America to live in a cottage in the Irish countryside. After writing a couple of plays there and finding them unsatisfactory, Iris decided to attend Chekhov's classes as an apprentice playwright, and Friedrich hoped that his prospects as an actor would improve with professional training.

At Dartington, which he later described as "paradise," Ivan had learned that respect for the individual was more productive than respect for convention, and listened attentively to Bertrand Russell, Bernard Shaw, and H. G. Wells, a notable trio of freethinkers engaged as guest lecturers. On a personal level, he had grown very fond of the Elmhirsts, who at times seemed like surrogate parents, and had also formed a rewarding friendship with a fellow student, Michael Young, whose first experience of boarding school had been very similar to Ivan's. Over the years, they continued to meet whenever Ivan was in England; and Young, by then a distinguished social historian, wrote a book about the Elmhirsts and their school.

At seventeen, Ivan was the product of two English educations, the first oppressively conventional, the second dedicated to intellectual and sexual freedom. Outwardly he appeared self-contained, with the almost stereotypical air of a young and privileged English gentleman; inwardly he was the opposite. The inwardness stemmed from long periods of childhood solitude, a lack of family life that often made him feel displaced and uncertain, and the formidable glitter of Iris's circle of friends, where infidelity, divorce, and even promiscuity raised no eyebrows. For the rest of his days Ivan's conversation, especially when he told a story, was full of startling and sometimes ruthless insights, delivered in a casual but very articulate upper-class voice; and throughout his life he tried to reconcile a persistent need for affection and sexual adventure with a fear of being caught emotionally off guard.

The Young Man About Town

As the child of parents who seemed to know "everybody" from Coco Chanel to Man Ray, Max Ernst to Max Reinhardt, and John Maynard

Keynes to Aldous Huxley, "I felt a need to overperform and to pretend," Ivan once told his son Jonathan. "Later I learned how to gain entry to important social situations." Gaining his first entry to the most important social situation of the time was not difficult, as David Tennant, founder of the legendary Gargoyle Club, had fallen in love with Ivan's cousin, Virginia Parsons.

The Gargoyle was basically a nightclub version of the society that Ivan had encountered through his parents. Its first press release promised members "an avant-garde place, where people can express themselves freely in whatever manner they please." Handsome, rich, well-born, and well-connected, Tennant had in mind people who were artists, writers, and intellectuals; and it was to Henri Matisse, whose daughter Tennant had met through a mutual friend, that he owed the extraordinary setting of the club's ballroom. When he told Matisse that he planned to install a gold-leaf coffered ceiling there, the painter suggested that its effect would be enhanced by covering the walls with mirrored tiles. And he even knew where Tennant could buy them, from the owner of a French chateau who was putting up the property and its contents for sale.

Although Tennant made Matisse an honorary member of the Gargoyle, he was unable to attend its opening night; but among the more than three hundred members who dropped by on January 16, 1925, were Somerset Maugham, Virginia Woolf, Noël Coward, Nancy Cunard, and Osbert Sitwell. Later the club's regular members would include H. G. Wells, Augustus John, Cyril Connolly, Stephen Spender, Anthony Powell, John Maynard Keynes, Frederick Ashton, Dylan Thomas, and two Mitford sisters, Nancy and Jessica. They guaranteed plenty of intellectual exchange, and some of them, according to Michael Luke in *David Tennant and the Gargoyle Years,* used the club as "a social and sexual gymnasium."

Two small groups representing opposite extremes also frequented the place: café society and a more interesting quartet of left-wingers, three of them queer. Tom Driberg, a journalist, later became an important Labour Party politician. Brian Howard, a brilliant high-camp dilettante, worked for British Intelligence during World War II until he was fired on account of reckless promiscuity. The equally promiscuous Guy

Burgess worked in the Foreign Office, became a Soviet agent, and defected to Moscow in 1949. Michael Straight from Dartington Hall completed his education at Cambridge, where he joined the Communist Party and was recruited as a Soviet agent. Back in America, he changed his mind, broke with the Party, and worked as a speechwriter for the Roosevelt administration. Later, married with children, he became editor of *The New Republic* (which the Whitney family owned). Later still he revealed his secret past in a book that exposed Anthony Blunt (leading art expert, recently knighted Surveyor of the King's Pictures) as yet another Soviet agent.

At the Gargoyle, Ivan established a foothold in all these worlds, but unfortunately he didn't live to write much about Howard and Burgess, or anything about Straight. Another unrecorded gap in his life is the year he spent at the London School of Economics, where Curtis (for reasons that remain unclear) decided that he should continue his studies.

Mark Littman, a law student who first met Ivan at the School, and later became a Queen's Counsel, remembers "the atmosphere at LSE was very left-wing, and it influenced Ivan's decision to join the Communist Party." Like Driberg and Spender, who also became Communists in the uneasy pre–World War II years, Ivan was more anti-Fascist than pro-Soviet, and joining the Party was a gesture of solidarity with the only political group in Britain that recognized the danger of what had happened in Spain and was happening in Nazi Germany. But by the end of Ivan's first year at the School, Curtis had heard reports that its professor of political science, Harold Laski, described himself as a Marxist, and informed the principal that he was withdrawing his son.

As an American citizen, Ivan (like Michael Straight) never had to obtain a visa and answer questions about his political past before entering the country. In fact he left the Party in the summer of 1939, two years after he joined it. A few months earlier, his father had decided to return to the USA. His mother was seriously ill with cancer, and as he believed that World War II was inevitable, he thought his new wife and infant daughter would be safer in New York.

The marriage to Kathleen Allan, his studio assistant, was so discreet that Ivan, living on his own in a modest apartment, never knew about it at the time. Enigmatic design or habitual offhandedness on his father's part? In 2002, Curtis's daughter Penelope recalled Ivan telling her that one day, after he hadn't seen or talked to his father for several weeks, Curtis said, "By the way, I've married Kathleen." She thought it "typical of his remoteness as a father."

When Curtis left England, he offered Ivan the use of his apartment on the top floor of 4 Fitzroy Square until the lease ran out. He had sold many valuable paintings and African masks, but a few remained, like the modernist furniture, the contents of his library, and the leftovers of his wine cellar. Shortly after Ivan moved in, he met an eighteen-year-old girl called Natalie Newhouse. Rebellious child of a conventional family, she was staying at the Cavendish Hotel, another outpost of sexual freedom with no questions asked.

Its owner, Rosa Lewis, was a remarkable self-made Cockney who entered domestic service when she was twelve and rose to the heights of kitchen maid at the house of the Comte de Paris. There she caught the eye of the Prince of Wales (later Edward VII), and became his mistress. With the money she acquired from him, and from the wealthy Lord Ribbesdale, who was soon sharing her with the Prince, she eventually bought the Cavendish because she "liked people, and if you make a place like the people you like, you get the people you like."

Rosa and Natalie liked each other, but Ivan didn't much like Rosa, and soon after meeting Natalie, he moved her to Fitzroy Square. The affair, his first on record, set the pattern for many that followed, sexual and temperamental attraction with no binding commitment on either side. They lived together until January 1942, when Ivan joined the U.S. Army. A few years later she married Robert Newton, the irredeemable alcoholic and talented movie actor, whose disorderly persona found a perfect match in roles like the renegade of the Salvation Army shelter in *Major Barbara,* and Bill Sykes in *Oliver Twist.*

The affair also established another pattern in Ivan's life. He was unfaithful to Natalie with at least two other women: Marcelle Quennell, formerly married to the literary critic (and Gargoyle regular) Peter Quennell, and Henrietta Law, known as "The Lady Brett of Soho" because she was as beautiful and licentious as the Lady Brett of Hemingway's *The Sun Also Rises.*

Soon after World War II broke out in September 1939, Ivan applied for a job with Strand Films. He needed money, and knew that the company atmosphere was congenial. Donald Taylor, who headed Strand, was an heir of the British documentary tradition, leftish like its founding father John Grierson (whose twenty-minute film about a fishing fleet, *Drifters,* shared a premiere at the London Film Society with Eisenstein's *Potemkin,* which the censor had banned from public showing). When the outbreak of war interrupted Taylor's plans to start producing feature films, his company made government-sponsored propaganda shorts for the home front. Although Ivan had no professional film experience, his intelligence and charm decided Taylor to pay him £4 weekly as an assistant in the cutting room.

He soon graduated from splicing celluloid to writing and directing scripts at £8 weekly. His first film as director was *Balloon Site 568,* aimed to recruit women to join the anti-aircraft balloon service, from a script by Dylan Thomas. Ivan originally met him at the Gargoyle, and as Thomas was equally in need of money, introduced him to Taylor. A day's work at the Strand office was seldom hard, leaving Thomas plenty of time to write poetry, and Ivan to perfect his skill at backgammon with another colleague.

The backgammon expert had also fine-tuned his talent as a storyteller. Natasha and Stephen Spender, who were friends of the Elmhirsts, went to stay at Dartington Hall soon after they got married in November 1941. During their stay, Ivan arrived for a weekend, and Natasha remembered "his dramatic account, in words and gesture, of how his girlfriend Natalie Newhouse fell from a balcony but wasn't seriously hurt. I was very struck by his sense of drama as he described exactly how she fell, then how she managed to escape serious injury."

Meanwhile, Beatrice Straight had arranged to transfer Michael Chekhov's theatre studio to Ridgefield, Connecticut. The students who followed him there included Iris and Friedrich, with twelve-year-old Boon, whom they enrolled at a local school. Soon after they arrived, Friedrich met Beatrice Straight at the studio, and they became lovers. "Private life is apt to spread so—sometimes into sloughs, sometimes into mazes," Iris wrote a friend, "and to find the perfect adjustment needs so much firmness and fierce will." Richly endowed with both, she found adjustment in a romance with Alan Harkness, a pacifist teacher at the studio. During the summer of 1941 they took Boon along for their first vacation together, in a rented house at Martha's Vineyard. Curtis was living on the island with Kathleen by then, but apparently the couples never made contact.

In December that year the Japanese attacked Pearl Harbor, America entered World War II, and with many of Michael Chekhov's students liable to be drafted, the studio closed. Chekhov moved to Los Angeles, where he founded his own acting school and resumed his acting career, playing character roles in Hollywood movies. Iris also moved to California with Harkness and Boon, rented a house in Ojai and enrolled her son at a nearby school. The couple formed a local theatre group, but within a few weeks Harkness had fallen in love with one of its young actresses, and they left together for New York. Once again in a slough of private life, Iris once again found adjustment. As if on cue, Friedrich reappeared. Beatrice Straight had left him to marry a journalist.

Concurrently, the Gargoyle had closed when the Blitz failed to bomb Britain into submission, but had shattered more than London nightlife. After the German air force suffered severe losses and the bombing subsided, the club reopened; but change and dispersal were in the air. On closing night, David Tennant had tried to explain to Ivan what it stood for, concluded that it hadn't really stood for anything, and Ivan realized that "the night had entered a darker phase for him." When the club reopened, Matisse's *The Red Studio,* which Tennant had bought in 1927, no longer hung in the dining room; he'd sold it to pay for repairs. Several former members arrived on leave in uniform, but most new members were refugees from German-occupied Europe; and after Pearl Harbor, Ivan knew he would soon be drafted into the U.S. Army.

And while the band played once again in the ballroom with its walls of mirrored tiles, some of them cracked or splintered during the Blitz, it occurred to Ivan that the Gargoyle's success was due to "the need to escape relevance to the times we were living in." He couldn't foresee, of course, until World War II brought him face-to-face with the times, that the night would soon enter a darker phase for himself as well.

The Soldier

Some of the most graphic pages in Ivan's autobiography describe his experiences in the U.S. Signal Corps, a film unit commissioned by General Eisenhower and attached to the Supreme Headquarters Allied Expeditionary Force. It was created to document the European sector of World War II from June 6, 1944, when Allied forces launched the invasion of France, to May 7, 1945, the day Germany surrendered after Hitler committed suicide and its army collapsed. Movie director George Stevens headed the outfit, soon nicknamed the Stevens Irregulars, and its members included William Saroyan, Irwin Shaw, Ernest Hemingway's brother Leicester, cameramen, sound technicians, and assistant directors, all carrying backpacks and semiautomatics.

Ivan's unit landed in Normandy a week after D-Day, and joined Stevens with his unit that had filmed the landing a few hours later. At first he was so impressed by the spectacle of so much "concentrated industrial power of the United States, projected across the Atlantic," and its "extraordinary logistics" on land and in the air, that he forgot to consider the human factors involved. But during the early months of the campaign, when the U.S. Army suffered heavy casualties, Ivan was emotionally overwhelmed by scene after scene of destruction and mortality, French towns gutted by air raids, vistas of ruined, deserted countryside, dead soldiers and civilians lying alongside almost every road—some of their faces weirdly peaceful, others contorted. Later, the liberation of Paris came as an emotional reprieve, but it was followed by the inferno of Dachau concentration camp with its piles of corpses and dazed, emaciated survivors.

The official footage of the war was shot in black-and-white on 35mm, but Stevens also filmed his own personal record on 16mm

Kodachrome; and as their friendship developed, Ivan became close to this side of the operation. After Stevens died, his son George Stevens, Jr., compiled a remarkable documentary from both personal and official footage. In *From D-Day to Berlin,* Ivan makes his first appearance, very young and very serious, in a photograph of the unit assembled for departure. During the slow, difficult advance toward Paris, he's seen occasionally conferring with Stevens, or lying on the grass and reading a book during a coffee break; later, he's smiling with a mixture of triumph and incredulity as he stands in a group of soldiers and civilians, and celebrates the liberation of Paris with his arm around a pretty French girl. Ivan also shares the voice-over commentary with George Stevens, Jr., and several Irregulars, but the account in his autobiography is inevitably more personal and more detailed.

The war was responsible for Ivan's first marriage with a Russian girl he met in Paris after the liberation, and more enduringly for his friendship with Stevens, which led to a screenwriting career in Hollywood. It was also an extreme kind of sentimental education that taught him the best and the worst that human beings were capable of; and June 6, 1944, became Ivan's private memorial day every year for the rest of his life.

The Husband

As many of his friends remarked, Ivan was definitely not the marrying kind. Yet he married twice. The first time, Natasha Sorokin became pregnant while she was still in Paris, waiting for permission to join Ivan in California, and refused to have an abortion. The determining factor was less her desire to have a child than her desire to get to America. The second time, as Ivan told their daughter Lorna, "it's because Kate is easy to get along with, good-natured, terribly nice—and people expect it." The Hon. Katharine Smith had also become pregnant, but he didn't tell Lorna that.

For very different reasons, both marriages proved disastrous. Natasha, who makes a brief appearance in the last completed section of Ivan's autobiography, had been a student at the Lycée Molière. There she fell in love with her philosophy teacher, Simone de Beauvoir, and became one of several young girls with whom de Beauvoir embarked on simultaneous affairs that she recorded in letters to her sometime lover and longtime companion Jean-Paul Sartre. Her characterization of Natasha suggests a portrait by Picasso with the same face painted from two different angles. There's the troubled, violently jealous and possessive creature who pummels de Beauvoir with her fists when she feels neglected; and behind that first image is a charming, attractive, intelligent girl with "lovely tragic and despairing expressions that wring my heart."

Those expressions had a similar effect on Ivan's heart, but when he agreed to marry Natasha, he warned that he had no intention of becoming a faithful husband. She accepted this without protest, and he left for California with a promise to send for her as soon as he found a place to live. In Hollywood he quickly acquired impressive credentials, thanks to his association with Stevens, and also to Iris, who introduced him to Salka Viertel and her famous salon of expatriates that included Chaplin, Garbo, Thomas Mann, and Bertolt Brecht. Iris was already a friend of Garbo, and in 1934, when she lived with Friedrich in a trailer, the star had allowed her to park it for a few weeks in the garden of her Brentwood home. Chaplin, a friend since Iris met him with Sir Herbert, had recently seen her play Lady Macbeth in a production at the Ojai Festival, and found her surprisingly powerful. Perhaps the months with Michael Chekhov were partly responsible.

Some time earlier, Friedrich had once again left Iris for a younger woman, but once again she found adjustment in an affair with Ford Rainey, who played Macbeth; and when Ivan arrived in California the lovers were dividing their time between an apricot ranch (bought with a generous assist from Friedrich) and a rented apartment above the carousel on Santa Monica pier.

Natasha arrived in Los Angeles in February 1946, a few months after Ivan had accepted an offer from George Stevens to work as associate producer on his next Hollywood movie. But his salary was relatively low, he told Natasha, and so was his bank account. She refused to believe it. You know so many famous people, she said, they keep inviting you to parties, you *must* be rich. And after she learned that her husband had a charge account at a department store, Natasha used it to indulge her love of expensive cosmetics. It took a serious row, Ivan later told Lorna, to bring her down to earth. But at a party given by Darryl and Virginia Zanuck, he was appalled when "Natasha suddenly started passing around a hat, asking guests for money for her poor husband. And she actually collected $500."

Husband and wife were equally unsuited to parenthood, and although Ivan at times tried his best to be fatherly, Lorna's birth did nothing to save the marriage from fairly rapid deterioration. As Natasha declined to breast-feed her daughter, she sent her to the house of a wet nurse; and on the evening of her parents' first anniversary, Lorna recalled, "my father left my mother alone and went out with another woman. She retaliated by cutting her long hair, which he loved, very short. Then she gave away some of his clothes and personal belongings to charity."

But it was de Beauvoir who provoked the breakup. The former lovers had kept in touch, and at Natasha's invitation, de Beauvoir stayed at the Moffat house on Barrington Avenue in Westwood when she spent two weeks in Los Angeles on her U.S. lecture tour. In March 1947, de Beauvoir wrote Sartre that she found Ivan "marvelous" and had "a lot, really a lot of affection" for him. The three of them visited Iris and Ford Rainey at their ranch, picking up Lorna from the wet nurse ("a bloated monster of obesity") on the way. Local actors filled the house from dawn to 2 a.m., de Beauvoir's letter continued, and Iris was "a fantastic bohemian."

Before de Beauvoir arrived, Ivan had read her novel *All Men Are Mortal,* and recommended it to George Stevens as the basis for a movie. Stevens was sufficiently interested to commission him to write a treatment, and if the film was made, de Beauvoir wrote Sartre, "it would mean at least $30,000 for me—doesn't that make your head spin?" But a week later, Stevens opted to film Dreiser's *An American Tragedy* instead, de Beauvoir decided to move on, and invited Natasha to accompany her on a tour of Arizona by bus. Ivan drove them to the depot, where "he quarreled with Sorokin and everything became heavy," de Beauvoir wrote in her last letter from Los Angeles. "Of course, our departure more or less upset what had been a peaceful, tender friendship."

It also upset a marriage that was no longer peaceful or tender, and until Ivan could afford to divorce Natasha three years later, they lived separate lives under the same roof. After her unsuccessful attempt to seduce Oreste Pucciani, a queer professor of Italian at UCLA, Natasha paid a visit to de Beauvoir in New York; and in August 1950 she went to stay with de Beauvoir and Nelson Algren, who were living together at his lakeside house near Gary, Indiana. This time Natasha brought Lorna along, looking to de Beauvoir "virtually like a battered child, due to a total lack of care and attention." Algren later commented that many of his friends had been struck, from the way Natasha kept fondling and kissing de Beauvoir, "by her lesbian side." But apparently he and his friends had not been struck by de Beauvoir's similar side.

Nine years later, when Ivan had become a highly successful screenwriter, Lorna was staying at his house on Bowmont Drive in the hills of Beverly, and her father had become seriously involved with Donna O'Neill. Handsome rather than beautiful, she had a high-bred, casual elegance, charm to spare, and a voice reminiscent of Katharine Hepburn's. She was married to a wealthy businessman, and although he owned a house in Brentwood, they lived mainly on his ranch near San Diego. To Lorna, her father seemed unmistakably in love with Donna, but when she asked if they planned to marry, he said: "No. That would be fatal, I think. Our temperaments are too different, and she'll never leave her husband."

At fourteen, Lorna was still in some ways very innocent. "If Donna's married," she asked, "why is she with you?" Her father shrugged. Then he said: "That's how life sometimes is, darling. One day you'll see."

A year later, the Hon. Katharine Smith from England, not beautiful or handsome but with an endearing supply of goodwill, came to stay at

Bowmont Drive; and early in 1961, when Ivan told Lorna they were going to get married, because "everyone thinks I should," she wondered why he'd given up Donna. "It won't work," he said. But Lorna was persistent as well as innocent. "Do you still love her?" she asked, and Ivan answered sadly: "Very much."

From his parents Ivan had acquired a taste for high society and the good life, and Kate offered both. Her father was William Herbert Smith IV, Viscount Hambleden (principal shareholder of the W. H. Smith chain of bookstores), her mother lady-in-waiting to the Queen Mother, and she numbered Princess Margaret among her friends. But as Kate had fallen deeply in love with Ivan, the marriage seemed

The wedding of Ivan and the Hon. Katharine Smith, who is wearing Merle Oberon's dress, in the garden of Lenny and Dominick Dunne at 714 Walden Drive in Beverly Hills, 1961; at left, Nick Dunne, Gavin Lambert, and the bride's mother, Lady Patricia Hambleden

unpromising from the start, and was fated to come unstuck when he deferred to her wish that they live in England.

Although there was another reason why Ivan agreed to move to England, apparently he never discussed it with anyone at the time. Many years later he confided to his son Jonathan that "he'd been having a casual affair with a girl who interested Howard Hughes, and two FBI men had called at his house to warn him to break it off." After he ignored the warning, an impending contract for a movie script was suddenly canceled. Then the FBI paid another visit, accused Ivan of having been a member of the British Communist Party, and took his passport away.

With the help of the British ambassador in Washington, whom he'd met at a party, Ivan had managed to get his passport back by the time he became involved with Kate. But as the long arm of Howard Hughes ensured that Ivan's services as a screenwriter were no longer in demand, there seemed nothing to lose by moving to London.

For a while, social diversions cemented the cracks that soon began to appear in the marriage. At their house in Kensington, Ivan and Kate gave lunch and dinner parties that his half-sister Penelope, then living in London, recalled as "distinctly grand." The guest list merged the couple's social-aristocratic and social-showbiz-literary backgrounds— Princesses Margaret and Alexandra touching elbows with Elizabeth Taylor and Richard Burton, various members of the titled (and interrelated) Hambleden and Pembroke families with Ivan's friends from the Gargoyle years, literary critics Cyril Connolly and Philip Toynbee (son of the historian Arnold Toynbee and another former Communist), travel writer Patrick Leigh Fermor, famous for walking, at the age of eighteen, from Holland to Constantinople.

The Moffats also entertained their friends at the house they often rented for the summer months in Sardinia. The well-heeled, fashionable British had begun buying houses on the island in the early 1960s, and among them was Lady Caroline Blackwood's mother, Maureen, Marchioness of Dufferin. She enlisted the help of her Anglo-Italian friend, the mildly scandalous real estate developer Raphael Neville (who entertained rough trade wearing a caftan), to find Ivan and Kate a house for rent near her own. As social arbiter of the expatriate set, the

Marchioness made sure that the Moffats met "everybody," and as an enthusiastic party-giver, encouraged them to follow her example.

Leslie Caron, who was building a house in Porto Raphael when they first arrived, recalled one of the Moffat parties as crowded, boisterous, and alcoholic, with the Marchioness and Ivan equally animated and witty. But he confided to actress Barbara Steele that Kate "just wasn't the type you dreamed of driving along the Riviera in an open convertible with her hair blowing in the wind." Steele found the comment even more devastating because he made it "so casually in that wonderful, charming voice."

Inevitably, Ivan ran short of money while living on the Hambleden-Dufferin scale, and although blacklisting was no longer the problem, he found it difficult to get movie work. As so often happened, he was taken off the list as secretly as he'd been placed on it; but he had left Hollywood at the peak of his career, and for any screenwriter who moved farther away than New York, out of sight was out of the studios' collective mind. Assignments on two World War II movies shot in Europe were all that he managed to secure, a few weeks as one of the writers on the forgettable *Heroes of Telemark* (1965), and as an uncredited script doctor on the successful *The Great Escape* (1963).

The marriage with Kate produced two sons, Jonathan and Patrick, but Ivan was no more at ease as a parent than his own parents, and Jonathan later recalled that "he hated the whole idea of family life." At the same time, when Iris wrote that she didn't have the money for Boon to complete his medical studies, and nor did Friedrich, Ivan felt obligated to provide it. But as his financial and career anxieties intensified, he felt increasingly trapped in marriage to Kate, and needed emotional compensation.

He found it in serial infidelity. While still involved with Donna O'Neill, Ivan had begun an affair with Caroline Blackwood; it would end and begin again more than once over the next twelve years, and although its total duration amounted to less than a year, he looked back on it, as he looked back on World War II, as one of the indelible experiences of his life.

Caroline and Ivan occasionally met as lovers while Ivan was married to Kate, and she suspected as much, having already heard about

Patrick and Jonathan visiting their father in Los Angeles in the 1970s

other infidelities, including an affair with Peter Quennell's second wife (whose husband, Ivan commented later, "surprisingly" bore no grudge). According to Jonathan, "after my mother heard about the fifth or sixth affair," her store of goodwill was exhausted. In late 1971 she filed suit for divorce.

The Lover

In childhood Ivan was emotionally neglected, but his senses were indulged. Growing up in his grandmother's country house, where she set a good table, servants were always on call and the surrounding gardens and grasslands were "paradisial," he soon became a connoisseur of pleasure. As an adolescent he was introduced to caviar and champagne at dinner parties by torchlight on an Austrian lake, as well as the steam yacht, swimming pool and fleet of luxury automobiles at his great-uncle's Long Island estate. By the time he was seventeen, the lonely boy had learned, in the presence of brilliant company, how to appear more self-sufficient than he really was. At Schloss Kammer he was always the youngest guest, holding his own with von Mendelssohns, von Hoffmannstals, and any visiting heiress or celebrity, among them Alice Astor, Cecil Beaton, Noël Coward, the English stage designer Rex Whistler, Winston Churchill's son, the Hon. Randolph, and Toscanini.

In 1936, when Curtis first invited Ivan to one of his lunch parties for artists and writers, the guests of honor and the menu were equally re-markable. Like Salvador Dali and Osbert Sitwell, he ate *turbot en papil-lote, pâtes au gratin, choux au lard, jambon, salade, fromage et fruits,* accompanied by *Hugel's Riesling Reserve 1923, Château de Cheval Blanc 1921,* and *Grande Fine Champagne Jubloteau 1906.*

Among the autobiographical fragments found among Ivan's papers is "First Love," about his first passionate crush on an American girl he had originally met on a visit to Schloss Kammer. Although the tone is light and charming, there's a subtext of disenchantment. When they meet again in New York, twenty-year-old Angelica Weldon has become a *Vogue* model. He's "in love" with her, she knows it, and although she "loves" him, her "real" love is for an older married man who will never leave his wife. It makes Ivan feel old enough, at nineteen, to suspect that he can never compete with this kind of "real" love. "There was no belief," he wrote of himself and Angelica at this time, "that in the end one would be loved by anyone we loved."

Was the situation with Angelica on Ivan's mind when he told his daughter that although he was in love with Donna O'Neill, the affair had no future because she would never leave her husband, then added: "That's how life sometimes is"? In any case, when he realized there was no future with Angelica, it took Ivan little more than a year to opt deci-sively for Eros. And no doubt his success the first time around made it clear where the future lay. Natalie Newhouse, fiercely independent, hard to please, and pursued by various wealthy and famous members of

the Gargoyle, dismissed them all and chose to live with the very mod-
estly salaried writer of documentary films.

In his autobiography, Ivan refers very casually to his extracurricular
affairs during the years with Natalie, but describes another kind of
episode in more detail. In the spring of 1943, he spent his first leave
from the Stevens Irregulars in London, and a woman who had previously rejected him suddenly changed her mind. At last, he realized, "we
were to be lovers and she was my love," and the moment of triumph was
so overwhelming that he failed to perform.

Yet the idea of "real" love continued to haunt him. Colin Campbell,
an English writer Ivan met in the mid-1960s, recalled: "He told me
about a love affair with a nurse when he was wounded in World War II.
He made it sound very *Farewell to Arms*, intensely romantic, especially
as he never saw her again after he left the hospital." But this "intensely
romantic" affair was a fantasy, as Ivan revealed in his autobiography,
and it became an ironic account of an incapacitated patient offered "a
form of therapy" at the hand of his "not unattractive" nurse.

In a biographical study of Casanova (published in 1928, on the bicen-
tennial of his death), Stefan Zweig described him as:

> An altruist in love. Unlike Don Juan, he never desires crude posses-
> sion; he must have a willing surrender. We have no right, therefore, to
> call him a seducer. He invites a woman to join him in a new and fas-
> cinating game, in which he would like a weary old world (burdened
> with inhibitions and scruples) to participate, and find a fresh impulse
> in Eros.

Years later, when Ivan began playing the game, it was no longer new
but still fascinating, because the same inhibitions and scruples bur-
dened much of the world. His adventures probably approached the two
hundred mark, and although not nearly as legion as Casanova's (whose
memoirs claim three thousand), were impelled by what the Venetian
called "a secret force that I was unable to resist."

From the early 1940s to the mid-1980s, this force impelled Ivan to the pursuit of erotic happiness with many kinds of partners, from a stripper at a London club to Ernst Lubitsch's daughter, and from a black housekeeper at a New York hotel to Van Heflin's wife, Frances (during the location shoot of *Shane*). He enjoyed spur-of-the-moment pickups as well as affairs that lasted a few weeks or several years, some of them open and others involving deception. But unlike Casanova, he was impelled on two occasions by another kind of irresistible force, and fell so deeply in love that he hoped (against hope) for a lasting relationship.

Ivan's relationship with the stripper (c. 1964) developed into something briefly more serious when she confessed to being a drug addict. It brought out the Pygmalion in Ivan, and he took her to a psychiatrist. But after a preliminary interview, the psychiatrist thought Ivan was equally in need of help. He agreed to one session, and at the end of it, the psychiatrist proposed that Ivan should continue seeing him for three weekly sessions at fifty pounds each. "I would gladly pay you double that amount," Ivan unhesitatingly replied, "for the pleasure of *not* seeing you three times a week." Although he also stopped seeing the stripper, he continued to pay for her treatment.

On the first morning of Ivan's stay at the Regency Hotel in New York (c. 1968), he was awakened around 8:30 a.m. by a knock at the door of his room. "Then I heard a key turn in the lock," he said later, "and this exceptionally beautiful young black woman appeared in the doorway, explained that she was the housekeeper on her usual round of checking the rooms, and apologized for disturbing me." Unable once again to resist the secret force, Ivan looked the beautiful housekeeper in the eye, and said he was very happy to be disturbed by her. "She understood at once, and we had some enjoyable times together until I left for L.A. three days later."

The episode with the stripper occurred while Ivan was not only married to Kate but involved with Patrice Chaplin, novelist, journalist and author of several radio plays. Their affair began in 1962, and was "easy because we agreed from the start it should be open on both sides. I never challenged the situation, or the identity he chose for me, so there were no surprises." One aspect of the "identity" that Ivan chose for Patrice was that they should be occasional lovers and long-term friends; and their relationship continued on this basis for twenty years, in London when Ivan came over for a visit, in Los Angeles when he invited Patrice to stay.

Two or three things that Patrice recalled about Ivan: "He was very astute about people, could sum them up very fast. Partly because, even when he loved or cared a great deal about someone, there seemed to be an invisible layer of glass between him and the other person. It created an emotional distance, he had a way of being *there and not there*. He also compartmentalized his relationships, lovers as well as friends. When we first met, he told me he was married to Kate, but not that he still felt seriously involved with Caroline Blackwood. He did tell me about the stripper, but then, unlike Caroline, she wasn't one of his first-among-equals affairs."

In 1974, halfway through Ivan's on-and-off affair with Patrice, he began another relationship that developed in a similar way. Linda Lane was first introduced to Ivan at a party at the Magic Castle, the magicians' club in Hollywood. Shortly afterward they met and "connected" at a party for David Hockney. At the time, Linda earned a living as a ghostwriter and selling concepts for TV pilots, but her avocation was holography, and she had recently organized the first exhibition of holographic art in Los Angeles. "This interested Ivan very much because his father and Man Ray had been interested in the same thing, and made some experiments together." Their affair began shortly afterward, and Linda found it "easy" for the same reason as Patrice: "He was never monogamous by nature, nor was I, and neither of us wanted a long-term commitment."

The romance played itself out after a few years, but they remained friends, and Ivan became godfather to Linda's daughter Lucy (the result of a one-night stand with an Australian, who quickly retreated Down Under when Linda informed him she was pregnant). The role of godfather brought out the Pygmalion in Ivan again, and he involved himself in every stage of Lucy's upbringing. "He really grounded her in the way of the world as well as the world of ideas," according to Linda (and Lucy agreed). "He also chain-smoked and drank too much, which she found unglamorous, so without realizing it, he taught her not to do the same. She took the best of Ivan and benefited enormously."

Linda, who also found that Ivan "compartmentalized" his relationships, believed "he did this because he was always at his best one-to-
one, even in simultaneous one-to-one relationships." And by always
focusing very intently on a woman he was close to, "he was rewarded
with adoration."

In 1978, soon after Ivan and Linda had evolved from lovers to
friends, he began his third and last on-and-off affair. Judee Flick met
Ivan when he was half-seriously involved with Ernst Lubitsch's daughter, Nicola. "When we started dating, we had to figure out how to prevent Nicky knowing. Fortunately the problem was solved when another
man got very interested in her, and she in him."

Judee was working as an apprentice film editor at the time, but two
years later she got a better-paid job in the sound editing department at
Paramount, and decided to move to a higher-rent apartment, "large
enough for two." By then her relationship with Ivan had reached the
stage when "you have to decide where you're going, and whether or not
we were going to get married." At first Ivan seemed to favor the idea,
and offered to help with the rent, then decided he didn't want to get
married after all, or move into her new apartment. But he still offered to
contribute $300 a month to the rent.

"What do you think would have happened if we'd gotten married
after all?" Judee wondered aloud to Ivan a year later. "Well, my dear," he
replied, "I think we'd be divorced by now."

By the early 1980s, Ivan was rarely in demand for movie work. As
Judee knew he was financially strapped, she always paid when they
dined out, "and later on I bought him an air ticket when he wanted to
go to London." When faced with a definite offer of work, he was either
unlucky or made what Judee considered "an incredibly bad career decision." Although Ivan contracted to write a movie adaptation of the best-
selling novel *The Thorn Birds,* the producer sold all his rights in the
property to David L. Wolper for a TV mini-series. The network rejected
Ivan's screenplay and brought in a new writer. Shortly afterward, he was
asked to write a TV-movie about Florence Nightingale, met with network executives, and learned that Jaclyn Smith, formerly one of *Charlie's Angels,* had been signed to star as the Lady with the Lamp. "Ivan
was appalled. He said that Florence Nightingale was not at all beauti-

ful, in fact famously plain, and he refused to create the 'love interest' they demanded because she never had one." Judee thought he should accept the job because he needed money so badly, but Ivan emphatically disagreed. "If I do what they ask, I could never set foot in England again."

By the end of 1984, Judee felt that the affair had run its course. Each time she drove Ivan back to his rented house on Mulholland Drive after they'd had dinner together, he asked: "You're coming in?" For a while she made excuses, but finally preempted the dreaded question by asking one of her own: "Are we lovers or are we friends?" He looked at her as if trying to read her thoughts, then answered: "Friends."

Two or three things that Judee recalled about Ivan: "Men don't feel a woman's pain," he once told her. "They just don't." When someone mentioned a person he considered nondescript, he often said, "There's no point to him." In the last years of their affair, he began collecting porn videos, but was very secretive about it. She couldn't understand why someone so sexually free should feel guilty or ashamed.

In the early days of her affair with Ivan, Patrice heard from Oona Chaplin that he'd acquired the reputation of *un homme fatal*. Patrice was formerly married to Michael Chaplin, one of Charlie and Oona's sons; and several people had told Oona that one girl committed suicide after Ivan left her, and another attempted it. But like so many rumors, this one bore a very skewed relation to the facts.

From 1949 to 1951, Ivan had been half-seriously involved with Joan Elan, a very pretty, very shy British actress who hoped to make a movie career in Hollywood. After she took an overdose of sleeping pills, it was rumored that she'd become pregnant by Ivan, who paid for an abortion. This was true, but the pregnancy and the abortion occurred in 1950, and as Joan Elan's death occurred in 1981, it seems far more probable that she killed herself out of loneliness and depression, like not a few unknowns who finally lost all hope of a movie career.

Between 1953 and 1954, Ivan had been half-seriously involved with another British actress, Patricia Cutts. But after a modest career in England, she failed to make headway in Hollywood, and returned home two years later. In 1957, when Ivan was deeply involved with Caroline

Blackwood, she came back for a second try at Hollywood. After a few unrewarding parts in unrewarding pictures, she went home again. Apart from a supporting role in a TV series, *Coronation Street,* she worked only sporadically in London, and was found dead in her home from an overdose of sleeping pills in 1974.

And yet, twenty years later, Ivan had remained uniquely important to her. A few hours before she took the pills, Cutts called him in California. He was not at home. She left an urgent message to call back as soon as possible. He didn't. Next day he learned of her suicide, and for a long time afterward felt agonizingly guilty.

Another rumor about Ivan circulated during the early 1960s. It was very "hush-hush," according to Barbara Steele, "and Ivan became extremely angry if anyone mentioned it to him." But geographical factors prove that Aldous Huxley could never have been Ivan's biological father. As Ivan was born in February 1918, he must have been conceived in the early summer of 1917; and while Huxley was living in England from 1914 to 1919, Iris left for America in November 1915 and remained there for three years.

In July 1956 20th Century-Fox sent Ivan to Greece, where his script of *Boy on a Dolphin* would begin shooting two months later, mainly on a wide range of exteriors. Director Jean Negulesco wanted Ivan to inspect the locations he'd chosen, then rework various scenes to accommodate them. Mission completed by late August, Ivan left for Rome, where Iris had touched down for a while, sharing a one-room penthouse apartment overlooking the Spanish Steps with her black Belgian sheepdog.

He stayed at the nearby four-star Hassler, and on his second day in Rome, encountered a fellow screenwriter with his wife on the street. They were also staying nearby, but at a hotel with only two stars. Ivan professed shock. This could lower your asking price in Hollywood if producers get to hear about it, he warned the writer, better move to the Hassler, at my expense of course.

Surprised and grateful, the couple accepted an offer that was not as altruistic as it seemed. Ivan had waited to make it until he learned that they were due to leave Rome in three days; and he "fancied a walk-out" (favorite phrase for an erotic adventure) with the writer's wife. Astute as usual, he judged correctly that she was willing.

A few hours after the couple left for the airport, Ivan dropped by his mother's apartment, and found several other visitors there, among them Caroline Blackwood. She was twenty-five and had just left her husband, Lucian Freud. Ivan was thirty-eight; and over the next forty-six years he spoke only once, at length and in private, about their relationship. A few months before he died, he recorded an off-the-cuff tape at the request of Caroline's daughter Evgenia, and a transcript appears later in this book. On the page, of course, it lacks the sound of his voice, with its ache of personal loss when he sums up Caroline's life, and their relationship, as "a series of unanswered questions: sorrowful, echoing, disappointing." Or when he remarks, with a mixture of pride and regret, "I'm just very glad I knew her. All of it."

Caroline's father, the Marquess of Dufferin and Ava, came from an aristocratic landowning family, the Blackwoods, who had lived in Northern Ireland since the late seventeenth century. He joined the royal horse guards in World War II and was killed when Caroline was thirteen. Her beautiful, snobbish, witty and unloving mother, Maureen Guinness, came from an equally wealthy banking and brewery family with estates in Ireland and a distant connection, through Charles II, to the royal house of Stuart.

Caroline was born privileged, with the twin gifts of beauty and talent; but the Marquess had been a heavy drinker, Maureen an even heavier one, until she cut back after drying out for a while in her fifties; and the Marquess's mother went incurably mad. Another shadow across Caroline's life was the Northern Ireland of her childhood, recalled in one of her series of autobiographical sketches as dour, bigoted, provincial, with an atmosphere of boredom that "seemed to be sweating out of the blackened Victorian buildings of Belfast." Cool on the surface, these sketches have a subtext of ferocious irony; and they provide a key to the adult's enduring distrust of the world.

Because it was conveniently near the family home, Maureen decided that her three daughters should become day-girls at a boarding school for boys, and Caroline's portrait of the school bully, a brutal, overweight semi-albino nicknamed Piggy, who forces younger boys to swallow his urine, is at once horrific, shrewd and absurd. When Piggy tells Caroline that he objects to the presence of girls in a boys' school, she's terrified that he'll make her a special target; and when this hulk with massive "thyroid-condition thighs" asks her to strip naked while he watches, she dares not refuse. But his reaction astonishes her. Overcome with prudish embarrassment and shame, he mutters, "I didn't know it would be like this," and she realizes that his "fear of me was now far greater than my longstanding fear of him."

In another sketch, Caroline's sinister, toothless riding instructor tells her that she'll never make a good rider unless she takes some special pills; and he promises to give her a bottle if she'll meet him in a forest clearing at night. (In daylight someone might see them; "How do you ever know who you can trust?") She agrees, then decides not to go, then changes her mind because she fears his reaction if he waits for hours before giving up hope. But he behaves so strangely when he hands her the pills that Caroline suspects he intends to poison her, and dashes away on her bicycle. Completely deflated, he can only call after her: "Please . . . Never breathe a word!"

When the bully exposes himself as a coward, and the reaction of the suspected would-be murderer implies his guilt, it's the potential victim who laughs last. As a novelist, Blackwood specialized in reversals of this kind, often when they occurred at the expense of a threatening male. This aspect of her work disturbed Ivan. He felt that the men in her novels were weak, selfish, "rather despicable" and "cardboard-like" characters, and pointed out that none of Caroline's real-life husbands resembled the men in her fiction.

Ivan once told her daughter Evgenia that he thought Caroline was "a better journalist than novelist, which I took as a competitive way of damning her with faint praise. He also told me he was so incensed by *The Fate of Mary Rose* [her third novel] that he threw it across the room. I think he recognized his own selfishness in the serial infidelity of the character of the husband."

Evgenia's reaction is well grounded, as there's no reason to assume that Caroline based any of her fictional men on any of her husbands; and did Ivan ever read *Corrigan,* whose eponymous hero is a wonder-

fully engaging, passionate and complex rogue? In this droll and touching novel, the game of reversal is so ingeniously played out that both
con man and apparently guileless female victim emerge as simultaneous winners and losers.

The Stepdaughter, equally surprising, is a seriocomic study in paral-
lel obsessions, the self-obsessed woman who feels she's left with "nothing in life except my apartment" when her husband leaves her, and the
enigmatic stepdaughter, obsessed with baking and eating cakes. In
Great Granny Webster, the Marquess's formidable grandmother became
Caroline's point of departure for the portrait of a grotesque family tyrant,
rich, miserly, unrelentingly joyless, with a murderous psychotic episode
in her past. But just as even the weakest or most selfish of Caroline's
male characters have moments of unexpected insight and sympathy, a
terrible loneliness underlies the often ruthless comedy of mother and
stepdaughter, and the family tyrant is not simply a gothic monster, but
pitifully brave in her acceptance of a slow, painful death from cancer.

In all these novels, there's a very original combination of lethal wit
and human wisdom; and although alcoholism made gradual inroads on
her life, Caroline remained Ivan's equal in intelligence, and matched
his adeptness in the game of love. She was also born into a superior
social class, a distinction that Ivan took seriously in spite of himself.
And like Ian Hamilton, Robert Lowell's biographer, Paul Theroux felt
that Caroline occasionally played the Blackwood card. Recalling her
talent as a writer, and her "strange, almost wild beauty" when they met
occasionally during the 1960s, he added that "there were moments
when she pulled rank and reminded you she was an aristocrat."

But Jonathan Raban, a close friend of Theroux and of Caroline, felt
that "her gruff shyness" could seem intimidating, and lead people to
mistake it for "the aristo stuff." Soon after Robert Lowell married Caroline, he took Raban to meet her at her house in Redcliffe Square. "She
was still a beauty, and her shyness, her bark of a voice, made her a commanding figure, especially in her long (sometimes agonizingly long)
silences. But in my experience it was always Cal [Lowell], never her,
who liked to stress the Blackwood ancestry and 'Lady Caroline' thing."

In his taped memoir, Ivan remarked that Caroline never told him of
"a man that she really, without any reservation, loved or worshipped."

Obviously Ivan was no exception. After divorcing Lucian Freud, she was free to marry him and knew that he wanted it. But she also knew him well enough to suspect that in the end he would always prefer freedom to marriage; and the twinge of sadness in Ivan's voice suggests that although Caroline was the only woman who prompted him to write a long, pleading love letter, he knew she was right.

The Father

In 1949, Curtis Moffat was depressed by his waning creative impulse and bank account, and had developed cancer. "I feel I'm a man of straw," he said. "There's nothing left for me except death." A few weeks later he killed himself.

Ivan's brief reference to his father's death from cancer in his autobiography didn't mention that he committed suicide; he only comments that it made him wish he'd known Curtis better. But to explore that relationship any further would have led to a confrontation with his own reluctance to accept his responsibilities as a father. Additionally, Ivan himself had undergone chemotherapy for colon cancer in 1992, and it was only after he learned that the disease was in remission that he began his autobiography with the loaded sentence: "Tomorrow was often a day to be afraid of."

Ivan had four children: Lorna, by his first wife, Jonathan and Patrick by his second, and Ivana, who was brought up as the daughter of Caroline Blackwood and her second husband, Israel Citkowitz. It was not until 1998, when she was thirty-two and Ivan had four years left to live, that a DNA test determined her paternity.

Because of her deranged and abusive mother, Lorna had a particularly bleak childhood. She later compared herself to the young boy in

George Stevens's *Shane:* "I understood, as a child of three, and I remember it clearly, that my father could no longer live with my mother Natasha. She had become violent and uncontrollable to herself and others. What I couldn't understand was how he could leave me with her. Almost every weekend he would come for me, and take me to the beach or a fair, and bring me a magical gift, like a kitten to comfort me in my terror, but when he left I cried and called after him, 'Daddy—come back, come back!' with all the intensity of the boy at the end of *Shane.*"

At first Lorna never told Ivan of the beatings, because Natasha had threatened more and worse if she did. But when she was finally unable to hold back, and described how she lived in daily terror of saying or doing anything that might provoke Natasha to an irrational outburst of rage and cruelty, Ivan explained that if a mother had legal custody of her child, the courts never revoked it without a witness to supply firsthand evidence of abuse.

Fortunately, when Lorna was eight, Natasha agreed that Ivan could send their daughter to boarding school if he paid for it. As Natasha insisted that she spend most weekends at home, it was not a total reprieve. But one evening, when Lorna returned from a weekend with her mother and went to change her clothes in the dormitory closet, the superintendent passed by. Shocked by the dark bruises on the child's back and legs, she asked what had happened.

Immediately after Lorna explained, the superintendent called Ivan, who asked her to testify in court. Her evidence convinced the judge to grant Ivan sole custody of Lorna, who went to live with him at his house in Santa Monica Canyon; and for the first time in her life Lorna felt truly loved. "He taught me the ways of the world without any pretense." Caroline Blackwood, whom Ivan "absolutely adored," was often there, "with her blazing blue eyes and her husky laughter in a haze of blue cigarette smoke and Ivan looking happy." Lorna also recalled the praying mantises that still fascinated her father, no doubt as symbols of one of the ways of the world. "He ordered sacks of their eggs, and when they hatched, thousands of baby mantises covered the picture windows overlooking the Pacific. He would choose one, put it in an aquarium, and we would watch it grow fat on captured bugs and flies."

By the time Ivan married Kate and moved to London, Lorna was a teenager. A cultural as well as geographical divide soon followed. While Ivan stopped over in an Establishment world for ten years, Lorna embraced the youthful anti-conformist rebellion in 1960s California, especially its believers in the need for shamanist/Buddhist spiritual transformation.

When Ivan returned to Los Angeles, Lorna had moved to Monterey, where she took temporary jobs to support her mainly volunteer work for environmental groups. One day she drove down to visit her father with the baby duck she'd recently acquired. ("He eyed it rather like a praying mantis eyes a fly.") She began talking about her spiritual experiences until he looked so bored that she interrupted herself in mid sentence. But although he hated "spiritual talk," or any mention of God, when Lorna asked if he'd ever had any kind of spiritual experience, Ivan reluctantly admitted that at the age of nine he shot a duck, and it died in such obvious pain that he swore he'd never kill another. Then he asked God to forgive him, "and as a sign of forgiveness, I asked that seven doves fly over my head. Soon afterward seven doves, exactly seven, did exactly that."

It was the only time that she heard him allude, unless skeptically, to "any kind of spiritual experience."

Ivan's sons were born almost twenty years after Lorna, who grew up an only child with a stronger need for fatherly protection. Jonathan and Patrick, raised by an affectionate (although increasingly unhappy) mother, became more grounded in "the real ways of the world," and could keep each other company. Although Jonathan also realized that Ivan "hated the whole idea of family life," each time his sons went to stay with their father after he returned to Los Angeles, "he was wonderfully kind and entertaining, as long as you weren't needy." He could also be casually devastating. Several years after Patrick had decided to live in the country and become an artist, his father remarked: "I'd hoped by now to have seen a flowering."

A remarkable aspect of Ivan's character was that almost no one who became closely but not always happily involved with him—son, daughter or lover—bore any lasting resentment. The notable exception (as will appear later) was Ivana, who never knew that Ivan was her father until it was too late to have or even want a close relationship with him, and who "didn't know whether to be angrier with Caroline or Ivan for hiding the truth so long."

"I found Ivana very attractive," Jonathan remembered, "and when we were both in our teens, we dated a few times without having any idea that we were half-brother and half-sister. Just as well nothing happened, or it would have been incest." In the same tone of voice so casually amused that one might think Ivan was speaking, Jonathan also recalled how his father ran very short of money after Kate divorced him, and she was obliged to pay their sons' school fees for a while. "But even when Ivan was almost broke," Jonathan added, "he managed to keep up his membership of White's," the exclusive London club that Cyril Connolly had introduced him to in the late 1930s.

It was Ivan's attitude toward human experience that seemed to have made the strongest impression on all his (legitimate) children; and it was essentially the same attitude that he inherited from Iris. "So much of the charm of life," she once wrote, "depends on chance encounter, on novelty, on odd association, and however much one thinks, 'I will read, exercise, write, think, sleep, concentrate, eat more fruit, learn the harp,' one is forfeiting the absolute nourishment, and perhaps avoiding the ultimate necessity to love, laugh and perhaps to suffer."

Obviously not everyone can afford to live that way, and perhaps the few who succeed have made an unconscious choice. They may not lack the talent or skill that life as a creative artist or scientist or doctor or politician demands, only the tenacity of focus; and they focus on "the charm of life" as an end in itself.

The Writer

"After Kate divorced him," Jonathan recalled, "Ivan had no alternative but to return to Los Angeles and try to revive his screenwriting career."

In fact he didn't go back right away. After *The Great Escape* and *The Heroes of Telemark,* his reputation as a World War II expert brought an offer to write three episodes of *Colditz,* an American TV series shot in England and Europe. Robert Wagner starred as one of a group of POWs planning to escape from supposedly escape-proof Colditz Castle. And although obliged to take a flat in less fashionable, lower-rent Fulham, Ivan soon managed to resume his man-about-town role.

He had always appreciated and charmed beautiful movie stars, including Merle Oberon (with whom he had a walk-out) and Elizabeth Taylor. ("I once began kissing her and she seemed to like it, but unfortunately there was no time for more, she's always so busy.") Now he charmed Wagner's wife, Natalie Wood. Part of Ivan's social success came from his genuine pleasure in giving pleasure; and Wagner remembered that "because he knew Natalie was Russian, he took us to an out-of-the-way, authentic Russian restaurant in London. She absolutely adored it and always remained fond of him."

As he finished writing a third episode of *Colditz,* Ivan's reputation brought him yet another World War II assignment. Max Reinhardt's younger son Wolfgang, a friend first met at Schloss Kammer in the twilight of the 1930s, was about to produce *Hitler: The Last Ten Days.* A polyglot movie jointly financed by Italian and British companies, with an Austrian producer, it would be shot in both English and Italian versions; and Reinhardt, who had collaborated with its director, Ennio de Concini, on the Italian script, offered Ivan the job of making an "English adaptation."

With Alec Guinness always less than formidable as the Führer, and often more comic than malign, and British or Italian actors playing all the main German roles, the result was predictably weird. Like *Colditz,* it improved Ivan's bank account before he returned to Hollywood, but neither project revived his career in a changed industry.

By 1973, the major studios had become part of various corporate empires, the roar of the blockbuster would soon be heard in the land, and the best of the decade's new generation of directors were making movies worlds away from *A Place in the Sun, Shane* and *Giant:* Martin Scorsese's *Mean Streets,* Robert Altman's *McCabe and Mrs. Miller,* Francis Ford Coppola's *The Godfather.* Like many screenwriters over the age of fifty, Ivan found himself increasingly sidelined, and although he managed to get occasional work for a while, only one project reached the screen. *Black Sunday* (1977), cowritten with Ernest Lehman and Kenneth Ross, was a melodrama about a terrorist plot to blow up the Super Bowl, raised a notch or two above routine by the energy of John Frankenheimer's direction. And like all of Ivan's movie work after he left Hollywood for London in 1961, it offered little in the way of personal satisfaction.

When a screenwriter derives genuine creative satisfaction from his work, it's because he's been allowed the last word; but he can only be sure of getting it by becoming his own producer and/or director, like Joseph Mankiewicz or Preston Sturges or Billy Wilder. In 1951 Ivan wrote Kathleen Allan, his stepmother, that Paramount had "tentatively" offered him a picture to direct, and "although it's not something I wholly like or believe in, I suppose I should take the opportunity." Either he didn't, or the offer evaporated. In any case, he never considered directing a movie again, and when interviewed about his career, the only unreserved enthusiasm Ivan expressed was for working with George Stevens.

On *A Place in the Sun* and *Shane,* he was credited as Associate Producer, although (as Stevens acknowledged) Ivan was creatively important to both movies, rewriting a few scenes and supplying ideas for others. On *Giant* he shared screenplay credit with Stevens's longtime associate Fred Guiol, but although they won an Oscar nomination, and Stevens won the award for Best Director, the movie looks less impressive today than its predecessors. The deliberate pace and rich detail of *Sun* and *Shane* worked so effectively because the material justified it. In *Giant* the same style too often seems as overloaded as Edna Ferber's Saratoga trunk of a novel.

But the movie remains indelible for the scenes with James Dean, when the dramatic temperature always rises; and after its huge popular and critical success Ivan found himself in great demand as a screenwriter. Between 1955 and 1961 he worked on three "serious" projects and three routine assignments. The factory jobs were for 20th Century-Fox, the first an adaptation of a World War II novel by Lionel Shapiro, *D-Day the Sixth of June* (1956). As Ivan had strong feelings about the subject, he imagined, after working for Stevens, that he was hired to express them. Instead, the task became his first exposure to the ways of the major studio world.

Harry Brown, author of *A Walk in the Sun,* had previously written a draft that failed to satisfy Charles Brackett, a Fox contract producer. He wanted more emphasis on the "romantic" element, less on the military campaign; and (apparently without argument) Ivan provided it. *D-Day,* so vividly described years later in his autobiography, became the backdrop for a standard triangle, American officer in love with girlfriend of British officer.

Ivan's contract gave the studio an option on his services for two more pictures, and his next assignment was the 1957 adaptation of John Steinbeck's *The Wayward Bus.* Charles Feldman (producer of *Red River* and *A Streetcar Named Desire)* owned the rights to the novel and a screenplay adaptation by William Saroyan. He sold the package to Fox, where it was handed to Charles Brackett, who rejected Saroyan's version as "uncommercial."

Formerly Billy Wilder's writing partner, Brackett had settled for the life of a well-paid company man. Unlike his movies, he was still entertaining and acerbically witty, and Ivan became a fixture at his Sunday luncheons. The regular guests were mainly Establishment, including Olivia de Havilland and Rosalind Russell, not the sort of movie stars that Ivan appreciated (they lacked the dramatic allure of Ava Gardner, Merle Oberon, Elizabeth Taylor, Natalie Wood). But he formed a lifelong friendship with a young charmer from Louisiana, Marguerite Lamkin. Voice coach to several actresses who needed help with their Southern accents for a movie role, Marguerite eventually married a man whom Ivan had known as a fellow student at the London School of Economics; and as the wife of Mark Littman, by then a Queen's Counsel, she became a leading hostess and some years later fund-raiser for AIDS charities.

The bond between Ivan and Brackett was not creative but social, and Ivan later admitted that his company-man script of *The Wayward Bus* was probably the worst thing he ever wrote. He did better with his next adaptation by taking a ridiculous best seller at face value, and turning it into a ridiculously popular movie. In *Boy on a Dolphin* (1957), an

American archeologist (Alan Ladd) and a wealthy aesthete (Clifton Webb, of course) compete for ownership of an ancient Greek statue that a sponge diver (Sophia Loren) has glimpsed in the depths of the Mediterranean.

That Ivan agreed to write to studio formula is not in itself surprising. In the past many writers with a high reputation—William Faulkner, John O'Hara, Dorothy Parker, Nathanael West—had done the same thing because they wanted or needed the money. They were pragmatists who believed, like Faulkner, that "you can compromise without selling your individuality completely." Only Scott Fitzgerald felt deeply humiliated, and damaged for life, when his work failed to please; unlike the others, he had dreams of "conquering" Hollywood.

But Ivan was not an established writer, and had never imagined any kind of writing career for himself until he began working for Stevens. His first writing credit was on *Giant,* prestigious enough to impress studio executives while the movie was still in the cutting room. Even before Fox offered Ivan a contract, George Cukor had asked him to rewrite Robert Ardrey's script for *Bhowani Junction* (1956). They had met socially, liked each other, and after listening to Ivan talk about love and politics, Cukor felt that he'd be "right" for the job.

It seemed like beginner's luck to work with Cukor after working with Stevens; but Pandro S. Berman, assigned to produce *Bhowani Junction* for MGM, was a cautious, insecure operative who agreed to hire Ivan on condition that Sonya Levien, an amiable and wily old hand under contract to the studio, collaborated with him. Although Levien's name appears first on the credits, there's no way of knowing which scenes each of them wrote, separately or together; but as he received successive drafts of the script, Cukor repeatedly asked his writers to strengthen the personal story.

The movie's source material, a novel by John Masters, is the story of a beautiful Eurasian girl who embarks on a series of affairs, with an Anglo-Indian, an Indian who wants to marry her, and a British colonel. Each affair reflects a stage in the girl's search for identity, and takes place against a background of violence and cultural confusion: the riots and undeclared wars that broke out after the British government partitioned India (80 percent Hindu) and Pakistan (90 percent Muslim).

From a story outline that Ivan wrote for Cukor before he began work on the script, it's clear that he was equally fascinated by the political and erotic elements of *Bhowani Junction*. But when he saw the completed movie, he felt that Cukor had underplayed the politics and spent too much time on "atmosphere." However, Ivan was working at Fox by the time MGM executives viewed Cukor's first cut, and unaware of the drastic changes they had imposed.

The studio not only ordered the picture recut, but in Cukor's words, "rearranged it in a most uninteresting way," and found "too much promiscuity" in the Eurasian's story. The seduction scene between the girl (Ava Gardner) and the British colonel (Stewart Granger) was stripped of its erotic details (almost certainly invented by Ivan), the political episodes were shortened, the powerfully directed riot scenes trimmed on account of "excessive violence." But in spite of what was lost, the movie holds on account of what remains: the sympathy that Cukor and Ava Gardner create for the girl, and an eye-catching response to the Indian scene.

After Stevens and Cukor, Brackett and Fox, Ivan had become fully educated in the creative challenges and pitfalls of a Hollywood screenwriter's life. There had been no real pitfalls during his apprenticeship with George Stevens, a director powerful and shrewd enough to resist studio pressure. Each respected the other's opinions, and as the cowriter on *Giant,* Ivan had a firsthand lesson in the problems of adapting unwieldy material to the screen. In retrospect it seems that they were not completely solved, although Stevens approved the final script. But they made their own mistakes, and never had mistakes imposed on them.

It was the first and only time that Ivan would work under such ideal conditions. Cukor, an equally talented and exacting director, was not powerful enough to resist MGM's every demand, especially when his producer's first loyalty was to the studio. At Fox, Ivan played Faust to Charles Brackett's urbane devil. It was not simply a case of opting for the rewards of easy money, and "the charm of life" that he'd learned to appreciate at Fitzroy Square, Schloss Kammer and a Long Island estate. A similar life, incidentally, could still be appreciated in Hollywood from the early 1930s through the 1960s, in spite of complaints from the disaffected. ("This place," wrote Nathanael West, "is just like Asbury Park, New Jersey.") But after the sudden demand for his services, Ivan was not "corrupted" by professional or social success. Potboiler assignments, in his view, were a necessary challenge to mastering the screenwriter's craft, and he learned that to make a polyester—if not a silk—purse out of a sow's ear, like *Boy on a Dolphin*, took as much skill to adapt as a superior novel like *Bhowani Junction*.

In August 1958, Ivan began work for David Selznick on a movie version of *Tender Is the Night*. He already knew and liked Selznick, whose reputation for bombarding employees with memos was famous. During the four months it took to complete a final draft that satisfied his producer, Ivan took the relentless paper war in stride. Selznick had always intended to produce the movie for his own company, with Jennifer Jones as Nicole, George Cukor or John Frankenheimer his directors of choice, but financial problems obliged him to sell the property to Fox. Henry Weinstein, the well-intentioned but inexperienced producer who took it over, smoothed away some of the script's sharp edges on executive orders, made one fatal mistake in casting Jason Robards as Dick Diver, and another in taking Selznick's advice to entrust the direction to an old-fashioned studio veteran nearing the end of his tether.

Too late, they both regretted it. Selznick favored Henry King because he'd directed one of Jennifer Jones's greatest successes, *Love Is a Many-Splendored Thing;* but King had no sympathy for the Jazz Age or for psychoanalysis (Dick Diver's profession), and although the movie took place entirely in the south of France and Switzerland, he insisted on paring actual locations to a minimum. A final nail in its coffin: By the time the movie started shooting, three years after Ivan started writing it, and seven years after Selznick had acquired the rights to the novel, Jennifer Jones was forty-two, and couldn't get away with playing twenty-five-year-old Nicole in the flashbacks.

Meanwhile Walter Wanger had joined Fox as a nominally independent producer with two projects, *Cleopatra* and the four linked novels of Lawrence Durrell's *Alexandria Quartet*. Ivan declined Wanger's offer of *Cleopatra* but agreed to write a treatment for a four-hour movie of the entire Quartet. The studio had approved the project on condition that a "happy ending" was devised for the heroine, Justine; but when it rejected Ivan's treatment, Wanger sold his rights to MGM. Ten years and many troubles later, an adaptation of the first novel only was released as *Justine* (1969).

When Ivan began his next screenplay at Columbia, he had just met Katharine Smith, and had no idea it would be fifteen years before he worked in Hollywood again. *They Came to Cordura* (1959) was an adaptation of Glendon Swarthout's best-selling novel, supposedly based on an "actual event" that occurred in 1916, when a U.S. Army expedition was sent to hunt down the Mexican rebel Pancho Villa. Although the mission failed, Washington ordered one of its officers to select five men to receive the Congressional Medal of Honor for bravery.

A minor episode of American history, but it allowed Ivan to draw on his World War II experiences more directly than for any of the movies he was contracted to write about D-Day or its aftermath. In 1916, as in 1944–45, war brings out the best and the worst in human beings. After the expedition raids and captures a Mexican outpost, subsequent events reveal that some of the officer's chosen heroes (as well as the officer himself) have been guilty of momentary cowardice in the past. A momentary coward, in fact, may finally become a hero; a momentary hero may finally turn out a coward. Apart from some awkward exposition in the first ten minutes, *They Came to Cordura* contains Ivan's best work, firmly structured, strongly characterized, with some ironic contemporary touches about the cynicism of journalists covering a war, and the way government manipulates public opinion.

But once again the result was flawed, first by casting Gary Cooper (old and tired, but still "star power") as the officer; then by the studio's insistence on sweetening Ivan's bitterly ironic final scene; and finally by Robert Rossen. Although he directs the action sequences very efficiently, he fails to convey the sense of danger and urgency that John Huston would have brought to the shifting tensions and allegiances within an isolated group, played out in a series of forbiddingly desolate landscapes.

Yet, as in *Bhowani Junction,* the story holds, this time on account of the writing, and two strong, surprising performances, by Tab Hunter as the coward with a heroic streak, and a wonderfully ambiguous Rita Hayworth as the American woman accused of "aiding and comforting the enemy." Taken prisoner and forced to accompany the unit on its long trek to the American base at Cordura, she at first resents and tries to manipulate the officer, but ends by respecting him as much as she despises his "heroes."

Ivan was never an obsessive writer. He was driven by circumstances, the friendship with Stevens that began in the Irregulars, and although he found movies fascinating, they never became a passion. Screenwriting, it seemed, was primarily a way to support the kind of life he wanted to live. Not that he didn't take "serious" projects seriously, but once he became skilled at his craft, he never took the next step, of creating his own original material without a commission.

In 1996, a producer paid Ivan an advance to write a screenplay that may or may not have been original. The only clue to its provenance is a photocopied sheet attached to the screenplay. Dated June 10, 1996, it contains the address and phone number of Irby Smith, in charge of "contact information" for Run and Gun Films, a long-defunct company based in Seattle. The screenplay itself is undated, and only "THE GRAND DEFIANCE by IVAN MOFFAT" appears on the title page. He described it to several friends as "a World War Two movie," but never mentioned whether it was based on his own or someone else's original story. Either way, *The Grand Defiance* is far more authentic and thoughtful than *D-Day the Sixth of June* or *The Heroes of Telemark* etc., but not truly personal. As narrative, it's convincing in a solidly traditional way, but fails to solve an enduring problem that began with the talkies.

How to write convincing dialogue for French and German characters in an English-speaking film, with actors whose first and/or only language is English? Should they assume foreign accents of variable authenticity, and sometimes (as in Ivan's screenplay) say things like "Gross Gott!" or "au revoir," as well as "Hey!" and "Right, sir!"? It's a problem that most movie writers and directors still fail to recognize (or ignore) today.

Patrick Leigh Fermor, Ivan's closest writer friend in England, wrote that "his most precious gift—a very rare one—was the spoken word." This was an obituary verdict, undoubtedly fair at the time, but he might have qualified it after reading the completed section of Ivan's autobiography. Here, finally, he began to write (so to speak) in his own voice, and for the first time without a commission. Although he was offered an advance, he declined it, saying he "didn't want to be tied down." But he made slow progress because of a laziness that he often confessed to, and was surely inherited from his father (who took fencing lessons in bed). In five years he wrote, by hand, only a hundred and seventy pages.

In conversation, Ivan rarely seemed introspective. He was too busy observing, enjoying, and being astonished by the world. But in 1995, after his cancer was pronounced in remission, it seems likely that the shadow of mortality impelled him to look back on a life that had lasted more than three-quarters of a century, and to discover what he felt about it. There was also another, longer shadow cast by Iris. In 1968, while Ivan was still married to Kate, his mother had died of cancer at their house in Kensington. Friedrich had arrived to be with her, and their son Boon, by then practicing medicine as Dr. Christian Ledebur.

A year earlier, Iris had started to write a memoir of the people in her life whom she particularly loved. She is known to have completed four portraits, of her father, her first husband Curtis Moffat, Augustus John and Nancy Cunard. The portrait of Cunard, with its account of a vanished era of "transition and danger" and "exultant, longing, laughing loves unspotted by respectable sin," was published in a collection of tributes to the great friend of her youth. But a young man who had offered to type Iris's handwritten pages unaccountably lost all the rest.

In many ways Ivan wrote as he spoke, with the same quick yet detailed talent for setting a scene, evoking a character and reenacting dialogue; but without, of course, the voice prints of the raconteur: the "pauses and changes of pace and pitch" that Leigh Fermor recalled, the interruptions of "all-consuming and infectious laughter." But in the autobiography a very personal touch of melancholy underlies the wit, especially when Ivan recalls the mystery and pain of growing up, his benevolently remote father and elusive, charismatic mother; and there's also a deep sense of personal involvement in his account of a world "turned upside down" by World War II.

At least once, though, the autobiography misleads. The night before D-Day, Ivan writes, a childhood love told him that she'd asked her husband if they could spend the night together, because "she feared she might never see me again." Surprisingly, the husband consented, and for "the first and last time in our long lives we held each other close, and more." It wasn't difficult to identify David Tennant as the husband, and the "childhood love" as Ivan's cousin Virginia, later the graceful and forthright Marchioness of Bath. There was no "more," she told me, just a chaste night of love; and she was clearly amused that Ivan, of all people, needed to indulge in a sexual fantasy.

As Ivan pondered how to write about his life after 1945, the cancer recurred; and he never began what he knew he would never finish. He also doubted that he could face all the self-examination it would involve. "How much should I tell?" he asked the last time we had dinner together. "Everything important, these days, if you want people to be interested," I said. "Apart, of course, from anything that might hurt people whose feelings you respect." After a moment he said quietly: "That was the answer I expected." Pause. "And was afraid of."

ABSOLUTE HEAVEN

As a child, my parents and the parents of other children I met were part
of the same social group; and every time anyone came back from a party
in Paris, or wherever, we asked, "How was it?" And they answered, "It
was absolute heaven, my dear, absolute heaven." It was the phrase ring-
ing in one's ears. And I thought of calling this book Absolute Heaven,
even though a lot of life in the 1920s *and* '30s *in England wasn't heaven,*
but the opposite, some difficult and bad times in the rotten years leading
up to World War II. I haven't finally decided on that title yet, it'll be a
long time before I have to. I'm lazy.

Tomorrow was often a day to be afraid of, because my grandmother,
with whom I lived, although witty and whimsical, was also unpredictable and sometimes became fearfully angry. What would be
expected of one tomorrow night might not be made known until it was
nearly over, and by then one could have become, yet again, a disappointing and even a wicked boy.

On this particular tomorrow I had become wicked before it was
even half over. Exiled and in disgrace, still shocked by her reaction to
what I had said to her at lunch, I stood alone in the dank greenhouse,
watching the tunnels at the back of the spiders' webs. The webs were
horizontal, thick and dusty. The tunnels were dark. To make happen
there what I was about to make happen, was to ward off anxiety. Much
that I did alone had become secret.

Today I was alone in a sense more than usual. My mother and
father were indeed alive and about—my mother vividly so—and some-

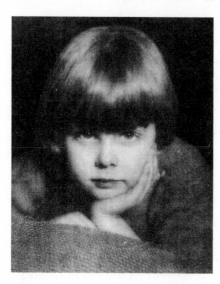

Ivan at age four

times came to see me, usually from America or France. Otherwise, except when my cousin Virginia came to stay, I was alone with my grandmother and my governess, Constance. I was eight years old. My grandmother's house was the only one I could think of as somewhere I "belonged"—and even that involved a question.

On that day, because of what I had said at lunch—and because, for a child, of the uninformed disquiet that lay between fear and curiosity—the question loomed larger. I should have known better, of course, but even on the warmest of summer days one was never quite sure of what was going to happen.

This was winter.

During lunch I had told my grandmother, Lady Tree, that she was ugly. We called her "Mameena," and—meaning to compliment her when, as I supposed, she contorted her face because she was about to imitate somebody—I had said, "Oh, Mameena, you *are* ugly!"

I had said it with a smile and was therefore all the more shocked at being ordered in a voice thundering with rage, which I had seldom heard before, to go out into the garden and stay there. "And then, may I come back?" I asked. "Perhaps never!" she said with another crack of thunder.

My grandmother, widow of the famous actor-manager, Sir Herbert Beerbohm Tree, had been a schoolteacher; and then, through him, had become an actress of no great fame. But she was famous all the same, as a wit, a mimic, a woman on constant display. In a moment of silence during lunch, she had momentarily lifted her chin, jutted it forward and scratched at the stretched folds of her neck. Then she happened to catch my eye. I had naturally seen this as a performance, a grotesque imitation or ridicule of some famous figure, or friend, or both. Her imitation of Margot Asquith (wife of the Earl of Oxford and Asquith, until recently our prime minister), involved grimaces not unlike those she had just made.

Even Constance, my governess, so usually reasonable and on my side, had failed to see the matter as I saw it when she came to the greenhouse some forty minutes later, in search of repentance.

"Will you go indoors now and ask Mameena, very kindly, to forgive you?"

"Yes, but I want her to know *why* I said it. Then she won't have to forgive me, because I thought she was just being funny."

Constance shook her head and left—unfairly, I thought, because my grandmother was nearly always being funny. This was not just my opinion, but a well-known fact of English life since Edwardian days. Once, protesting Somerset Maugham's early departure from one of her supper parties in the Dome, Sir Herbert's apartment above His Majesty's Theatre, she had said: "But surely, Willie, you can at least stay and have coffee with us?" "No, Maud, I h-have to g-go to bed early—it's the only way I can hope to k-keep my youth." "But then why didn't you bring him?" said Lady Tree. "We *love* those kind of people!"

In those days my grandmother had been not only funny but beautiful. Now she was only funny; and I had apparently caused deep offense by thinking her funny when it was not her intention. After Constance left, I inspected the glass panes of the greenhouse again and found a fly, an old and dry but live bluebottle. I caught it, held it among one of the largest of the dusty spiders' webs, and dropped it. It had hardly touched the web when a huge spider, with a fierce tearing energy made even more frightening by its hunger and its eight thin legs, rushed out of the tunnel to seize the fly and drag it back in. In the greenhouse silence I could hear the dragging sound it made. As always, I was shocked by what the spider—and I—had done. But it was my betrayal of the fly, as well as the spider's ferocity and swiftness of execution, that shocked me. Mameena's sudden rage had been scarcely less appalling. I decided to apologize by saying that I thought she had intended to imitate Lady Asquith.

"Ah, that may well have been," said my grandmother forgivingly at teatime, when I had been allowed to make my reappearance. "But don't ever, *ever* let anyone know that you thought my imitation of Lady Asquith made her look *ugly*, dear! She used to be one of the most beautiful women in England. Some—though, alas, not her husband—think she still is." Lady Tree addressed this last tidbit to Constance, who glanced up gratefully from her darning needle. "One of the most beautiful," my grandmother continued, "and perhaps the *most* brilliant."

I had never heard Lady Asquith so described by my grandmother before, and suspected her of exaggeration. As if sensing this, she said to me, "Remember Lord Ribblesdale, dear?"

Today I remember this man, known as the Picturesque Peer, mainly because of his clothes. Sitting on a chair in the garden of my Aunt Viola's country house, he had worn a soft rakish hat, a long jacket buttoned only at the top, and underneath it a vest unbuttoned all the way down. I was five at the time, and thought him oddly untidy for a grownup. Aunt Viola had said that he was the most beautiful man in England, but the man I saw was old, and his long face with its tracery of fine lines seemed made of cobwebs.

"Even Lord Ribblesdale," my grandmother said, "thought Margot Asquith one of the most beautiful women in England."

All very well, I thought, but because some people thought Lord Ribblesdale beautiful, did that mean he could pronounce Lady Asquith beautiful, with her horse's jaw and ferocious smile? And if so, was this—in my grandmother's phrase—the way of the world, dear? It was the answer she had given when I asked why women wore hats in church, and also when I asked why it was "improper" to serve egg dishes at dinnertime. On the other hand, when I asked why it was wrong to pour milk into the cup before the tea, she had said, simply, that it was "common."

Ivan at age six

Lady Tree's clothes, which were complicated, always seemed to be coming apart at some point: to one side below her bosom, or directly in front of her midriff.

"Coming apart, Mameena," was the warning I had been told to whisper to her when this happened, as it once did when we stood on the steps leading to the front door of a country mansion she hoped to rent for the autumn. Its owner stood above us, dressed in checkered jacket and mustard-colored vest, and looked down at her visiting card. "I'm awfully sorry, Lady Tree, but I'd really wanted a tenant who—well, who liked shooting and hunting and that sort of thing, you know."

Mameena took him up on it eagerly. "A hunting squire?"

"Yes, if you put it like that."

"I am he!" she said, extending her arms wide, with a gesture that parted silk over lace, in its turn parting to reveal the bare skin at my grandmother's middle.

The squire stared at her.

"Coming apart," I whispered.

The squire cleared his throat. "Yes, well, all the same, Lady Tree, I'm afraid I'll have to disappoint you."

Mameena turned back mournfully to our car, an Essex somehow not really big enough to justify being driven by a chauffeur.

Mameena had dark, symmetrical nostrils. I told my cousin Virginia that I believed she darkened them artificially. Although we were the same age, Virginia usually knew better and told me grown-ups never do that. "Shall I ask her all the same?" I wondered.

"Whatever you do, don't."

I didn't. And for fear of offending Mameena, I never asked why my morning lessons were always canceled on the day she heard the first cuckoo in spring. Not that Con's daily lessons were exacting, I only learned to read just before my ninth birthday. All the more vivid, then, were the readings out loud from Dickens every night, as I lay on the bear rug in front of the fire, scribbling block in front of me. All the more terrifying, too, when Mameena would "enact" in trembling tones the murder of Nancy by Bill Sykes. Or when tiny Great-aunt Harriet, so gentle and soft of voice, once came to visit and sat beside my bed to read by lamplight from a book called *The Red Redmaynes,* by Eden Philpotts, so bloodthirsty that when Mameena happened to overhear a particularly lurid passage, she ordered my great-aunt to stop at once. And forever.

Nowadays, in this age of murder, it is hard to understand how dreadful, how almost impossible it seemed to a child, living quietly in the countryside, that in real life anyone could commit a murder. Or how even more dreadful it seemed because, in those days, it happened so rarely.

A few years before I was born, as the press widely reported at the time, Police Constable Gutteridge had been shot in both eyes. The event was still spoken of in terms of such outrage that it seemed unlikely such a terrible thing would occur again in one's lifetime. As for the hushed, reverential tones in which the deaths of so many gallant soldiers in the recent Great War were mentioned, they only served to make it seem remote from any actual killings, let alone murder. In any case the War was something hard to conceive; it lay in a dark tunnel at the back of the imagination. It was an appalling event that seemed to have passed forever in the long hush following our "victory" in 1918, the year I was born, even though it was solemnized by two minutes of silence at eleven o'clock in the morning, on every November 11, for as long as I could remember.

My grandmother had been a widow since Sir Herbert died a year before I was born. I knew nothing of their marriage, and later, when I learned of its tribulations, it was only by an occasional anecdote or oblique reference. For instance, a slogan coined during the War had urged "respectable people," on account of food rationing and shortages, "to learn to stand in queue." When my grandmother was asked to explain the gap of several years between the birth of her second child, Felicity, and her third (my mother Iris Tree), her answer referred indirectly to Sir Herbert's notorious and prolific philandering. "By then," she said, "I had learned to stand in queue."

Her chief rival, and long-loved object of Herbert's affection, lived in a south London suburb across the Thames River. Mameena made light of her bitterness by never mentioning her by name. Instead, she called her, "Herbert's confinement in Putney." But although I never heard my grandmother speak openly of her bitterness, I was all too aware of her affectations.

I used to think it affected when she would call out, or rather sing out, "Water, tra-la-la!" to the twin red Irish setters, Sunset and Dawn, as the gardener filled their drinking bowls. The dogs responded instantly from somewhere in the paradisial grounds, bounded back to lap noisily, then raced off across the grass uplands and vanished over the horizon.

When Dawn was run over and killed by a car, we mourned her with slow, long tears; but Sunset soon forgot her, played and raced on.

There was a deep pool in the grounds, deeper and clearer in spring and summer, with water weeds and gliding newts. I learned to lie dead-still on its banks, observing the mottled black-and-green surface of its depths. At first you saw nothing, then perhaps a water beetle heading erratically downward, and then, as a darker outline on the mottled surface, the first oily-black newt would appear, wriggling upward, and finally exposing an orange belly as it rose and sipped the air before floating listlessly down again.

I used to find a worm, drop it in the water, and watch as it sank twisting to the depths. It lay there for only a moment before it was seized and dragged into darkness, carried off to invisibility by something invisible. My grandmother gave me a glass tank, where I planted water weeds and sand, and kept newts and water beetles. As I never closed the top, they could escape at will. And if the tank was empty of life in the morning, I never minded. The pond was the true wonderland, and when revisited at dusk, the most exciting place I knew.

One day, when my mother as well as Virginia had come to visit, we went for a picnic in the country. We had just settled down, and my mother had started to recite "Ode to a Nightingale," when a harsh voice suddenly interrupted her: "This is private property! Can't you read?"

A gamekeeper, stick in hand, wearing cap and leggings, glared at us as we sat among the bluebells with picnic things spread out all around us.

"We aren't doing any harm," my mother said calmly. She lay back, cigarette in hand, yellow stockings below her orange skirt.

"That's not for you to say, is it?" The gamekeeper pointed to a tree. "That sign there says, 'Private Property, Trespassers will be Prosecuted.' And it applies to all of you as well as the gypsies round here."

The gamekeeper glanced at my mother's stockings, which matched the yellow-gold helmet of her hair. She wore them, I decided, to attract the attention of strangers, and to draw particular attention to her legs. They were achieving both purposes now.

I had tried to warn her about the signs and the legendary fierceness of Mr. Crisp's gamekeeper. But she was fresh from a long visit to America and scoffed at my fears. "Who's afraid of gamekeepers? Besides, it's Sunday. And look at those bluebells, it's years since I saw bells as blue as that!" And she had led the way over the gate, helping Sunset to scramble over, while Virginia, Con and I held the picnic baskets, handing them to her on the other side, then climbing over ourselves beside the tree with the dread warning.

Pheasants rose whirring in front of Sunset's quick-foraging nose, and the gamekeeper turned his head sharply. "If I had a gun with me, I'd have a mind to shoot that dog. You've got five minutes to leave here before I fetch the police!"

"Fetch them!" said my mother as he turned away. And then, loudly, as he walked on: "Awful, awful man!"

He stopped, glanced at her, then turned back and walked on fast toward Mr. Crisp's house, invisible just beyond the wood.

"Come on, Mother, let's not stay," I said. "Please let's find somewhere else. *Please.*"

Con, always so tactful, suggested "a nice little place among the rhododendrons in the back of Mameena's house."

"All right," said my mother, and turned to me. "But I hate to see you so timid."

"It's all very well," I said. "But we live here."

My mother turned to Con. "Who is this Mr. Crisp?"

"We've never met him," said Con, "but Ivan's been to tea with his children."

My mother got up slowly. "Darling," she said gently to me, and helped Con to start packing the picnic things away. "I really do hope you won't grow up a timid boy."

"He isn't and he won't," said Virginia. "I promise."

My heart bounded to her and my mother gave her a quick hug.

After we finished our safe little picnic by the rhododendrons, Virginia and I were delegated to pack everything up and take the baskets back to Mameena's house.

"It's your turn," Virginia said.

"Let's do it together," I said.

"No, it's your turn."

"No, I did it last time while you were burying the magic amulet, remember?"

She remembered. And started to quote, " 'Here, here I put . . . ' "

"Yes," I said. " 'Here, here I put a letter to Lady Tree.' "

"But what did we mean?"

"I don't know. Anyway, you made it up."

Virginia stood there, afternoon sunlight on her blond curls. "We'll decide who does it," she said, "by seeing whose pee is darkest."

I found that strange, and somehow untypical of her, but I pulled down my shorts and she lifted her skirt. Then we compared the streams, and Virginia's was darker.

Ivan, age seven, with beloved cousin Virginia, age eight, in Mameena's garden

"So you have to do it," I said.

"All right. But you have to help."

I loved Virginia. I love her still. Now the Marchioness of Bath and mistress of Longleat Palace, her hair is a cloud of thick gray, her nature kind, her imagination gentle. But she always had a strong will.

"Those yellow flowers, you must eat them," she told me when I was five and Virginia one year older, and I was staying at another house in the country. It had been rented for the summer by Virginia's mother (Iris's sister, and an actress) and her husband Alan Parsons, a civil servant.

"Why must I eat them?" I asked.

"You must."

"But why?"

"Because Joan of Arc did."

I didn't really know who Joan of Arc was, but ate the bitter flowers for Virginia's sake.

When she came to stay at Mameena's house, we often shared the same bed at night. And if, once or twice, after the lamp had been put out, our hands strayed with quick light movements to each other's thighs, swiftly exchanged movement for giggling, then withdrew, it was less an act of exploration than of a night conspiracy against the grown-ups' world of day.

We had learned, of course, that darkness brought not only revelation but fear. For that reason, when we lay in the same bed—or later, after it had been forbidden, in separate ones—I would tell Virginia a story that terrified her. It was about the death of a bunny rabbit when it came out of its burrow in search of food.

"Don't let it happen! Please let the bunny live tonight!"

And I would pretend that I planned to let the story end happily. But with a fierce change of voice at the last moment, I would bring death upon the rabbit as usual. Those night stories were the only power I held over Virginia, otherwise bolder and more precocious than me.

Once I was lying in the bath while Virginia dried herself. "Know what Mameena said today?" she asked.

"What?"

"You ought to play the 'Kid' in that new film Charlie Chaplin's making."

"Why?"

"Because of the way your hair's cut, and your large eyes."

I shook my head. "I'd hate to do that."

"Get out of the bath and I'll help you dry."

I got out and she dried me. But our innocence was soon shattered. Sweet Constance had been given two weeks' holiday, and replaced by a woman whose name seemed as remarkable and apt at the time as it does today. One winter's night in the nursery, when Mrs. Feline wasn't there and the fire blazed brightly, Virginia said: "Let's take our pajamas off and dance round the table before we go to bed."

No sooner said than done. Naked around the table we pranced. There was a lightly curtained window overlooking the passage outside, and from the violent way that Mrs. Feline flung open the door, I guessed she must have been peering through it.

Virginia and I (always so ecstatically close in laughter, love and conspiracy) were now wicked, vile, disgraced, forbidden. Mrs. Feline
would report us instantly to our grandmother, and we were to go
straight to bed, no warm milk, straight to bed and not only to separate
beds, to separate rooms. Forever.

When Mrs. Feline pointed to the door, I held my pajamas against
my body and stood aside, as I had been taught, to allow her to precede
me through the portal of our vanished Eden.

"No," she said, and pushed me through with a slap. "From now on
I'll have no more mischief in front of me."

My grandmother's house, formerly a priory, stood all too close to the
village church; and on Sunday morning its jangling bells became a sum-
mons to boredom—and once inside, to giggling. I had come to dislike
the resonant tones of the clergyman who read the Lesson, and much of
the meaning of the service was (and would forever remain) unclear. We
were warned, in the text of our Book of Common Prayer, to "beware of
false doctrine," which I thought meant "doctoring," and also to beware
of Jews, Turks, Infidels and Heretics.

I asked my grandmother what Jews were.

"The Chosen People, dear. Though more by their choice than mine."

"And Turks?"

"*Very* wicked men with turbans and scimitars, dear."

"Infidels?"

"People who have seen the light—but a very *different* light."

As she intended, I was none the wiser. Once I refused to go to
church and was locked in the nursery cupboard for two hours.

But I not only hated to go to church, I hated to be *made* to do anything. Although I liked going for walks with Constance, I didn't like it
when anyone else said, "It's time for your walk now."

"Shall we go for a little walk?" was better, because it was a polite
suggestion that I could politely refuse. But if I refused, it became an
order. "Don't be silly, Ivan. Run now and put on your gumboots quickly!"

When Constance addressed me by name, it was a sign of impatience. But when my mother was impatient, she said: "Oh, *darling!*
Really! You're being too boring for words!"

I learned that being wicked was preferable to being boring. But while wickedness was readily forgiven, being boring incurred no punishment, but no forgiveness either. In that world, it seemed, there was a spectrum stretching from the heaven of one end to the hell of boredom on the other.

"How was the party, Alan?"

"Absolute heaven," Virginia's father would answer in his husky voice.

"How was the weekend at Christabel's?"

"An awful bore, really."

"Oh, come on, Alan!"

"But it was. Matter of fact, it was absolute hell."

The clergyman had spoken of hell and its fires. If sufficiently prolonged, I wondered, could they become boring, too? It was a question I asked my father, who had driven down for the day with Alan.

"Do you think hell could become boring in the end, Daddy?"

"Immensely, I should think," he answered without hesitation.

My father, Curtis Moffat, American by birth but brought up partly in France, was a man of charm and enormous taste who disliked action. Supine upon a rug, he would decline the country walks that Iris proposed, then embarked on with her long stride and her legs cased in blue jeans, a garment then unknown in England.

And my father, his fingers gently twisting a lock of hair beside his brow, would walk out to the lawn, lie down and watch my mother and me with a smile as we set off on our walk. As I disliked being *made* to walk, I half envied and half despised him.

Although in later years he took up golf in a very leisurely way, my father abhorred all exercise. At one stage, on the recommendation of his doctor, he also took up fencing. But it came to an end one morning when he greeted Monsieur Bertillon, the instructor, from his bed. I was a witness to the instructor's astonishment, and his concern for my father's health.

"Are you not well?"

"No, I'm very well indeed."

"Alors, au debout!"

"No, I can just as easily parry and thrust from a lying-down position."

He held out his hand for the foil. Bertillon, with that long expository gasp beginning with "Ahh!" that only a Frenchman can make, handed it to him, followed by the mask and protective jacket.

My father merely draped the jacket across his torso, but put on the mask. Bertillon did likewise. My father raised his foil, and Bertillon took a step or two backward—or, rather, above him.

For a moment the foils crossed and recrossed.

Bertillon thrust. My father parried *carte,* and nimbly whipped his foil into Bertillon's thigh, just below the protective jacket.

Bertillon stepped back and removed his mask. "Monsieur Moffat, I regret very much, this has been our last lesson."

My father extended his hand like a victor, shook Bertillon's and bade him farewell.

Although he had never, I believe, taken to horseback riding, my father had a taste for clothes. On a visit to England in 1912 he had ordered and even paid for a pair of riding boots from Peel's, the fashionable store in Oxford Street. But he never called to collect them, never asked that they be sent anywhere, and it was not until 1936, after twenty-four years of paying an annual fee for their storage and nourishment, that he dispatched me to go and get them.

At Peel's I was escorted upstairs to a loft, a dim and dusty morgue for unclaimed boots and shoes. The Peel's employee in his green apron consulted a piece of paper, and found a pair of boots engraved with my father's name on a small, bone-ivory plaque above one of the trees. Nourished or not, they were badly cracked. I took them back by bus to my father's elegantly "modernistic" flat in Fitzroy Square.

Somehow the whole procedure had depressed me, and I could tell from my father's face when he examined the boots, that he was also depressed. As he thanked me, his warm brown eyes met mine.

"Futility," he said, returned to his bedroom and stowed the boots at the back of one of his many clothes closets.

I wandered back toward my own bedroom. Seemingly, my father never had any money, and his uncle Robert Graves, from whom he used very occasionally to receive a handout, had committed suicide in 1934 after losing most of his millions as a result of the Wall Street crash. Yet a profusion of antique West African masks and figurines of ebony, ivory and bronze stood on glass shelves in several rooms. A large Braque, a small Picasso, three Matisse drawings and a Cézanne decorated the living room. Its walls were surfaced in cork, and a table with chromium metal legs and a top of black glass stood exactly at the center. White leather banquettes, long and wide, were built against two walls. A bar made entirely of black glass was inset into a third wall. At night, a large backgammon table, bordered in white leather, lit softly and indirectly by glass panels, was usually the sole source of light.

My father's apartment extended through the two conjoined buildings that formed 4 Fitzroy Square. With its innumerable combinations of concealed and indirect lighting from various sources, it was remarkable for its proclaimed "modernity." Today it would be an antiquarian's wonder, but at the time it was a wonder to my father's friends, who knew him to be perpetually and hospitably broke.

But all that was in the future as I waited, at the age of eight, to be sent to boarding school.

"Moffat, what on earth is that thing on your shirt?"

I had never been called just plain "Moffat" before. I was visiting

● GO INTO THESE ROOMS

YOU CAN BREATHE THERE AND WALK ABOUT ●

NO LONGER DECORATION SICKLY WITH CHARM FROM WHICH THE SPIRIT TURNS ● HERE THERE IS NOTHING OF DECEPTION ● THE LIE IS A TRUE ONE ● THE MACHINE WORKS

CURTIS MOFFAT

● FOUR FITZROY SQUARE LONDON WEST ONE

Advertisement for Curtis Moffat Ltd.

the school a week or so before I actually became a boarder, and remember the visit because the shirt I wore, in the eye of the masters and boys who saw it and spoke to me that day, branded me as peculiar, spoiled, effete or rich, or maybe all four. In fact none of those qualities was necessarily a reason to be despised or ill-treated at that school, brutish and an eternal winter as it was in many ways. But my kind and protective older cousin David Parsons (Virginia's brother) was still at the school, and took me aside to suggest that my shirt was "perhaps not *absolutely* the best one to wear today."

Why? I asked myself. Could neither Mameena nor Con have foreseen what would happen? The shirt being stared at by boys in gray-and-blue uniforms, and two schoolmasters in tweeds and gray flannels, was of bright scarlet silk, with a large green praying mantis embroidered across the front.

None of the boys had ever seen a praying mantis, alive or embroidered, none knew what it was when I informed them, and only one of the masters professed a vague knowledge. I proceeded to tell them, brightly and defensively, everything I knew about praying mantises. I told them that the mantis represented on my shirt had been captured the previous summer in America. I explained its habits, the way its long serrated forelegs fastened on its prey and held it up to the mantis's mouth, which usually bit first into the joint between head and thorax, or devoured its eyes.

I did not tell them of my joy, gratitude and initial disbelief when my mother had come running across Fairmount Park in Philadelphia that summer, holding a straw hat upside down and shouting excitedly that she had caught a live praying mantis. Or how the sight of that large specimen with pale green wings, exactly like the photographs I'd seen in the book by Jean-Henri Fabre, had overwhelmed me not only with the excitement of possession, but the unexpected kindness, sweetness and imagination of my mother, who had recognized the mantis from my description when she saw it in flight, ran after and captured it.

All this she had done when she'd been lying on the grass on a hot afternoon, rehearsing her part before the opening night of *The Miracle*, the extravaganza based on a medieval legend that Max Reinhardt had first brought from Germany to New York, where it took audiences by storm.

My mother had been asked to take over the part of the Nun for its American tour, even though she had never acted before. But neither had the beautiful Rosamund Pinchot, daughter of a former governor of Pennsylvania, and a "discovery" of Reinhardt, who originally played the part in New York and London. As she was not available for the tour, my mother's great friend Lady Diana Manners, who had already dazzled both cities as the Madonna, had suggested to Reinhardt that Iris replace her. And so, only a few hours after she captured the mantis, that night would be the first opening night of her life.

My mother had promised too many things before, too many things that had fallen through, too many false hopes of her arrival from abroad, too many toys that had arrived broken, clockwork boats with their keys missing, castles lacking a drawbridge or a tower, visits to the zoo arranged but canceled—and now, without request or promise, she had brought me a praying mantis!

Even my father waved happily from his distant rug. And my mother, hand on my shoulder, smiled with excitement and triumph on this of all days, not for her opening night but for the mantis and me!

I took it back to my room at the Mayflower Hotel, placed it in a dry washbasin, found a small cockroach (not very difficult there) and dropped it in as well. The cockroach had run only twice around the basin when the mantis turned its head (no other insect was capable of this) and moved upward. As the cockroach came within range, the mantis snapped its barbed forelegs with the speed of a spring. The prey was seized in a serrated grasp held up lengthwise and then, corn-on-the-cob-wise, instantly devoured.

Everything had happened exactly as Fabre described in his book, which I had been given a year earlier, when I had just learned to read.

That night I watched my mother on the stage for the first time; saw her in nun's habit kneel gracefully before the Madonna in a great cathedral, where a thousand candles burned; heard her recite the Lord's Prayer; saw her courted and then sinfully caressed by a marvelously handsome knight in iridescent armor; saw her captured and torn, to the beat of gypsies' drums, by a band of cruel robbers; and finally saw her mock coronation at the court of a mad king, where she sat on a throne in a robe of flowing gold, with a gold crown upon her golden head.

For the first time in my life I saw Iris, my mother, as beautiful. I wished suddenly that she would always be dressed in gold, or even in the simple gray and black of the Nun, instead of the blue jeans, multicolored jerseys with (now and then) bits of looking-glass sewed on them.

As she rose from the throne to holy music, and was blessed by the Archbishop, gasps and whispers came from the audience all around me. Constance, seated next to me, gripped my hand and leaned close to repeat, in a whisper, a remark she'd overheard: "Miss Tree is even more beautiful than Rosamund Pinchot was in the part."

As I gazed at my mother, I felt grateful all over again for the mantis, and life was suddenly all joy and expectation.

At the end of *The Miracle,* a rapturous audience stood to applaud both my mother and Diana, and so did I. My mother's false coronation stays more vividly in my memory than any actual royal event of the time that I witnessed—far more than the funeral of Queen Alexandra, widow of King Edward VII, in 1925. Virginia and I had been privileged to watch it from the balcony of the Foreign Office as the dark procession, led by several actual kings, moved down Whitehall toward Westminster Abbey.

One moment of that day, however, made a deep impression. As the first dead-slow notes of Chopin's Funeral March sounded (I had never heard it before, yet knew instantly what it meant), and at the same moment, the various heads of state appeared behind the cortege with its black-plumed black horses, a thick early snow, the first of the year, began to fall. The flakes were so dense and soft that they formed an almost opaque canopy between Virginia and myself, and everyone below. It seemed both miraculous and appropriate, as if a heavenly hand were drawing a sheet across the scene.

Afterward, Virginia and I went to St. James's Park and rolled crumpled balls of snow along the walks. Then we were taken to have tea with our great-aunt Constance Beerbohm, Sir Herbert's sister, and report on the funeral. Tall and pale, a shawl invariably around her shoulders, Aunt Constance lived in a flat in Upper Berkeley Street with her companion, Miss Dreyfus. Swarthy, lightly moustached, and harsh of voice, Miss Dreyfus always wore the same hat, indoors and out. A bunch of shiny imitation cherries decorated it, bobbing and glowing in the curtained gloom of my great-aunt's drawing room.

Miss Dreyfus pronounced her "f's" as "p's." She often had a convulsion during our visits, as she suffered from epilepsy. The warning sign came when she began to say boastful things and her voice rose to a strident climax—then the gasp and sudden straightening of the limbs.

Aunt Constance would say quietly, "Don't pay any attention to Miss Dreyfus, dear."

On this occasion, it began when Miss Dreyfus bared her smile at me. "And are you learning to speak French?"

"A little," I said.

Her smile broadened and her voice rose. "When I was at school I learned to speak perfect French quite early. I was by far the best in a class of some thirty girls! So far and away the best at speaking French that I was awarded—"

A gasping sound, an exhalation from her mouth. It became as rigid as her body. Only the cherries on her hat continued to bob and glow in the wake of paroxysm.

Aunt Constance said, "Pass me one of those chocolate biscuits, dear, then take two for yourself. Then, if you like them, I'll send you some as soon as you start school."

And she did.

At English boarding schools, boys were usually too accustomed to cold, and their own tears, to give much sympathy to fellow sufferers. But when the crying would begin after "lights out" in the dormitory, they understood and offered a few words of condolence.

"Bad luck, Davis," a quiet voice would say in the dark.

The sobs would increase, and everyone knew that Davis, "a new boy," was desperately homesick.

"Bad luck, Maconchy."

We knew that Maconchy's parents were in India and he would not see them for a year or more. He was eight, and his wracking, uncontrolled sobs grew louder.

I lay listening. I was not exactly homesick, but I thought first of Con during that past autumn in New York, where we went after *The Miracle* opened in Philadelphia, and of how we used to pause in front of the windows of the Automat on Lexington Avenue, that glowed so invitingly at night, then sometimes insert a coin and take out a Jell-O or a pie.

Then I thought of my mother. My father had written me from London that she was in a faraway part of America called California. I remembered her yellow skirts and bright stockings. I thought of her hugs. She only gave them on greeting me, but they were warm. I remembered, with longing, the time when my father took me to visit his uncle on Long Island for a few days during that previous summer. Robert Graves owned a private steam yacht, had a huge estate with many cars, and a huge swimming pool that was being dug by men who could only speak Italian. I remembered taking swimming lessons at the Huntington Bay Club, and last and most of all, the sandy roads and giant butterflies beside the dunes. I thought of the picnics on those sand dunes; and then, as an antidote to longing, of the mocking laughter when a tall black Ford drew up, and Prohibition officers like Keystone Kops got out to search the cove for bootleggers—while my great-uncle and the other grown-ups winked as they sat around drinking whiskey from paper cups.

I had started to love America, wildly excited by the little I knew of it, and at that moment it seemed to me wrong, almost like blasphemy or treason, to laugh and scoff at the law against alcohol. Besides, I had never been with grown-ups when they were drinking gin, whiskey or whatever, and now I had to listen to gusts of empty laughter, and to Mrs. Barclay—rather beautiful, I thought, in her big hat—who began to imitate my English accent, and mock my longish words, even though (only an hour before) she had pleased me by telling my father that I was going to be as good-looking as him one day, maybe even better.

During her imitation, my father had merely smiled wanly and gazed out to sea. I looked at him critically. Was I wrong to think badly of him? He was distant but always kind. And he had ordered, especially for me, the live baby alligator that was brought to our suite at the Ambassador Hotel. So perhaps I was being treacherous for thinking badly of my father when he didn't come to my defense.

On the other hand, there he was, lying on the sand, drinking whiskey even as the tall officers perched like birds on a nearby dune and scanned the sea. My father, who had been a little treacherous toward me, was now being a little treacherous toward his country.

Then he turned his warm eyes in my direction. "Ivan?"

"Yes, Daddy?"

"Are you having a nice time?"

"Yes, thank you, Daddy."

"Good." He smiled at me, patted the rug beside him. "Come sit next to me."

I ran over, sat beside him, and he put an arm around me.

In the dark of the dormitory, I listened to the crying, then closed my eyes tight. In the morning there would be mathematics class, I hadn't done the sums because I didn't understand them, and I would be pun-

Ivan at Earleywood School

ished. I snuggled deep into the sheets and imagined I was in an igloo. Snow and cold raged all around me, but in the igloo the snow was warm.

At Earleywood School near Ascot, Berkshire, our chief diet comprised football, cricket, bad food, facetiousness, and cruelty. In the so-called "Latin classroom" next to Dr. Pitkin's study, where I often did my homework, the routine torture of younger by older boys was something I couldn't avoid observing, although I was seldom made to suffer it. The favored victims were ugly little boys. The creased, tear-stained face of little Woods as he was set free after being forced to squat on half-bended knees while his thighs were beaten with a ruler every time he moved or wavered—this disgusted me as much for the expression of helplessness and agony on his face, as for the smirks and giggles of the three boys responsible for it.

Woods was ugly, his ears stuck out, and his family (as far as anyone could determine) was nondescript. Therefore he was fair game, not to be pitied. Whether he had just been beaten by Pitkin or tortured by the prefects known as "captains," his face was so often crumpled in tears that its permanent expression became one of pain. His ears offered a convenient handle to be seized by the under-matron, Miss Cope, as she dragged him off in his pajamas to the captains' dormitory next door, where she stripped him and made him bend over in front of each captain's bed in turn. They beat him with whatever came to hand, ruler, knotted cord, hairbrush, and then Miss Cope pulled Woods back to the dormitory by his ear, pajamas dragging around his ankles, dark red weals and bruises across his behind, while the boys jeered.

An ugly boy's frequent tears were not only thought unworthy of sympathy, but completely disgusting, unlike the far less frequent tears of a pretty boy. But the most sadistic of our teachers, Mr. Honeyball, enjoyed provoking the latter.

Honeyball, who taught French, used to summon one of the best-looking younger boys from his desk, make him lie across his knees, then spank him, keeping time with each spank as he repeated: "Humphries, the more I beat you, the more I like you." Of course we had never even heard of the word *sadist,* and although we thought it very strange, perhaps on the verge of some obscure area of indecency, we had no idea what Honeyball was really feeling or doing.

Our chief weapon, against such teachers as we dared employ it, was to play the fool. And if you were no good at sports, playing the fool was an alternate way of buying popularity. There were different ways of playing the fool, and being facetious, making bad jokes in class, was the way I and two friends, Pratt and Lyon, chose to play it.

When tall, thin Mr. Williams, who taught history, drew his threadbare jacket across his midriff with both hands, it signaled a change of mood and subject. "Now!" he said. "We come to one of the turning points of the war between Oliver Cromwell and the Royalists—the battle of Worcester."

I raised my hand.

"Yes, Moffat?"

"Is that where they make that very excellent sauce, sir?"

Giggles and sniggers from lowered heads. I kept a straight face.

"Moffat, come and see me after class."

The lesson continued, but cheeks bulged with suppressed laughter at any further reference to Worcester. In his study, Mr. Williams told me that the very next time I played the fool he would see to it that I got a caning from Dr. Pitkin.

So I was being let off. "Sir," I said, and as I thought about the very excellent sauce and my cheeks started to bulge, I managed to keep my lips tightly pursed. Then Williams turned to flick ash from his pipe into the ashtray, and missed. A squelching sound escaped from my cheeks. Williams turned and gave me a sharp blow on the face.

"I trust you'll find that equally amusing, Moffat."

"Sir."

He started to pull the thin jacket across his midriff. "You may go."

"Thank you, sir."

In the continuing battle for popularity, a tiny victory was likely to reduce our masters to the level of the boys, and it elevated the boys to a heroic stature that we never granted even the most fair or athletic of our masters. Among them was Mr. Griffith, a kind, ordinary, decentminded man with an open face, a sympathetic gleam in his eye, and fingers permanently stained with red ink and white chalk. But fair and decent as he was (or even, perhaps, *because* he was), we considered him a bore. And when it was Mr. Griffith's turn to take charge of our long dull afternoon walks, we never sought his company.

Before starting out, it was the custom for us to ask for a "side," to be allowed to walk on one side or the other of our master, who walked at the rear of the two-by-two columns of boys in gray and blue uniforms. Some of our masters, even the cruel ones, even Honeyball, could be entertaining, and the more sophisticated older boys sought their "sides." In fact, a master knew his status in the school by the number of boys who asked for a side before the walk. But dear Mr. Griffith would glance in vain toward Lyon or Pratt or me as we assembled, until finally one of the smaller boys would ask for and be granted the privilege.

Although I did not enjoy witnessing the social humiliation of Mr. Griffith, I was unwilling to alleviate it, on those interminable walks past damp bramble bushes on the roads around Ascot, by sacrificing the company of Pratt and Lyon. But I hit on a scheme. As we chatted and milled about, we would watch and wait unobtrusively until David Tertius or Woods had asked for and been granted a side. Then we would run eagerly up to Mr. Griffith.

"Please, sir, can I have a side, sir?"

"Ah! No, er, I'm sorry, Moffat—Pratt—but I'm afraid, er, Woods and Davis have already spoken."

Delighted by our show of compassion, we would take our places near the head of the column, which formed in order of height. But before long Mr. Griffith saw through our scheme, and greeted our requests coldly, staring above our heads instead of looking us directly in the face.

After that, Pratt and I thought it was probably too late to ask Mr. Griffith for a side in earnest, but we decided to try; and when everything turned to smiles and cheerful decency again, it felt worth the try.

Honeyball, who shared teaching mathematics and algebra with Griffith as well as taking French class, was tall, blond and athletic, with pale shiny skin stretched tightly over his cheekbones, and deep-set dark eyes. He was also in charge of sports, and played a hard game of rugger and football.

One day in algebra class, Honeyball stared down at the exercise book belonging to Leese, who sat next to me at the long, scarred table.

"Leese, you've botched it. You've got until I've walked around the room once, and come back, to get it right. Or it'll be the worse for you."

As I was even worse than Leese at algebra, I dreaded the moment when Honeyball might pause and look at my own page. The classroom was dead silent, heads bent over exercise books as Honeyball made a slow, casual circuit. On the way, he glanced over the shoulders of a couple of boys, and pointed out an error on Henderson's page.

Meanwhile Leese's hand shook slightly as he appeared to try and solve the problem. He was a fairly tough boy, good at rugger, and although his snub-nosed profile was bent over his exercise book, I knew he wasn't really thinking about the problem, but of what Honeyball might do.

Honeyball strolled past me and stood for ten seconds behind Leese, whose pen made a few movements on the page. Then he shot out his hand, gripped Leese's hair, pulled his head back as far as it would go, and banged it hard, facedown, on the table. He did this three times. Blood, not a usual sight at the school, ran from Leese's nose and mouth, covering a few ancient scars of chalk and ink on the table.

The room was very quiet as Honeyball returned to his high desk. He perched there, looking down at us, then flicked back his shirt cuff and looked at his watch. "Time," he said quietly, and strode out of the classroom.

There was a general murmur of sympathy for Leese, who said nothing, but pressed a sheet of pink blotting paper against his face, then got up and left the room. My pent-up dislike of Honeyball boiled into hatred, and at the same time a sense of guilt fueled that hatred. Although I was even worse at algebra than Leese, he was victimized while I had been spared.

My anger soon began to spread toward our other masters. They talked constantly of "fairness" and "decency," qualities they defined as "essentially English." They crowed over English victories in battle, invariably "glorious" and "just." They exulted over the map of the world, the British Empire spread wide and red across it.

Next day I discussed the treatment of Leese with Pratt as we lay watching, with no interest, a cricket match between Earleywood and a neighboring school. "Why can't we go to Pitkin and tell him what Honeyball did?" I asked. "Or tell our parents?"

"We're not supposed to sneak," said Pratt.

I knew that, of course. But surely there was a difference between sneaking on a schoolmate and sneaking on Honeyball? And surely the rule against sneaking didn't apply to a grown-up who violated the terms of his authority? I reminded Pratt that a previous headmaster had been dismissed, shortly before our time, for notorious and excessive cruelty to boys. But Pratt believed that to tell Pitkin might be more dangerous than useful. "Suppose he just gives Honeybags a ticking-off? Then Honeybags will have it in for us the rest of our time here."

"So let's tell our parents."

"We'd be up against the same thing, unless they just came and took us away from the school. And that's sort of a disgrace. My father's a major in the army, you know."

"But surely you don't *like* Earleywood?"

"No," Pratt said, and smiled. "But I might dislike another school a jolly sight worse." Then, turning his head: "Oh, look!"

A large, black, thin-waisted wasp had descended nearby on the grass and seized a small green caterpillar. It flew off, holding the caterpillar with its legs.

"I liked that," said Pratt. "Gave me a nice funny feeling."

"What sort?"

"Sort of tingling up and down inside."

I suspected that I knew the feeling he was talking about. But when I made it happen to me, lying on my stomach at night, it was a good deal stronger than a tingling up and down inside.

"I get the same feeling when I think about slaves," Pratt continued. "Do you?"

"No, not exactly about slaves." I thought back to a time when I was seven years old, and my mother had taken a cottage for the summer on the Devon coast. Although Con came with us, it was still the only time that I felt my mother and I had been really alone together.

I loved it while it lasted. We had a picnic on a hilltop, and my mother wrote a poem with the burnt end of a matchstick on a piece of thin paper. She placed it in a flat cigarette tin and buried it at the foot of a nearby pine tree. I went early to bed that summer evening. Sunlight still shone through the curtained windows, birds sang outside. Restless and hot, I felt an undefined sense of emptiness and longing.

Con had brought with us, as a present from Mameena, a children's encyclopedia. It stood on my bedside table. It contained full-page photographs of Greek and Roman marble statues, men, women, young girls and boys, many of them naked. They represented Adonis, Apollo, Venus, Cupid, a bearded man and his two naked sons struggling with a giant snake, a naked boyish St. Sebastian tied to a stake, his body pierced by arrows.

As I lay in bed I thought of St. Sebastian, then of Virginia, then of the white marble body of a girl in one of the photographs in the encyclopedia. Eyes closed, I turned on my stomach; and as I moved, the bodies became alive with movement in my head. I could almost touch them. I moved with their movement, thinking of Virginia, of touching her. A growing feeling of delight flowed all through me, then a hardening, and a sudden violent surge unknown or felt before.

Then calm and wonder.

What had happened, what had I done, was it even I who had done it? Was it usual? Wrong? Who should I ask or tell? I decided to ask or tell nobody, and wait to see if it happened again. Afterward, there was always a hollow somewhere, a constant unquenched yearning— although, much later, when a girl first held me tight and close, it seemed for a long moment of bliss as if that hollow had been filled forever. But forever was only a long moment.

Earlier, when I stayed at my aunt Viola Tree's London house, there was a Columbine doll in the room where I usually slept. It wore a stiff dusty dress, its face (including lips and eyelashes) was painted marble, and I would take it to bed with me, kiss it and stroke it to sleep.

Lying on the edge of the cricket field, I wondered if I should tell Pratt about the violent tingling sensation I could bring about at will, just by closing my eyes, turning on my stomach, moving rhythmically, and thinking about naked bodies close to me and touching them.

Halftime was called on the cricket field. It meant tea in the pavilion, so Pratt and I got up. I went to the lavatory in the school buildings and met Honeyball coming out, in open white shirt and cricketer's blazer.

"What's the score?" he asked.

Panic. I had no idea, and to have no idea of the score at halftime, when our school team was playing another team, was an almost punishable crime. "I think, sir," I said, "that Heatherdown's scored seventy runs for six wickets."

Honeyball's deep-socketed eyes stared at me. "Rot! They'd already scored eighty-six when I left the field five minutes ago."

For a moment I thought he was going to seize me by the hair and bash my skull against the nearest wall. But he merely shook his head. "Moffat, you're about the most useless individual in this entire school," he said, and walked briskly past me.

I considered the judgment he had just pronounced; and thought, in fairness to Honeyball, it probably contained a large grain of truth.

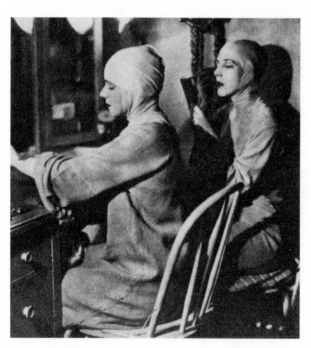

Iris (left) and Diana Cooper making up for their roles as the Nun and the Madonna during the American tour of The Miracle

. . .

During my first year at Earleywood, while my mother was touring America in *The Miracle* and I was staying with Mameena for the summer holidays, she wrote me a letter in the form of a poem:

> *In Cincinnati,*
> *Everyone asked us to a party,*
> *Because we act in The Miracle,*
> *And Americans are so hysterical;*
> *In Boston I lost and found all my week's profit.*
> *Here is a dollar of it.*
> *I wonder what you and Mameena*
> *Are having for deena.*
> *I eat octopus and buffalo and hyena,*
> *Cooked by Red Indians in a circus arena.*
> *I lasso my lunch and fish for my breakfast,*
> *Eat a whole whale but always have an egg first.*
> *I live on a frozen lake*
> *In a frozen house like a wedding cake.*
> *Then seven bears came up to sup,*
> *Each had his plate and cup,*
> *But nothing to eat for tea,*
> *Nothing to eat but me.*
> *The bears are gone, the ice is gory,*
> *That is the end of my story.*

At the end of my first year, my mother came back from America and I was summoned to meet her in the gloomy presence of Dr. Pitkin. Only the briefest of hugs would be right and proper in front of him. My mother wore a blue linen jacket, a man's jacket with silver buttons. In his heavy brown tweeds, Pitkin poured tea. I had never been in his drawing room before, only to his study for a reprimand.

My mother flashed me a look that said, what an awful place to meet. As a matter of form she asked if I was well, and as a matter of form I said that I was, thank you. Then, to my dismay, she asked Pitkin how I was getting on. He tapped out his pipe, and said in the solemn voice he used for preaching a sermon: "For the first two or three terms, I don't think he found it easy to get into the school spirit."

"Oh?"

"But that's not uncommon." Pitkin looked at me through his heavy bulldog glasses. "However, I'm told you're settling in a bit better this time, Moffat."

"Yes, sir."

"It's not easy for some boys at first." He turned back to my mother. "But I think he's starting to get into the school spirit now."

So that was it. You got into the spirit or fell by the wayside. There was no middle ground. The nature of the boy was immaterial, although if he fell by the wayside, it was entirely his fault. The school itself had nothing to do with it. Its only responsibility was to continue to be the school it had always been, and always should be. The school was immutable, the boy a malleable object. But this object, if made of anything approaching the right stuff, could be molded and polished so that it reflected well on the school. In a few cases it could even be polished brilliantly. Like Henderson.

Henderson shone. He shone at Latin and Greek and French, on the rugger and football fields. He was also extraordinarily nice. He later won a scholarship at Eton College. Later still, I heard, he committed suicide.

My mother and I went for a brief walk. I could have told her what I felt about the school in a hundred vivid ways. Instead, I told her very little. In a sense, to complain too much about school was to confess failure; and failure, in its multitude of greater or lesser forms, was apparently a possibility that a boy at an English prep school faced every day of his life. And as one of our masters had said, to complain unless you were successful was to be a worm.

Better, I thought, to stick it out quietly. After all, it wouldn't last forever. And my older cousins, who were now at Eton College, told me that by the time I went there, or wherever, I would most likely begin to *enjoy* school. Even so, in their urbane way, they threw off a few complaints about Eton. Certain aspects of it, they said with supercilious relish, were pretty much hell. But one got used to it.

"Darling, you aren't being bullied, are you?" my mother asked quietly as we walked through the drizzle.

"No. Compared to some of the boys, in fact, hardly at all."

"You seemed awfully timid in front of Dr. Pitkin. He doesn't beat you, does he?"

"No. I've really been jolly lucky up to now."

Later I would learn that luck was not the reason, and I would pay for it. But for the time being, I felt lucky.

"How's Daddy?" I asked.

"Very well. He sends you his love. Yes, he's really pretty well though he has his problems, poor darling." Then, more to herself than to me: "Money's such an awful thing. If only Curtis were a millionaire, he'd be the most generous man in the world!"

"Yes," I said.

"He was brought up to be rich, you see. That was his problem. His darling mother, who loves you so, inherited quite a fortune from her Graves father. But your grandfather Moffat spent it all, alas, squandered it on those Canadian gold mines. He had a black beard, Black Jack Moffat as they called him."

I didn't like the sound of my grandfather. "Is he still alive?"

"I believe so. I never met him, of course. They were divorced long before I met Curtis."

We walked in silence for a moment longer, then turned back. The winter evening was drawing in. "Who do you like best?" my mother suddenly asked. "Me or Daddy?"

I waited before answering, not because I had any doubt, but I thought the answer deserved a pause. "You," I said.

She nodded. "Yes, when they're young, boys often feel closer to their mothers. But when you're older, you'll get to know Curtis and become terribly fond of him."

We were approaching the long gravel drive that led to the school. I stared ahead without answering. Perhaps my mother sensed something in my posture. "I love Curtis and always will," she said very deliberately. "He's the most original man I know. And he has enormous warmth. There are three men I admire most of all, and Curtis will always be— always be . . ." Her voice trailed off.

"Who are the other men you admire?"

"I told you about Denys Finch Hatton."

"The one in Africa?"

"Yes, he'll be coming to England again soon, and wants to meet you."

"How do you know?"

"I told him you were interested in animals and insects and reptiles. He wants to tell you about the birds and insects and animals in Africa."

"He flies his own aeroplane there, doesn't he?"

"Oh yes. I wrote him a poem last year. It was called 'Wild Geese Are Flying.' "

"So who's the other man you admire?"

"Someone I met in California. An Austrian, very tall and a wonderful horseman. He was a mounted lancer in the Austrian army during the War."

From Mameena, and our history master Mr. Williams, I had heard bad things about the Germans and Austrians in the War, although more bad things about Germans than Austrians. Williams had adopted a sinister tone when he described our former German and Austrian enemies as "The Central Powers." It had a forbidding ring.

"His name is Friedrich and he gave me this jacket. It comes from Austria and its buttons are old silver coins."

I examined them closely.

"By the way," my mother said, "would you like to hear the poem I wrote for Denys? It's quite short."

By then my mother had published two books of poetry, and although she normally had a beautiful voice, she recited this poem in an affected way that I didn't care for. But I remember its opening lines:

> I saw gray geese flying over the flatlands
> Wild geese vibrant in the high air—
> Unswerving from horizon to horizon
> With their soul stiffened out in their throats . . .

In spite of her affected voice, I liked "Wild Geese" and asked my mother to say it again. Then we reached the front steps to the school, and I asked: "Will we be spending the Christmas holidays together?"

Of course, she said, we'd be spending a good deal of the holiday time together at Mameena's. Then, as her taxi was waiting, she hugged me close and left.

I went indoors, dreading the bedlam gaiety of the dormitory, its bullies and show-offs, the deceptively placid face of Miss Cope, and the eventual darkness.

From the small wooden bracket that held my "things" above my bed, I had hung a tiny Stars and Stripes. It was a talisman of sorts. None of the boys begrudged me my flag. They were curious about foreign places, and often asked me about America. But tonight the subject was my mother.

Cooper said: "We were all at the window and got a good look at her kissing you, Moffat."

Davis said: "Oo-er!" And gave his famous smirk. "She's not bad looking but she had on a pretty funny sort of jacket. It's for a man, isn't it?"

"No, it's an Austrian jacket."

"A whatta?"

"An Austrian jacket. Haven't you ever seen one before?"

"Never."

Lyon said: "Then snubs to you," and Davis went back to brushing his teeth. Pratt, who was reading *The Boy's Own Paper* in bed, looked up and said: "Tell us some more about New York, Moffat."

Other voices: "Yes, come on!"

I told them about the Automat with its pink lighting on Jell-O and pies, the taxis that raced up and down Park Avenue, the drugstores that sold club sandwiches with tiers of crisp bacon and chicken and mayonnaise that dripped from each one. All these things were completely unknown to English boys, like the wild turtles crossing the sandy roads of Long Island that I also told them about.

They listened until Miss Cope entered the dormitory in her starched uniform, put her hand on the light switch and stared at us, waiting for silence. It fell instantly. If not, she'd have marched straight to the offending boy, stripped down his pajama trousers and beaten his behind with a leather strap.

Tonight there was no offending boy. She switched off the lights and closed the door.

But that kind of discipline awaits a safe pretext to be defied, and most of us were adept at providing one: hurled anonymously through the darkness, a slipper (preferably someone else's) would create an uproar that brought a furious Cope back to the dormitory. Switching on the lights again, she demanded to know who had made all the noise.

"Someone threw a slipper, Miss!"

"Let me see it!"

"Here, Miss."

She held up the slipper. "Whose is it?" Silence. "Come on, quick now!"

"Mine, Miss. But I'd lost it. And anyway, I was asleep."

Cope: "You're lying, Maddox."

"I'm not, Miss. Honestly. Word of honor."

She stared. "One more sound out of any of you, and the whole dormitory goes straight down to Dr. Pitkin!"

Lights out. A faint giggle from somewhere in the darkness. But no slipper thrown again. Obviously a better pretext had to be found, and next summer I found it.

Cockchafers, a species of scarab beetle, are seldom seen in England anymore. But in those days they used to fly in great numbers at dusk, with a sound like a swarm of giant bees. In the late afternoon, when I tapped the branches of trees, sleeping beetles would fall into the can I held out to collect them. After lights out in the dormitory, I would open the can and cast one beetle after another across the room. They instantly took wing and started to buzz clumsily against walls, beds, ceiling. Uproar, of course, and Cope entering in a rage. But the cry, "Cockchafers, Miss!" was undeniably true.

Cope cast an angry glance at the open windows, enveloped a beetle or two in a towel, threw them out and closed the door.

I opened my can again. Another cockchafer, another moment of uproar in the otherwise dull summer of 1930.

The following November I was awakened from the claws of a dream. In the dream, I was bound with my back to a blinding, burning sun, bent and twisted against its fiery surface, while a sickening sound like the blare of a horn assaulted my ears. The head matron, Miss Jenkins, was hitting my face and throat.

"How dare you make such a noise?"

I tried to speak, but my throat felt on fire. She slapped my neck again, and I was astonished. Even Miss Jenkins, with a black velvet ribbon around her neck, and famous for cruelty, was not given to gestures like that.

What had I done?

"Shouting out in the middle of the night for water! Woke up Miss Cope and half the dormitory! You're a very naughty and selfish and spoiled little boy, and I've a good mind to give you a good spanking!"

I tried to speak.

Jenkins, with her white powdered face, stared down at me. Was the burning in my throat due to her slaps? Surely not. Then why had she slapped the part of my body that hurt so much?

Her hand touched my forehead, followed a moment later by the cold hand of Cope, who had just arrived at my bedside. "Anyway," said Jenkins in a slightly more gentle tone, "go back to sleep now and I don't want to hear another sound. All right?"

I nodded. The light hurt my eyes until Jenkins and Cope were gone, and darkness fell. Soon I was bound again to the burning sun, smaller, harder and brighter than the real sun, twisting slowly to the same hideous blare of a horn. I supposed I must have cried out again, because Jenkins and Cope were back at my bedside at break of dawn, angry but less accusing.

"Come on, get up, quick now!"

While some of the boys watched, I got out of bed, dazed and unsteady. In the dispensary, a hand sticks a thermometer in my mouth, then I'm laid gently to bed in the sickroom with its green walls, single naked lightbulb burning overhead, and a glass of water on the bedside table. I fall asleep, until I'm woken by the doctor from Ascot with his ginger moustache, and a thermometer is stuck in my mouth again.

"We're going to take a swab. Open again."

I had never heard of a swab, except in the sense of swabbing the decks of a ship. And in fact, I thought, the wooden stick with its ball of cotton-wool did resemble a miniature version of the kind of thing used by gunners to moisten and tamp the guns in Lord Nelson's day.

Days and nights passed in fever and dreams. But now Cope would sit beside me, even offer water, and miraculously, as I got better, barley water and lemonade. Was she perhaps a nice person after all?

"You've been quite ill, you know."

"What was it?"

I thought it strange that neither Lyon nor Pratt had come to see me, only Pitkin, the doctor, another doctor from Ascot, Jenkins and Cope. And now Cope wouldn't answer my question, only said that my throat had been very sore.

My last day in bed, Lyon came to see me. "We were all told not to make any noise below the sickroom," he said, "because Moffat was up there dying."

I felt suddenly important. "What was I supposed to be dying of?"

"Didn't they tell you? You had diphtheria."

"What's that?"

"Haven't the slightest. But that's what they said you had. And you missed some pretty awful maths classes with Honeyball. So if I were you," Lyon gave the peculiarly sickly grin that he reserved for conspiracy or undeserved good fortune, "I'd consider myself lucky." Still grinning, he asked: "Didn't your parents tell you what you had?"

"I haven't spoken to them."

"I expect Pitkin wanted to keep it a secret."

"Why?"

Another grin. "Typical Earleywood."

If Pitkin had not told my parents, I thought, in one way it would have been "typical," in another way unlikely. But I never found out whether he did or not.

Early one evening, my mother arrived unexpectedly for a visit, accompanied by one of her admirers, Ian Campbell-Gray; and we went to have dinner at the Berystede Arms, "grandest" and dreariest of the nearby inns. Ian was the champion fencer of England and (equally to my mother's fancy) a painter. He was also a man of exquisite manners, quiet charm and high temper—qualities, as my mother told me later, sometimes at odds with..

Ian had taken her to a party, and at one point sensed that the host had been less than polite to her. He preferred not to make a public scene, but waited until they were ready to leave. After saying an icily correct goodbye on the doorsteps and murmuring, "Thank you *so much*," he took the hand their host held out, pressed it with his fencer's thumb and fractured it.

As Ian was also a bon vivant, wine, brandy and coffee flowed very freely that evening, and when I reminded my mother for the second time that I was supposed to be back at school by 7:30, it was almost 8:30. Unconventional though they were, my parents shared with many others a vague contempt for the school system coupled with a strong desire to see their son do well within the system. At the same time, my mother showed a blithe indifference to school regulations. "Don't worry, darling," she said again. "I'll tell Pitkin it was our fault."

We returned to the darkened school at 10 p.m., and rang the doorbell. An assistant master eventually opened the door, drew me into the dark hallway, and propelled me abruptly up the polished wooden stairs to the dormitory, where all the boys were asleep.

A few days later I was summoned to Pitkin's study and informed that my conduct was unsatisfactory. Specifically, I had been reported for talking in the dormitory just as Miss Cope switched out the lights. When I said I could explain it, he offered me a choice: Accept two strokes of the cane now, or take the chance that he'd find my explanation inadequate. In which case, six strokes.

I accepted the two, hardly a fearsome punishment.

"Knowing boys as I do," Pitkin intoned in his hollow voice, "I think you're wise." And reached for the cane.

At the start of Latin class a week later, Pitkin gazed at me balefully. "Moffat, I understand you can't take your punishment like a gentleman."

"I don't know what you mean, sir."

"I think you know very well."

Truthfully, I did not. And only learned much later that my parents enrolled me at Earleywood on condition that I must not be given corporal punishment. But after Pitkin's two strokes of the cane, I had written my father in a purely incidental way that, among other things, I had finally been "whacked." Although I wrote in no spirit of complaint, the damage had been done. From that day forward I was made to feel like a spoiled and coddled mother's boy, a kind of "untouchable," so tainted by privilege that, morally speaking, I wasn't worth touching anyway.

The staff had been informed of my parents' prohibition, but it didn't stop them from hitting me when they saw fit. On occasion, I suspect it may even have provoked them to harsher treatment, as I became the only boy at the school to receive a blow on the jaw hard enough to send me crashing into the row of desks behind him, and falling to the floor.

In those days there was a degree of anti-American feeling in England, caused by jealousy of America's rise to the status of world power after 1918, as well as a feeling that because it entered the War "late," it had no right to boast, as some Americans did, that their country had "won."

Our military drill master, absurdly named Sergeant Buckle, also taught (compulsory) boxing. He once told us during physical training that we had better get used to drill, because "in ten years' time you'll be walking around America shooting Americans." This struck me, and most of the other boys, as only marginally more fatuous than many other pronouncements by our masters; and besides, Buckle was not even a master. But thin Mr. Williams, of course, was a bona fide schoolmaster, and as he sat at his desk a few days later, he drew his threadbare jacket more closely around his midriff and suddenly proclaimed: "After the last War we had two and a half million men under arms, and we could have taken America by the scruff of the neck and—"

I hit the ceiling and said loudly: "Excuse me, sir, I don't think you could!"

Silence. Nothing like this had ever been heard before.

"Moffat, come here!"

I got to my feet. So did Williams, and as I approached, he delivered that blow to the jaw. After I picked myself up, I saw a fleck of foam at the corner of Williams's mouth. He never looked at me during the rest of the period, and I could sense his unease.

Technically, only Pitkin was supposed to mete out corporal punishment, although the regulation never seemed to deter Honeyball. But at the end of class, Williams followed me into the corridor.

"Moffat. I'm, er, sorry about that."

"Sir."

"I understand your feelings about your country."

"Thank you, sir." I felt the corrupt symbiosis of master-pupil-good-fellowship starting to form.

"On the other hand, Moffat, you know we just can't have boys flatly contradicting us in class."

"No, sir."

"So I hope you understand my position, Moffat. And I'm, er, sorry if I went a bit far."

"I understand perfectly, sir."

"No hard feelings, then?"

"No, sir, none at all, sir."

"Thank you, Moffat."

By that time I felt sorry for Williams, and in some faintly odious way, grateful to him. He had proved how easy it was for masters to become boys, and vice versa.

A single figure stood in calm contrast to Williams, Honeyball, Pitkin, Cope and the others: tall, gray, thin, awkward, sixtyish and scholarly Miss Sandwith. Full lips trembling, eyes averted, she spoke to the classroom in a shy cultured voice and held it in respect. Miss Sandwith taught (when she chose, which was not always) classes in Greek, Latin and, occasionally, English poetry. She had an aloofness that added mystery to the rumor that in some way she was a "partner" of Dr. Pitkin, although she seemed too unworldly for that.

Her personality was withdrawn to the point of self-extinction. She could show pleasure without ever smiling, and gave the impression of appearing out of nowhere, out of a hole. Although I wondered at her calm and gentle reasonableness, I couldn't help being reminded, against my will, of those gaunt, dry spiders in the dusty greenhouse at Binfield Priory, my grandmother's country house. Yet there was no trace of ferocity in Miss Sandwith, whose kindness and modesty (qualities otherwise unknown at Earleywood) made her the only member of the staff from whom one had nothing to fear.

Her only boast (or, more accurately, half-mumbled admission) gave Miss Sandwith a connection, as wispy as her gray hair, to an obscure event in British history. She was related to one Captain Sandwith, a nineteenth-century medical officer and the sole survivor of a British expedition against Afghanistan. An engraving of the good doctor, inscribed with his name, hung in one of the school corridors. It showed him arriving alone and tattered at the gate of Kandahar, head bent in exhaustion, seated upon an equally weary horse.

Miss Sandwith had another less obscure but more curious connection to fame. She was a close friend of Miss Moberly, who had collaborated with her friend Miss Jourdain on a best-selling book called *An Adventure*. It described how they went walking in the park at Versailles in 1901, and encountered the ghosts of Marie Antoinette and her court.

An Adventure had created excitement, controversy and skepticism of a high order, especially since both spinsters were respected members of academia, and Miss Moberly was the Bishop of Salisbury's daughter. Although their integrity was never in doubt, their tale was strongly doubted. I used to see Sandwith and Moberly walking closely together in the school grounds, equally tall, wearing similar hats, dry as pressed flowers. And Sandwith herself, remote and revered but not loved, seemed to me in a way as ghostly as Moberly's "vision" at Versailles.

Miss Jourdain, whom I once glimpsed many years later in London, was a more solid presence. By then she had met the formidable and formidably gifted novelist, Ivy Compton-Burnett, and become her companion for life.

Apart from Sandwith, the holidays provided the only other respite from "normal" school life. I remember them most of all for my enormous feeling of relief at waking up late on that first morning, in a bedroom instead of a dormitory, and for the dread I felt on the day the holidays ended.

Summer holiday memories during those earlier school years: the dunes at Brancaster swept by a dry wind, and the sound of curlews over the marshes, and the calling of nannies to my cousins, the children of Cory-Wrights and Parsons, to come out of the water and have their tea. Winter holiday memory: Con and I searching for shrimps or shells in pools of cold rippling water at Littlehampton, where my aunt Viola had rented a house on the Sussex coast. Spring holiday memory: riding over the Downs with my mother, who had rented a house at nearby Rottingdean, where we played word games with Viola, Ian Campbell-Gray and the once-celebrated-now-forgotten author Maurice Baring. Out of a possible twenty-six words in the game, Baring managed to squeeze only two from his exquisite vocabulary, and uttered them in a high-pitched Bloomsbury voice: "mollycoddle" and "namby-pamby."

During another winter, at Mameena's house, she received my mother late on a New Year's Day. "How was the Chelsea Arts Ball, darling?"

"Absolute heaven."

"How late did you stay?"

"Till past dawning, I fear."

"And who did you dance with?"

My mother started singing the refrain of a sinister medieval ballad. "'And who did you dance with, Lord Randall, my son? Oh, what did you dine on, my honey-man?'" Then, answering in the words of the ballad: "'On stickles and eels, mother! Oh, make my bed soon, for I am aweary and would fain lie down!'"

Then she smiled her open, generous smile. "Who did I dance with? Well, with Ian, and Dick Wyndham [another painter-athlete], and Napier Alington [a bisexual baron] and—a multitude!"

But I could only think of the cruel ballad, in which Lord Randall is poisoned either by his sweetheart or his mother—I was never sure which—for the sake of his castles and lands. My mother told me that she believed Lord Randall's mother did it, to prevent his sweetheart from getting her hands on them first.

When I was six years old there had been an accident, or mishap, and my mother had caused it. She went very pale when the doctor said that if the rope had been drawn only a fraction tighter, it might have been a very serious business indeed. He had said this supposedly out of earshot, but I heard it all the same.

We were playing "pirates," my mother and I. She had woven a red scarf around her head and placed a noose of coarse rope around my neck. Then she ran to a nearby tree and started winding the rope around it as she bound me to the tree trunk. We were laughing, but as I struggled to free my arms from the rope, it suddenly tightened around my neck. I gestured frantically with my hands and arms, but my mother was still laughing, pulling the rope tighter.

Then she saw my scarlet face, ran over, and loosened the rope. The skin around my neck was scorched and raw, and a ring of yellowish scabs developed there over the next few days. There was no one more tender and gentle in her actions than my mother, I doubt if she ever struck another person or an animal in her life, and even though I was only six, I sensed what the incident would cost her.

Very little was actually said about it. Mameena had sent for the doctor, who bandaged my neck with gauze and ointment. Emotionally, the accident had cost me nothing. But because I was so aware of my mother's innocence and kindness, her sometimes distant yet constant way of loving, I could afford long afterward to remind myself, playfully, of the sudden astonished feel of that rope when my mother sang, " 'Lord Randall, my son,' " the son who was perhaps being poisoned by his mother's hand.

John Raynor, a journalist on the *Daily Express,* said to me years later: "Your mother is a romantic, and romantic love idealizes, but it's not always warm."

When my mother moved away from my father, my loyalties were divided, mainly because I could tell he wanted her back, even though he said little about it. But although I began to understand him more, my feelings for my mother remained no less strong.

As I grew older, my loyalties at school were also divided. What did the school, and the British Empire that its attitude echoed, stand for? The question would grow more important as the 1930s moved closer to an end, and to another war. The British Empire was something toward which all of us, even I who was only half-British, could feel loyalty. But, unlike the other boys, I felt my loyalty waver in the face of flagrant injustice at Earleywood.

Injustice at a British prep school was part of a system that the British Empire ultimately embodied, in theory and practice. At one end of the spectrum of Empire stood the proud mass of red on global maps, the exotic postage stamps from Sarawak, Sierra Leone, Tanganyika. I was proud of my collection of stamps from these colonies, today (like so many others) no longer red on global maps: the first a member of the independent Federated Malay States, and the other two independent republics, with Tanganyika renamed Tanzania. When you were twelve, the British Empire was something to be proud of. It was the biggest empire in the world, the biggest the world had ever seen, even if a tiny silk Stars and Stripes seemed to contradict this by drooping from the wooden bracket above my bed.

But at the other end of the spectrum stood Honeyball, dogmatic and stupid drill sergeants, and the starchy army colonels so despised and wickedly mimicked by my mother. I had also seen the cartoons of my great-uncle Max Beerbohm, that so delighted my mother and her friends Augustus John, John Maynard Keynes, Lytton Strachey.

And on the evening of the day that I had watched Honeyball bang Leese's head on the scarred wooden table, I had gone to the small library adjoining Dr. Pitkin's study, taken the *Encyclopedia Britannica* from its cabinet, and opened it at a section devoted to a history of the USA. Not long before, I had heard Mr. Williams refer in class to the defeat of Lord Cornwallis's British forces at the hands of the American rebels under George Washington.

That was nearly the extent of my knowledge of the War of Independence until I opened the *Encyclopedia,* and what I read thrilled me enormously. Here were the starchy, stuffy British colonels and drill sergeants being overwhelmed by a band of freedom-loving citizens. Here was the battle of Saratoga, the Green Mountain Boys, Valley Forge. As the story unfolded to its triumphant conclusion with Cornwallis surrendering at Yorktown, it seemed almost too good and too apt to be true. I had moved on to Benjamin Franklin negotiating peace with the British when Pitkin entered the room and asked what the dickens I thought I was doing, taking down his *Britannica* without permission.

To answer truthfully I'd have said that I was immersed in a story of rebellion against *him*. In fact I said, "Reading history, sir."

"Well, Moffat, when you wish to consult my *Britannica* in future, you will ask my permission first." His tone became even more sepulchral than usual. "The way boys handle books, they become dog-eared in no time. I don't want that to happen to my *Britannica*. Its pages are made of rice paper, you know."

"Yes, sir." I closed his *Britannica* and replaced it on the shelf of the cabinet with glass doors. Pitkin turned the key and pocketed it.

But it was too late to stop me from imagining, after lights out in the dormitory, that I was in a line of skirmishers at Lexington in 1775. And during the next school holiday, I asked my father if our American ancestors had fought in the War of Independence. They certainly had, he told me. Then I asked when our forebears first came to America, and my father found the date, 1699, in a book called "Moffat Genealogy." It also recorded that our direct American forebear, John Moffat, became the thirteenth student to graduate from Princeton sixty years later.

Back at school, I was armed for rebellion. Yet my heart melted again in chapel when we sang of England's green and pleasant land, of chariots of fire and arrows of desire. The loyalty of boys is easily won and lost, regained and seduced again.

After lights out some weeks later, I led the fourteen boys of our dormitory, all wearing pajamas and dressing gowns, down the wide staircase to the double doors of the dining room. I opened them without knocking, and found the entire staff at dinner, with Dr. Pitkin at the head of the table. Looks of speechless outrage greeted our sudden appearance.

Honeyball leaped to his feet. "What the devil d'you think you're all doing?"

I explained that one of the boys had just been unfairly and harshly punished, for no reason at all, in the captains' dormitory. There had been too many cases of unjust punishment recently, I added, and we had come to protest.

A long moment of silence. The eyes of the staff were fixed with a guarded expression on Pitkin. And when I look back on the incident, it seems certain that he was thinking of the consequences of expelling an entire dormitory from the school.

When he spoke, he sounded calm. "You will all return to your dormitory this instant or be caned on the spot."

I hesitated, then asked, "But, sir, what about all the unjust punishments that—"

Honeyball cut me off with a roar. "Didn't you hear what the headmaster said?"

"Yes, sir."

"Then return to your dormitory *at once!*"

"Sir."

"Moffat!" said Pitkin. "Are you responsible for this?"

"We all are, sir."

"I'll see you in my study tomorrow, Moffat."

Although his tone didn't sound very threatening, as we trooped upstairs I felt that we had all failed. But Nathan Minor pointed out that at least there had been no immediate expulsions or canings. In fact, as I learned later, our demonstration had caused a few tremors. I was not called to see Dr. Pitkin next day, and for the rest of that term there were no more beatings in the captains' dormitory or even, so far as I know, by Honeyball.

A great change, a sudden leap, takes place toward the end of one's last term at an English prep school. The four and a half years that lie behind seem a disproportionately long and painful period of one's life; and they signal the beginning of a kind of Dark Ages of one's later childhood and adolescence. One has become less of a person, more of an object, more fearful, more rigid, less confident, less happy, less loved, a hostage to sudden fate, irrational and arbitrary rule, torture.

In retrospect those years still seem like an eternal winter. But in that final summer we experienced a completely new feeling. Pratt, Lyon, Somervell, Jacobson and I, now in the captains' dormitory, decided there would be no more bullying of boys there, no more punishments; and as far as our masters were concerned, we were now grown boys on our way to a real and future world.

The masters we were about to leave behind became the prisoners we had once felt ourselves to be. They no longer seemed fearful, with the power to threaten, cane or expel. In a matter of months they had been transformed, almost invisibly, into human beings: some bright, some cruel, some foolish, some weak or even kind. And so, along with them, we had come to resemble human beings ourselves, with a vocabulary equal to theirs, and in some of the words and expressions we used, more free-spirited.

David Jacobson had signed his end-of-term essay, "Yours truly disillusioned, D. Jacobson."

On the last day of school in that summer of 1931, I sat next to an unusually silent Mr. Williams.

"You're very taciturn today, sir," I observed.

He gave me a questioning smile. "What on earth does that mean, Moffat?"

Then Mr. Griffith asked: "Where are you going for the holidays, Moffat?" His worn tweed jacket smelt as usual of pipe tobacco smoke and boiled sweets.

"First to Austria, sir."

"To *Austria?*"

"Yes, sir."

"Well, Moffat, you're a lucky dog, that's all I can say."

"Sir," I responded, deliberately gracious.

A few days later Virginia's father, Alan Parsons, was having a whiskey and soda in my father's flat at Fitzroy Square. "So you're off to Salzburg for the summer," he said in his husky asthmatic voice.

"Yes, to a castle about thirty-five miles away."

"It'll be absolute heaven, I imagine."

Since *The Miracle* my mother had become friends with Max Rein-

Max Reinhardt's palace, Schloss Leopoldskron, in Salzburg

The library at Schloss Leopoldskron, where Iris auditioned

hardt, and visited him several times at Schloss Leopoldskron, his baroque palace in Salzburg. She had first met Eleonora von Mendelssohn there, and formed a mutually admiring friendship with the pale, romantically beautiful actress whose father headed the grand and famous von Mendelssohn family of bankers. My mother had confided that Eleonora was in love with Reinhardt, but her love, alas, had not been returned.

Reinhardt had blazingly dark eyes and a slow, resonant voice. Short and proud of bearing, he always dominated the company around him, and his ironic wit produced much laughter, as well as a few tears in Eleonora's case.

I was constantly looking at Eleonora's face. I didn't yet know, or know how to use, the word "vulnerable." Had I known, my search for a word to describe her face would have ended there. Reinhardt's elder son Gottfried, who became a good friend, once described Eleonora as "valiant to the point of self-destruction" in the way that she fell unhappily in love time and time again. She owned a castle, Schloss Kammer, on nearby Lake Attersee, and we had been invited there for what became a wet and in some ways dismal summer.

My father had predicted, correctly as it turned out, that because of the excessive rain, 1931 would be a year without vintages. And as I listened uneasily to the grown-ups talking, I learned that it was also a year of financial turbulence.

"What's wrong, Daddy?" I asked.

"We're going off the gold standard."

I didn't like the sound of that, even though I knew my father had more immediate cause for financial anxiety than anything so far beyond his reach as gold. Or, whatever that might be, its standard.

Max Reinhardt made a dry joke by calling the situation *"Die Sparkasse Volkabruck,"* which meant that the savings at the nearby railroad junction of Volkabruck might be a little unsteady. When everyone laughed, it summed up the castle's light-hearted attitude to signs of the gathering storm.

Schloss Kammer stood below a range of high mountains on a promontory at one end of Lake Attersee. Once a gigantic medieval fortress, it was still entered through a vast courtyard with a fountain. Eleonora was presently married to a Hungarian cavalry officer, Emmerich von Jessensky. (Her previous husband had been the sexually impotent Swiss pianist, Edwin Fisher; after Jessensky, her next would be the Austrian movie star Rudolf Forster, who played Mackie Messer in Pabst's film of *The Threepenny Opera;* her fourth and last, in America, the Russian-born actor Martin Kosleck, who played Goebbels in no less than three anti-Nazi Hollywood movies during World War II.) Jessensky attributed his prematurely white hair to the two days he spent floating in the Adriatic after an Allied airman shot him off his horse in 1917. He was tense, courteous and formal, with lips so thin as to appear nonexistent, and an infrequent smile that, according to my mother and other women who admired him, betrayed a streak of cruelty in his nature.

Jessensky, I soon learned, expected men younger than himself to live up to his own high standard of courtesy and so-called "exquisite" manners. Cruel or not, he belonged to a now-vanished world that gave him the right to slap the face of a young man who failed to stand up when a woman entered the drawing room of his apartment in

Eleonora's castle. It was a dark room with barred windows overlooking Lake Attersee. The walls were hung with huge dark paintings of fish caught in the lake a hundred years earlier: fish so fierce and enormous, with underslung jaws and sharp protruding teeth, that they resembled extinct prehistoric creatures.

I dreaded the idea that such fish might still be lurking in the depths of the lake, and asked Jessensky (whom I had been told to address as "Herr Rittmeister," meaning Captain of Cavalry) if he thought it possible. He did, although he believed that none of the biggest, darkest and fiercest specimens had been caught there for at least fifty years.

My father and Constance both stayed at Schloss Kammer, also a Scottish nanny engaged to look after the latest addition (in a manner of speaking) to our family. My new brother Christian, whom I met for the first time that summer, was three years old. I only learned much later that Friedrich Ledebur, my mother's Austrian friend who had given her the jacket with silver buttons, was Christian's father; and that my own father had gracefully acquiesced in the fiction that the boy was his own.

At the time, then, I attached no great significance that a giant of a man with silver coins for buttons, and rings of turquoise and silver on his fingers, was a frequent visitor to the castle. Count Friedrich, considered by many to be the handsomest man in Europe, had dark wavy hair, skin that years in the South Seas had turned the color of mahogany, and eyes blue as the turquoise on his rings and silver belt. He had a deep, resonant, almost echoing voice. He sang songs, Austrian peasant songs and also American cowboy songs that he learned when he worked as a horse-trainer on ranches in the Far West. My mother had first met him at a party given by Elinor Glyn, when the tour of *The Miracle* reached Los Angeles.

Friedrich described Tahiti to me, the crunching sounds of land crabs crushed under foot at night, the smell of their rotting bodies in the tropical heat of the following morning. And I remembered, when I first met him, that my mother had once sent me a complete coconut, shell and all, from Tahiti. French postage stamps had been stuck on the shiny brown shell with my address written in black ink. When I asked Friedrich if he and my mother had been in Tahiti at the same time, he cleared his throat resonantly—in a way that I later became familiar

LEFT: *At Schloss Kammer, Lake Attersee, summer 1931: Michael Erleigh, Virginia, and Ivan*
BELOW: *Summer 1937, Schloss Kammer on Lake Attersee: Ivan with Randolph Churchill*

In the garden of Schloss Kammer, left to right: Raimund von Hofmannstal, Friedrich in shorts, Ivan, Rudolf Kommer (Max Reinhardt's assistant), Iris in chair, and Eleonora von Mendelssohn in chaise longue

with—and mumbled something evasive that began with "No," and ended by seeming to imply "Yes."

With children, even the most apparently innocent things have a way of going wrong, for reasons not always clear. In the early evening, Constance and I occasionally walked to the crude little wooden cinema in the nearby lakeside village of Seewalchen. Once we saw a German movie without subtitles, and although I already knew some German, it was often difficult to follow. (In fact, it was about white slavery.) About two-thirds of the way through, Constance decided it was time to leave, and back at the castle, I was sent to the great dining room to say goodnight.

Eleonora and "Herr Rittmeister" were having coffee with my mother and father, and about eight other guests.

"Did you see a nice film?" my father asked.

"Not really. We left before the end."

"Why?"

"Con said it was boring. It was, actually."

Herr Rittmeister asked: "What was this film called?"

"Das Weg Nach Buenos Aires," I said. *"The Road to Buenos Aires."*

Everyone's attention was suddenly focused on me.

My father gave one of his short puffs of laughter. "What's wrong?" I asked.

"Nothing, darling," my mother said. "Off to bed, sleep well, see you in the morn."

Eleonora beckoned me over and gave me an impulsive hug. It was not only welcome, but seemed like a hug of forgiveness. As I walked to my room, I felt the same hollow unease that overcame me so often at my grandmother's house: a sense of having proved myself a fool, a failure in the company of older and wiser people.

My mother and I used to take walks in the green rounded hills above our end of the lake. I had a toy glider to fly from higher up, an expensive German thing with a short wooden body and wings six feet wide. But it didn't glide well in the still, drizzling air.

Far below, we could see Nanny with little Christian along the edge of the lake.

"Why did you name him Christian?" I asked.

"Because I loved the character of Christian in *Pilgrim's Progress*," my mother said.

"And why did you call me Ivan?"

"I was reading *The Brothers Karamazov* before you were born. I loved it, particularly the brother called Ivan, so that's why I decided to call you Ivan if you were a boy."

"You wanted me to be a boy?"

"Yes, and knew you would be, too."

"Did you know Christian would be a boy?"

"I wasn't sure, but hoped so." She looked thoughtful for a moment. "Sometimes the first-born is jealous of the second-born, but you mustn't be."

Her remark irritated me. It had never occurred to me to be jealous; but now, suddenly, she had put the idea into my head, and it would be all too natural.

"Nature takes care that a mother has strong feelings about her second-born," my mother continued, "because she wants to make sure it's not neglected or overshadowed by the first-born."

Now this I mistrusted. Her tone had become too consciously "lyrical." I said firmly: "I am *not* jealous of him."

My mother laughed.

"Why are you laughing?"

"Your tone of voice reminded me of a few years ago, when I was in bed one morning, writing, and told you to leave the room. And you said, 'You can *ask* me to leave the room, but you can't *order* me to leave it.' Remember?"

"No. Absolutely not."

"Anyway, I liked you for saying it. And I never asked you to leave the room again. Nor, may I say, will I ever ask you again."

I smiled.

Friedrich rode up and dismounted. Leather jacket with wide lapels and round silver buttons. A flower in his hand, which he gave to my mother.

"It's lovely," she said. "But a little past its prime, I fear."

"True," Friedrich said. "I picked it for you yesterday. What was it you once said? 'Lily da Festa smell far worse than weeds'?"

She laughed. "Ulan!" (She sometimes called him Ulan because he had served in the Austro-Hungarian army's famous cavalry regiment of that name in 1918.) "It's 'lilies that fester smell far worse than weeds.'"

"I thought there was a film star called Lily da Festa, and you meant that like old flowers, she smelled far worse than weeds." Friedrich looked at me and grinned. "You see, it's my bad English, always."

"When Ulan says something that's not too bright," my mother confided in a stage whisper, "he always says it's his bad English."

"Iris!" He moved to grab her, but she eluded him, and he turned to me again. "You mother always, always tease!"

"I know," I said.

And then she looked at Friedrich, kissed the flower, and threaded its long stem through the buttonhole of her Austrian jacket. Friedrich put his gloved hand against her cheek. (He wore embroidered chamois gloves from Santa Fe.) He bent and kissed her hand, mounted his horse and rode off at a gentle canter toward the woods.

"Where does he live?" I asked.

"Sometimes in castles, sometimes in caravans."

"But where is he staying now?"

"At a nearby inn in Schnortling." She looked thoughtful again. "I think I prefer the caravans to the castles."

At teatime my father was playing chess with another Count named Berchem. When my father played chess with me, he had a way of gently nudging a piece into position with his forefinger, instead of picking it up and placing it on a square. This irritated me, especially when he made a winning move. Now, I noticed, he did not move his pieces like that with Count Berchem—but soon checkmated him.

Berchem laughed and offered my father one of his Austrian cigars. My father felt obliged to respond by offering Berchem one of his precious Cuban cigars. Although Berchem relished the exchange, and my father confided later that he did not, he was careful not to catch my eye during the exchange. He was not the sort of man who winked. He gave, and gave with apparent pleasure, even when he didn't feel it.

That first summer at Schloss Kammer, I had no way of foreseeing dark years ahead for some of its present and future guests. (For my father, death from cancer at sixty-two. For Max Reinhardt, after the

Nazis came to power, exile in New York, then Hollywood, a mainly frustrating career in both places, and a fatal stroke in 1943. For his assistant, Rudolf Kommer, a fatal heart attack in his New York hotel room only a few months earlier. For Rex Whistler, a German bullet in the head shortly after D-Day. For Eleonora, the castle's owner, exile in New York, a fourth and last unhappy marriage, morphine addiction, suicide in 1953.) But even in 1931 the castle seemed to possess a pervasively ominous power and exotic gloom of its own.

As for the towering mountains at the far end of the lake, Con and I, often accompanied by my mother, used to take the graceful white steamer to the little town they overshadowed. From there we set out on strenuous hikes toward the highest peak, seven thousand feet above, and stopped at small inns on the way. Con and my mother drank coffee with a topping of thick whipped cream, and I sipped raspberry syrup and soda through a straw. At the last inn, I left them and walked the final mile to the summit alone. On the way down, my mother's brave high spirits soothed leg muscles that ached to the verge of collapse. Back on the steamer at dusk, looking at the cloud-covered peak we had climbed, I experienced something that I very rarely felt: an exhilarating sense of accomplishment. My mother, Constance, and I had become companions in adventure, and although Dr. Pitkin had often pronounced me rotten at games, for once I had not been found wanting.

At the end of that summer, my mother and I went to stay with two of her closest friends, Alice Astor and Raimund von Hofmannsthal, who had rented a villa at Celigny, near Geneva. A year later they would take over half of Schloss Kammer, and then, like so many others when the Nazis came to power, leave for America. Raimund was the son of Hugo, poet and librettist of Richard Strauss's *Rosenkavalier;* Alice (the daughter of Viscount Astor by his first wife, Ava, who later married the "Picturesque Peer," Lord Ribblesdale) was still legally married to Prince Serge Obolensky. One of the more exotic heiress-beauties of her day, she had a pearl-white skin, dark hair with a marked widow's peak, arched and pointed eyebrows above eyes that slanted downward, mouth that drooped slightly at the corners. There was an aura of sorrow about her face, even when Raimund's wit, youth, charm, and good looks provoked her to frequent and (I guessed) unaccustomed laughter.

She was gentle and kind with me, but I was instantly enchanted by Raimund's high spirits and joy of life. He was the first grown-up to treat me as an equal, with no trace of condescension. He responded to laughter as eagerly as he caused it, and after a surge of remarks in his unique, famous brand of Austrian English, he used to pause and utter remorsefully, "Ach, Gott!" as if atoning for the pleasure life gave him, a pleasure he seemed to feel was greater than he deserved.

Raimund and my mother would go riding early each morning, and return to a breakfast of wine, coffee, grapes, croissants and cigarettes. Alice, delicate and shy, would come down from her bedroom and join them. The mild scandal of her liaison with Raimund had put her in a light-hearted, rebellious mood. Her childhood, my mother told me, had been difficult. The early death of her father, followed by her mother's second marriage to Lord Ribblesdale, as raffish and promiscuous as herself, had left Alice needy and insecure.

Then, of course, there was always the fear of being loved for her money; and although Alice and Raimund were both still young, Raimund was the younger.

My mother told me how she had first met him during the American tour of *The Miracle,* when Raimund was nineteen. As a gesture to his famous father, Max Reinhardt had hired him to play two small parts, a pilgrim and a wounded soldier. He quickly incurred the jealousy of Reinhardt's assistant and gray eminence, Rudolf Kommer, whose plump catlike looks and feline subtlety earned him the nickname of The Kat.

The Kat made sure that Raimund was paid a minimal salary, and traveled on *The Miracle* train in the section reserved for extras in the crowd scenes (two men to a bed). My mother and Diana took him under their collective wings, and he became "our boy, still rather shy then, often hungry for food and romantically in love with Diana, whom he worshipped. But we always had to hide Raimund from The Kat's jealous and watchful eye."

At Celigny Raimund was far from starving or shy, and introduced me not so much to caviar itself, which I'd often been given in small amounts, but to whole drums of fresh beluga, eaten without stint or shame by the silver teaspoonful. He owned a pale brown Chrysler convertible and drove my mother and me, very fast, along the lakeshore road to Geneva. He wore gloves when he drove, even in summer. Not quite as tall as he wished to be, Raimund seemed even more debonair in consequence, and was going to Geneva to try on some new suits he had ordered.

"Made of vicuna, like this jacket," he said. "Feel it."

"Gosh, it's soft."

"Vicuna comes from llamas, those animals in the Andes that look like camels. Wonderful soft, yes, but *frightful* expensive."

"Raimund, naughty!" said my mother.

"Yes. I know, I know."

"Letting Alice spoil you is all right so long as *you* don't let it spoil you. Know what I mean?"

"Yes, I know exactly." Raimund lit a cigarette, driving with one hand

Raimund von Hofmannstal, whom Iris and Ivan stayed with at Schloss Kammer in Austria

on the wheel and taking the sharp curves even faster. "On the other hand, as you would say," he went on, "I'm not so easily spoiled."

"Because you have such an appetite," my mother said. "And that, you know, could be the trouble."

"Only if I take myself seriously. I take life and other people seriously, but not myself. And of course I take Alice and you seriously."

"And Diana as well, surely?"

"I take Diana more seriously than I will ever take anyone in my life." Raimund sounded very serious about that.

We avoided an oncoming bus by two inches. "I'm sorry," he said. My mother said nothing. Then Raimund smiled. "Speaking of llamas, they say that's where syphilis originally came from."

"*Pas devant,*" said my mother, with a nod in my direction.

"Ah yes. Ivan is so grrrown up. I keep forgetting."

Naturally I wondered what syphilis was, and how we caught it from llamas.

While Raimund went to his tailor, my mother and I sat in a café overlooking Lake Geneva. At the next table was a man with a huge hairy dog. Its hair covered its eyes and seemed so thick and tangled that I wondered if the man took proper care of it.

"It's supposed to be like that," my mother explained. "It's a Hungarian bundasz, a sheepdog bred on the grassy plains of Hungary. It's probably got the thickest coat of any dog in the world." She turned to the man. "*C'est un bundasz, Monsieur, n'est-ce-pas?*"

"*Bien sur,*" said the man. "*Mais c'est une elle.*" My mother asked if she could stroke the she-dog, then talked a long time with its owner about sheepdogs of various breeds and countries; and I got bored. The man offered my mother a brandy, and she accepted. She was forever talking to strangers as if she'd known them forever, and whoever they were, servants, dukes, children, princesses, she always spoke in the same relaxed way.

Yet my mother often said she was shy, and I knew it must be true. Shy as a child, she told me, and it had stayed with her. Shy, I thought, yet open and warmly, beautifully forthcoming with strangers.

This stranger raised his glass to her, and she raised hers in return. "You have a beautiful mother," he told me with a smile.

"Yes," I said.

But I wasn't sure. Was Iris, my mother, beautiful? I had never really defined to myself how she looked. Although people often said she was beautiful, I wasn't sure, and wasn't even sure that it mattered. Sometimes she's beautiful, I thought. In the coronation scene of *The Miracle* she had certainly been beautiful. Also, now and then, before going out to a party at night. But not always, I thought, as I turned to look at her.

Unusual, yes. Striking, with her helmet of yellow-gold hair. But as we sat in the café, I began to wonder if I knew anything about beauty anyway. My mother knew Greta Garbo well, had taken me to a Garbo film, and said she was beautiful. I had agreed without real inner conviction, and said that I thought the dancer Tilly Losch was beautiful.

"*Tilly Losch?*" my mother scoffed. Tilly had been "discovered" by The Kat, and played the Nun in the London production of *The Miracle.* My mother did not like her. "She's *pretty,* I suppose, in her way. But *nothing* like the beauty of Diana. Or, of course, Garbo." She shook her head. "No, Tilly isn't really beautiful at all."

I thought she was more beautiful than Diana Cooper or Garbo or my mother, but kept it to myself. "Last holidays Virginia and I saw a film in Brighton called *Just Imagine,*" I said. "The star was called Maureen O'Sullivan. Have you ever seen her?"

"Never even heard of her," said my mother.

"I think," I said confidently, "that Maureen O'Sullivan is *very* beautiful." In fact, the night after seeing *Just Imagine,* I had fantasized being kissed by Maureen O'Sullivan in the way she had kissed the hero on the screen. I had been hugged, but never kissed. Never, until that moment, even fantasized about being kissed. But I had bought my first movie magazine in the hope of finding a photograph of Maureen O'Sullivan inside.

"I love dogs, I've had so many dogs," my mother was saying as she gazed at the departing bundasz and its owner. "And I miss Pi."

Pi was a dalmatian, left behind in England because of quarantine.

"I had a strange dog once," she went on. "A very strange dog indeed. In Paris, with Ian Campbell-Gray. We were on our way back to the Ritz when Ian saw a man selling tiny fluffy dogs at a street corner. Sweet little things covered in fur, running about on leashes and getting tangled up with each other. Ian asked if I'd like one, and I said yes. The man said they were miniature Chinese poodles, and they weren't very expensive, so he bought one and we took it back to our room at the Ritz."

"*Our* room?" I wondered, but that was a detail clearly not uppermost in my mother's mind. She told how they had ordered a bowl of milk from the maid and how the tiny, nervous, frightened creature lapped it up. Then, as my mother and Ian were due to go out to a dinner party, they reluctantly left their new pet with more milk and a little chopped meat. When they returned three hours later, there was no sign of it in the room, not even under or in the bed.

They summoned the maid, who said she had never entered the room while they were out. As she left, they heard a curious scrabbling noise that seemed to come from above the window curtains. They looked up and saw the furry little thing perched up there, eating its own leg.

Then something emerged from behind the furry leg it was eating. A rat's foot. And they realized that they hadn't bought a miniature Chinese poodle, but a large rat sewn into a furry coat. Now it was eating its way out, a quivering nose already protruding from the last snout of fur that had covered it.

"What did you *do* with it?" I asked.

Ian got up on a chair, she told me, managed to capture the rat with a towel, and when they cut it free from its coat with a pair of scissors, it tried to bite him. They put the rat in one of my mother's handbags, carried it down to the street and let it go. "Probably not the kindest thing to do, but we didn't know what else." Next day they went looking for the man on the street corner, but never found him.

"What an awful story."

"Yes," my mother said mildly. "But in French circuses, I've heard, the wolves' mouths are sewn up before every performance to stop them from biting. I don't know whether it's true, but I wouldn't be surprised. One night in a Paris suburb I overheard people shouting and a hoarse voice coming from a garden somewhere in the dark. '*Attrapez-lui, il est aveugle!*' someone called. 'Catch him, he's blind!' They'd cornered a blind rat, or some animal that had escaped in the dark. I'll always remember that cry of shrill ignorance, *Attrapez-lui, il est aveugle!* as typically French in a certain way, typical of the cruel dark provinces and Paris suburbs at night."

My mother gave me a gentle look, and a smile. I smiled back. But somehow the story had made me uneasy. It sent me back to Earleywood, and cruel scenes of boys being caught and cornered.

Then I thought of something else that made me uneasy.

"When are we going back to England, mother? It's September, I'm supposed to be going to school at Stowe, the term begins on the fifteenth."

"I don't think you're going to Stowe, darling."

"But I've taken the exam and everything."

"I know, but we're not sure any longer about Stowe."

"Then where will I go to school?"

"Curtis and I are still discussing it. I didn't want to tell you till I was sure, but I'm going to America in three weeks and thought of taking you with me."

"America?" My heart leaped, but with fear as well as joy.

"Until we decide about school. You loved America last time, didn't you?"

"Yes, and I often think about it. But if I don't go to Stowe now, I'll miss a whole term. Then I won't be allowed to go there for another year, because I'll be superannuated."

"Superannuated, indeed! I never heard of such a thing."

"That's what they call it. It's true, I promise."

"Then you'll be superannuated, my darling."

My mother smiled again, then saw the look on my face. "Don't *worry*! First you'll go to Paris with Curtis, and stay at the Ritz. That'll be lovely. Then he's taking his sweet new American friend, Marion Hall—who adores you, by the way—on a motoring trip to Provence. So you'll go on to London by yourself and join Con at Fitzroy Square. Then you'll join me, Alice and Raimund on the *Mauritania* at Southampton. Don't you think that's an exciting idea?"

My mother, Alice and Raimund traveled first class on the famous ocean liner, while I shared a small tourist cabin with three men. One of them, a middle-aged American named Doherty, walked about the cabin in the kind of one-piece underwear we used to call "combinations." I thought it embarrassing and common, although I had liked Mr. Doherty when he said with a slow, very un-English deliberation: "I have traveled over the years in many wonderful places in this world, but—not withstanding—I prefer America the better."

I had never heard anyone say "notwithstanding" before, and found it agreeably quaint. I had also heard my father deride excessively patriotic Americans as "hundred-percenters," without being sure whether I shared his dislike of them. But if Mr. Doherty was a hundred-percenter, I thought I liked them.

When I mulled over the way he'd said, "I prefer America the better," I wondered if it was proper usage. Then I thought, no matter, because Mr. Doherty was a good man. Soft-spoken and kindly, he had been all over the world and found it exciting, but notwithstanding, preferred America the better.

Each morning, with the help of a steward, I found my way by small narrow doors and passages up to first class, and sought out my mother. She would always be on the promenade deck, reading or writing in a deck chair.

"Darling, you *are* a clever boy to find me. Come and sit next."

A steward would serve us cups of hot beef tea and *pâté de foi gras* sandwiches, cut very thin. After a game of quoits or Ping-Pong, we would go to Alice's stateroom for lunch; and when Raimund arrived from his own cabin in silk pajamas and dressing gown, we shared caviar and champagne.

"I feel frrrightful guilty," he said to me. "I mean, you know, about *you*."

"But why?"

"Because you're not with us in first class all the time, you know."

Raimund made me feel like a grown-up because he always considered my feelings. I told him there was no reason to feel guilty, I was perfectly happy in tourist, in fact felt very lucky to be on the *Mauritania* at all. This was true, even though I also felt uneasy about it. As my mother had promised, it was exciting, but I had been nagged by a sense of displacement long before the journey began.

I was going to America, but where was I *going*?

The first evening on board, I didn't return to my tourist cabin until long after the four of us had dinner together. Doherty was in his long johns, playing cards and drinking with his cabin mates.

"Where you been?" one of them asked me. "Up in foist?"

"Yes," I said. The first time I heard "first" pronounced that way, I savored it. And thought to myself, Raimund will enjoy that.

"What they give you to eat up there?"

Without really knowing why, I realized that I wanted them all to like me, and I said: "Club sandwiches."

"Well," the man said, "you don't have to go all the way up to foist to get a club sandwich."

"He doesn't go up there for the food," Doherty said. "He goes because his mom's there."

Grateful for the half-truth spoken on my behalf, I undressed and climbed the ladder to my bunk.

"Where you gonna be staying?" the third man in the group called up.

"In New York," I told him. "With my grandmother."

"Where's your grandma live?"

"On Park Avenue."

No answer. The three of them went on playing cards for a while. Then the second man asked my grandmother's name.

"Graves," I said. "She's my father's mother and used to be Mrs. Moffat, but went back to her maiden name."

"How come?"

"I don't really know. Something to do with my grandfather, I think."

"Graves," said Doherty. "That's a good Irish name."

I never thought of that before, and wondered about the difference between a good and bad Irish name. I imagined that Doherty was probably an Irish name, and a good one.

Diana Barrymore and I had been "betrothed," by our respective mothers, the year of our birth. Diana was the daughter of John Barrymore and his then wife, who called herself Michael Strange. She was one of my mother's closest friends and, like her, a poet.

I had never met Diana or her mother before. Now my mother and I were on a train to Montauk, at the far tip of Long Island, where Michael Strange lived in a large, beautiful house. Divorced from Barrymore, she was now Mrs. William Tweed, but if he lived in the house, we never saw Mr. Tweed.

All my mother had told me about Diana was that she looked like "a lovely Japanese dancer." I discounted this as one of her endless allusions to things I knew nothing about. But when I saw Diana standing beside a yellow roadster outside Montauk station, with her dark silken hair in a pageboy cut, her lightly tanned oval face, full mulberry-colored lips, almost black eyes and slender, mobile body, the standard was set in my mind for what a lovely Japanese dancer should look like.

Michael Strange had a bolder kind of beauty. As she drove to the house with my mother in the passenger seat, her thick mass of hair billowed in the wind. Diana and I shared the dickey, or rumble seat as I learned to call it. We jounced uncomfortably over rutted roads, but the discomfort was only partly due to the jolts and the hard metallic sweat.

Diana was showing intense personal interest in my life, and I felt underequipped to satisfy it. Our "betrothal" I had always regarded as whimsy or fantasy on the part of our respective mothers, but Diana seemed to view it in a more immediate light. Twelve to my thirteen, she snuggled close and held hands and asked precocious questions. Did I love to dance? I said I wasn't very good at dancing. Then what was I good at? I couldn't think of anything. No hobbies or interests? Oh yes, I said, I liked animals and insects, lizards and snakes.

"Bugs? Snakes? I never heard of anyone liking them!"

I tried to explain that they were not to be feared, and really very interesting, even beautiful. Praying mantises, for example.

"Don't they bite?"

"No, not human beings. If I can find one, I'll show you."

Diana was silent for a while. Then she took my hand, shyly enough, and whispered that if I'd stay on through Thanksgiving, she'd persuade her mother to let her skip school and stay on as well.

Impossible, I said. I had to go back to England before Thanksgiving. "Why?"

"School. I should be there already, I'm late."

"Why don't you come to school in New York? Then we could see each other all the time."

"Thank you," I said. "That's very nice of you, but I'm afraid it's out of the question. School began the first week of September and it's early October now."

"So what? What can they do to you?"

"They can superannuate me."

"They can *what*?"

"If you miss the first term at a new school, it's like missing a whole academic year. So I'll be superannuated."

Michael Strange glanced back at me. "You'll be *what*, Ivan?"

"Superannuated, I'm afraid."

She burst out laughing.

"Darling." My mother sounded irritable. "Don't go on and on and *on* about that."

Michael was still laughing. "Superannuated at *thirteen*? It's Iris and me who'd better worry about that—not you, kid."

I had never been called "kid" before, and wasn't sure I liked it. But I liked Michael's eyes and voice and brave shoulders.

"Come," said Diana as we entered the hallway of the enormous house, "I'll show you your room."

But first she showed me hers. It contained open closets with masses of shoes, dresses and jewelry. Photos of John Barrymore in profile everywhere, all signed to Diana with love and kisses, and photos of other movie stars, all signed with love and kisses as well. Then Diana led me by the hand to my own bedroom, with its adjoining bathroom, and told me to come down to dinner "in any old clothes" after I'd taken a shower.

Obediently I took a shower, changed into my Earleywood jacket (too small by now) and gray flannels, and went downstairs.

Diana took one look at me. "You don't have to wear a jacket, English schoolboy! Take it off."

I took it off. She gave me another look. "Your shirtsleeves are too short. Roll them up a little."

"How?"

"Like this." She undid the cuffs and rolled the sleeves halfway up my forearms. "That's better. You look fine now." She took my jacket and dashed upstairs.

"Well," said Diana at dinner. "When shall we do it?"

"Do what?"

"Get married. Shall we say, when we're nineteen?"

Our mothers laughed.

"I'm serious," said Diana. "It's a long time, six years, but I'll wait. Okay?"

I stared at her, feeling foolish and not knowing what to say.

"Come *on*, Ivan! You don't have to look so unhappy. Smile!"

Michael laughed. "Diana's so pushy."

"If I am, Mother, it's your fault. Because Robin's pushy too, and he's only my half-brother."

"You're probably right," Michael said. "Come to think of it, I *am* kind of pushy."

"Michael," my mother protested, "you're one of the least pushy people on earth."

Diana turned to her mother. "Well, if you have to do something as crazy as betrothing me at age zero, at least you betrothed me to a good-looking boy." Then, turning back to me: "Now don't I get a compliment, too?"

"Yes," I said.

"Come on, then. I'm waiting."

"Diana, watch your manners!" said Michael.

"*My* manners? What's so hot about *his*?"

I felt myself blushing. "You are too," I said.

"Too what?"

"You're . . . pretty."

"Bravo!" my mother said quietly.

"Well, finally!" said Diana. "What else?"

"Diana," said her mother. "Don't you *ever* get enough?"

Next morning I got up early to explore. The great house was isolated, overlooking ocean and rocks and wild grasses blowing in the wind.

There were large windows everywhere, and warm polished wood. The high wind rattled noisily around the house, and I thought it odd that no one else was out and about. Because of the wind, the house seemed empty; or, rather, I began to feel empty inside the house.

I went down to the shore, and felt a curious mixture of loneliness and exhilaration as the wind swept around me. Diana had challenged me, and I had been unable to meet her challenge. Although a year younger, she seemed like a grown-up in comparison. At the same time I felt older than just a "boy."

At bedtime Diana had said with a smile: "Don't worry about that school. I never worry about things like that. Mother never lets me, nor does John—my father. John always tells me everything's going to turn out wonderfully for me, and I'll be a star."

"I expect you will," I said.

She shrugged. "Either I will or I won't. I don't worry about it."

Perhaps Diana was right, I thought, staring at the sand as it sucked in foam from the rising tide. Perhaps I shouldn't worry about school or anything else. But then, what was the point of those long years at Earleywood, with its insistence on preparation, discipline, punctuality, hard study, if it led to nothing except happenstance and the half-shared pleasures of this new, careless adult world?

On the train to Montauk, my mother had said: "Diana never had a real childhood." Without being sure what this meant, I felt sorry for her. But after meeting Diana, I wasn't so sure. She was so exquisite, confident, energetic, complete.

"Ivan! Breakfast!"

My mother was calling from the house. She wore blue jeans and the blue Austrian jacket.

"You've never had griddle cakes, have you? Griddle cakes and maple syrup?"

I hadn't. "Delicious," I said when I tasted them, and I meant it.

After breakfast Diana announced that we'd leave at noon for a picnic on the shore, several miles away. Later, when we were alone, my mother said she planned to go back to New York in four days, but I could stay on at Montauk if I liked. She thought that would be best, although I could go back with her to New York if I preferred.

"I'll go back with you," I said.

"Diana will be awfully disappointed."

"I like her, but . . ."

"I know. She's a little old for you, although she's a little younger."

"It's not that. Anyway, she said she'll be coming to New York herself soon."

"Well," said my mother. "Nona will be so happy to have you back staying with her."

Nona was the name we always called my American grandmother, Mrs. Graves.

"She's so sweet and generous. And loves having you *so* much."

"I know," I said. But there was no gratitude in the way I said it.

My grandmother's musty apartment on Park Avenue, in spite of its sweet and generous tenant, had come to symbolize for me the lack of form and direction that my life had assumed since the summer. It was emphasized by Nona's habit of changing plans every morning. If she decided we would go to the Central Park Zoo, we'd end up merely walking to the Lexington Avenue drugstores.

"Don't deviate!" I had exclaimed angrily one morning, when a change of plan was sweetly announced.

She nodded her dewlaps, and became suddenly grave. "You're right, Ivan. Absolutely right. I must not deviate so much."

From then on, in fact, she began to deviate less often. But my life, it seemed to me, went on deviating and drifting further and further from the life I had been brought up to believe was right for a thirteen-year-old schoolboy, even if he was neither strictly British or vaguely American.

The uncertainty about where or whether I would continue my schooling troubled me less than where my life was heading. I lacked any sense of purpose or destiny, and although the certainties of Diana and her half-brother Robin were exciting, they only served to increase my doubts and fears.

Robin, enviably spoiled like Diana, was a year or two older than me. Soon after I first met him, he gave me an obviously expensive, gilt-edged leather wallet. Later, in New York, he embarrassed me when we went to the movies together. There was a long line outside the theater, and he went up to the doorman at the head of it. "I'm John Barrymore's son," he said, "and I don't have to stand in line."

I thought it an insufferable act of bad manners, but it was rewarded. We were let in ahead of everyone else, with Robin tenaciously holding my arm. The shame of it! And he wasn't even Barrymore's son, only Michael's by her first marriage!

I had begged him not to do it, but he smiled as we entered the lobby. "See? I told you it would work."

"That's not the point," I said.

"It's the whole point," Robin said. And he went on smiling.

The first section of Absolute Heaven *breaks off here. Manuscript Notebook #1 begins in mid-sentence nine years later; and presumably Ivan's account of the years between 1932 and 1940 was lost. It would have covered his education at Dartington Hall and the London School of Economics, as well as another kind of education after Iris divorced Curtis and married Friedrich in America. Curtis, who also married again, remained in London for a while; and Ivan began spending more time at Fitzroy Square than at Mameena's country house. Although it brought him no closer to his father, he gained a startling amount of self-assurance, and became a precociously fashionable member of London's High Bohemia in "the rotten years leading up to World War II."*

. . . to rejection but the loss of our friendship and shared laughter. London shared a lot of laughter in September 1940. Was it because of the gloom that laughter had become a way of life?

Pamela Trask—who was born with the curious family name of Silvertop, and married to (but estranged from) an Air Commodore in the RAF—had shining smart curly blond hair, and cunning cat's eyes of bluish green. She was cleverer than I, and a year or two older. Though I would have dearly liked to be her lover, I was (so far) too in awe of her to make any move.

She wanted to go to the East End to see the fires caused by German bombs. I had misgivings but was too captivated to voice them. Since my father left for America with his new wife and their baby daughter, I had been living permanently in his top floor apartment, and we went out into Fitzroy Square, then headed for the Underground station. The shining barrage balloons had gone up, taking the last of the light.

"Silver-tops!" I said, and she put her arm through mine.

"Aren't you clever?" she said, and I thought so.

At Warren Street station I asked the ticket seller if the trains were still running. "They are now," he said. "But if the sirens start up again— well, they'll tell you anything, won't they?"

This ambiguous assurance changed our plans. We decided on Piccadilly Circus instead of Wapping and the East End. On the train I asked Pamela if she was still seeing her dashing friend Captain Philip Kindersley.

"Of course I'm seeing him. I love Philip."

"I know," I said.

"I love him. Mmmm." She made a soft cooing sound. "I love him and I love you in a different way."

Whatever that difference was, I was jealous of it, and this prompted me to say: "Does he know about the Sicilian fishermen and their 'hard, direct and uncomplicated ways,' as you put it?"

She laughed. "What a memory you have."

"Unfortunately, it's just for your words."

Pamela turned away. I'd broken my own rules. Jealousy to the prejudice of reason can still be strong.

Like everywhere else, Piccadilly was in darkness. One sensed rather than saw people as we bumped past them on our way to the Café Royal. Inside, not many people, a few familiar faces but faces not known to Pamela.

Brian Howard, a failed literary exquisite with a soft mouth and dark eyes, cocked an arch eyebrow and fixed me with his octopus eye. "Hmmm, my dear!" he said in his challenging yet velvet voice.

Guy Burgess, seated next to Brian at the bar, had lips of a peculiar red, as if he had just been eating a spoonful of cherry jam. He gave me a schoolboyish grin. "Hello, Dubbie!" he said.

Cyril Connolly and Peter Quennell, both with new girls, waved to me. Earlier that year, returning from a weekend in Cornwall, Cyril had tapped the knee of a total stranger who, sitting opposite him in the

Virginia and Ivan enjoying a mock fight, 1939

train, was reading a morning newspaper that announced the German invasion of Denmark and Norway.

"Who," he had asked the stranger with genuine curiosity, "do you think is actually going to win the war?" The man was too astonished to reply.

As Pamela and I sat down at a table, the sirens started again. People started to leave.

"So what do you want to do?" Pamela asked.

"Now?"

"No, with yourself. In the end."

"I suppose I'd like to be a journalist. Or maybe even a politician."

Although not right-wing, Pamela was far from Left. "Then I'd be on the other side from you, wouldn't I?"

"I'd hope to have you converted by then."

The waiter had produced two small ham sandwiches and a lager. While I fumbled for change, Pamela quickly gave him a ten-shilling note.

"Please," she said. "It's my air raid present."

Bombs were sounding.

Pamela stood up. "I'm going now."

"No, please."

"Yes! I see in the dark."

"But your change."

"You can give it to me next time."

"When?"

"Mmmm." Pamela bent and kissed my cheek. She had pretty, bit-terly curved lips. I got up to see her out, but she waved me away. "I'm going to the loo, then I'm off. And as I told you, I can see in the dark." She pointed to the sandwich. "Better finish that off or someone else will."

But the place was closing its doors. I ate the rest of the sandwich standing up. The waiter brought Pamela's change, and I pocketed half of it. An evening of climax had ended in anti-climax, although my wish to go to bed with Pamela was to be fulfilled a year or two later, but as if by a wicked fairy.

Even if a taxi had been available, I couldn't have afforded it. So I guessed rather than saw the blacked-out streets on my way home. A few guns thudded in the distance, a sound as familiar as the sound of sirens; and how different my feelings that night from the sense of dan-gerous yet exhilarating finality on a Sunday morning little more than a year earlier—when sad wailing sirens had risen above London for the first time, all its pigeons with them, and time itself had felt like a giant page torn in two.

Next Monday, although I'd be at my job as an assistant editor on documentary films, Natalie Newhouse would be coming back to Fitzroy Square from her mother's place in the country.

Natalie, rebellious, slight and pretty, with hot china-blue eyes, gen-erous laughter and a tongue that acted like a slingshot for deflating words, had been living with me since I first met her, and at dead of night rescued her from the claw-like clutches of Rosa Lewis, mistress of the Cavendish Hotel.

I'd been prepared for Natalie to stay a day or two. That was five months ago. On her second day she developed chicken pox, and when

Virginia, Ivan (age twenty-two), and Natalie Newhouse (Ivan's girlfriend) at East Knoyle, the country house of Virginia and David Tennant

I finally braved the danger of Rosa at the Cavendish, she only said (with a click of false teeth), "'Ow's yer spotted dick?"

My welcome to Natalie on Monday would be streets of shattered glass. But the welcome needed to be warm, for where else could she go? So far, the question had been as unspoken as it was unanswerable, considering our meager resources. In fact it would not be answered for three fond but unfaithful years, and only then by the one certainty that had made everything else uncertain since September 1939—and even more uncertain since December 1941, when America entered World War II.

I stood smartly at attention as I saluted: "Private Moffat—one-o-six-o-one-four-eighty-six—reporting for duty, sir!"

"At ease, soldier."

Thus, in London, I met an American who would become a vital part of my life for the next ten years.

On that February morning in 1944, various strands had intertwined to fix me into the rigid posture that I surely presented to Colonel George Stevens. One strand was that I had graduated from lowly assistant film

Charades at The Schools, left to right: David Parsons, Virginia Parsons, Elizabeth Powell, Ivan, Donald Maclean, Viola Tree (Ivan's aunt), Pat Gibson, and Pamela Gibson

editor to full-blown (although still fairly lowly) director of several short "documentary" films for the British Ministry of Information. They were not documentaries in the noble sense of Robert Flaherty, but propaganda films designed to raise the somewhat gray morale of the British public, and to show the brave smiling face of Britain to the world.

Admirable objectives that I fervently believed in, and did my inexperienced best to serve. So did our whole brotherhood of Soho pub-going filmmakers, some of them idealists, others small-time operators.

One of them was not strictly speaking a member of that brotherhood, although undoubtedly a Soho pub-goer, and his talent would soon raise him high above the rest of us. Dylan Thomas and I had become drinking pals—in both our cases, something easy to become—and I had introduced him to Donald Taylor, the boss of our little film company, who offered him a job as a writer.

Dylan had a deep sonorous voice in which he recited poetry by himself and others, and it could create a roomful of silence. He didn't necessarily have to recite poetry. All he needed was an idea and an audience of five (or even less); and once, I remember, this audience was of five fellow passengers in the car of a suburban train on its way to Wimbledon and our studio.

He had braced himself for the morning commute with a couple of Bloody Marys. The other passengers were reading their newspapers as Dylan chatted to me about a publisher friend named Charles Fry.

"What a pity he's so queer!"

The tops of several newspapers lowered slightly.

"But is Charles *really* queer?" I asked.

"Oh," Dylan intoned, "Charles is queer as the devil!"

"But is the devil *really* queer?"

"Oh," Dylan intoned again, "the devil's as queer as heaven!"

The tops of newspapers were quickly raised.

In those days I had started doing imitations, of other people's voices and idiosyncrasies of speech. It never goes down well in the presence of the person imitated, but all the same I once did Dylan to his face. Unsmiling, he took a used envelope from his pocket, scribbled on it with a pencil stub, and handed the result to me. "What a pity there's nothing in Moffat for Moffat to imitate," I read. "Nothing for Moffat to scoff at, in all that juvenile spate."

Dylan died so young in 1953, but only a week before his death at thirty-nine, this insignificant bundle of a drunken rag on a New York sidewalk could react almost as quickly as he did when I imitated his voice. Forty-eight hours later the bundle had transformed itself, and acquired the shape and aura of a famous poet giving a public reading of *Under Milk Wood*.

There was another strand in the skein of circumstance that led me to the laid-back American colonel. In October 1942 I had volunteered to make a documentary about the Norwegian Merchant Navy. Although Norway had been occupied by the Germans in 1940, its merchant fleet, the fourth largest in the world, had escaped to ports in Britain and joined the Allied cause. In my documentary I planned to follow one of its ships on convoy from Liverpool to New York and back, a voyage considered to be particularly dangerous; but as well as relishing the idea of making the film, I looked forward to seeing New York again.

I especially looked forward to seeing Angelica Weldon again. Beautiful, with lazy sapphire eyes, a voice that seemed to me like a soft south wind, she had a scar on her forehead from a car accident, and I liked the fact that she was proud of it. Angelica came from a rather grand Southern family, and was two or three years my senior. I had been in love with her when I was nineteen, and in a way I still was.

We had first met in the summer of 1937, on one of my visits to Eleonora von Mendelssohn's castle. One night we all had dinner on a barge in the middle of Lake Attersee, with music, torches burning, fireworks shooting out of the darkness, and the gleam of Angelica's sapphire eyes.

The voyage from Liverpool to New York was known as the Northern Route. It took three weeks, a long time to be at sea, especially a sea where so many ships had been torpedoed. Our cargo was whiskey, the voyage invigorating and without danger. And after the London blackout, the first sight of New York harbor ablaze with light was even more amazing than usual. Angelica and I drank champagne at El Morocco, and I tried to tell her about London and the War and all that I had felt. She ended up passed out on a bed in a room at the Plaza.

In New York the draft caught up with me, but my induction was deferred, at the Norwegian Consul's request, until I finished the film. All too soon our ship was ready for the return voyage: another three dark weeks at sea after the bright delirium of Manhattan. We left on a Saturday, the doleful midday sirens bidding us farewell. Because all our cargo holds carried naptha, a more volatile and explosive fuel than high-octane gas, the mood of the crew was less cheerful. And the ship's black cat was missing.

The nightmare of torpedo attacks began at dawn, ten days after we sailed from New York. Ships exploded all around us, an orange glare circled the horizon. This is something I never dream about, because it's always there.

And another image is always there. At three in the morning I stood on the bridge as our sister ship, just astern and carrying the same cargo, blew up literally sky high. The chief engineer, who was standing next to me, started to flick his flashlight on and off. The captain, staring straight ahead, saw this out of the corner of his eye. He half-turned toward the engineer, slapped him hard across the forearm, then resumed staring straight ahead.

By the spring of 1943, the mood of London had changed from deep uncertainty to confidence in eventual although bloody victory. American privates smoking cigars lounged around Piccadilly Circus, filled restaurants and pubs. At night an air of almost feverish carnality pervaded streets and alleyways, not just in London, but in provincial towns. Free-spending Yanks spilled across the kingdom with a cargo of American music, dollars, jitterbugging and venereal disease.

My friend Cyril Connolly launched *Horizon* in 1940, and by 1943 it had become the most admired magazine in Britain. It published poetry by W. H. Auden, Louis MacNeice, Stephen Spender and Dylan Thomas, essays by George Orwell, reproduced photographs by Cecil Beaton and sculpture by Henry Moore, and sponsored new talent from Lucian Freud to Denton Welch. Cyril himself, plump and attended by women, was still querulous of speech but less so of heart.

Peter Quennell, another contributor to *Horizon,* bore me no grudge for having had an affair with his first wife, and would be similarly tolerant of my indiscretions with his second; but because there were no more air raids, he no longer sought refuge in my Fitzroy Square flat at night. It had never been safer than anyone else's, but thanks to my father it could offer a superior supply of wine.

Natalie, alternately loving and accusing, had gone to stay with my much-loved cousin Virginia Tennant. Soon after I got back, Pamela Trask dropped by my flat after dinner, as she had often done in the past, talkative and fondly aloof. But this time, as soon as I switched on the lights, she disappeared toward the back, and I assumed she was on her way to the loo adjoining my bedroom.

Time passed. I went to look for her. In my bed, sheets pulled up to her shoulders, Pamela stared at me with her blue-green cat's eyes. No smile, but we were to be lovers and she was my love. Aroused, I undressed and lay beside her. I embraced her. She stayed still. I moved to kiss her. She deflected her mouth. I moved my hand to her breasts. She stayed still. I remembered the Sicilian fishermen, "direct and simple," and started to become soft. We lay in silence for a few moments. I touched her again. A slight shake of the head, she stared up at the ceiling, a moment or two of nothing, then she got out of my bed and started to dress.

Months afterward I thought: How shallow I must be to have gotten over what I had thought, suicidally that night, I would never get over.

Meanwhile the draft loomed. My mother was then living in California, and Captain John Huston had met her there. He and his screenwriter friend, Captain Anthony Veiller, told me that if I enlisted with their recommendations, I could get into a special film unit that General Eisenhower had created to record a military operation, already in the planning stage: the Allied invasion of France.

So I enlisted, and in due course was sent for thirteen weeks of basic infantry training to the U.S. Army 10th Replacement Depot at Litchfield, Staffordshire, in central England. My first day on parade, there was a roll of drums and a lieutenant's voice began calling out sentences: "Private Abelino, absent from duty 14th to 19th November 1943. Eleven years!" Another drumroll, and "Fourteen years!" rasped in my ears.

What sort of an army had I gotten into? Those savage sentences for relatively minor offenses, I learned, were meant to discourage any of us from trying to avoid doing our part in the coming invasion. I soon got to know the mood of the men I drilled and messed with, played craps with, went to the local pubs and on route-marches with, exchanged doubts, fears and sometimes reminiscences with. No one was gung-ho about the invasion. Conscripts in the infantry and the safer Supply Services all agreed that they had no choice.

And I soon became aware that very few of the soldiers around me ever had much in the way of choices. One corporal had worked at a gas station, and was determined to make buck sergeant by the end of the war, because it would mean a better job in civilian life. In fact everybody was angling for extra stripes, although nobody wanted to become an officer. None of the officers at 10th Replacement was liked, respected or admired.

Our principal instructor was a young blond lieutenant. Smart, gleaming and articulate, he explained very clearly things that I knew nothing about. But when I said that he seemed pretty okay, I was met with, "Shit, he's just a cake-eater."

For a long time I didn't know what that meant. (Finally I learned it could mean a number of things, smooth operator, la-de-da, tomcat, stud.) But I knew the lieutenant was disliked because he belonged to the group of officers and non-coms who ran the Depot. The GIs called them "the cadre," and their dismissive contempt was tinged with envy.

There was also, of course, a kind of raucous camaraderie, a reluctantly shared sense of involvement in a huge, vaguely heroic adventure. It was something beyond their control, on a far bigger scale than anything they had previously glimpsed, or even wanted to feel.

At the same time it was confining, boring and corrupt. For those who by pure chance might end up in an infantry regiment or the backwater of Supply Services, the stakes could be very high. It depended on temperament, orientation, pride. Someone drafted to an infantry regiment would probably have refused to trade places with a clerk in a supply depot, even though it promised relative safety and easy routine. There were plenty of men who knew what they had crossed the Atlantic to do, and were resigned to risking their lives doing it.

We went on regular twelve-mile marches with full field pack and rifle, we walked along wet lanes lined with bramble bushes to local pubs, we saw movies and played marathon crap games on billiard tables wrist-deep in pound notes. I sent Natalie three pounds in a letter that a fellow trainee promised to mail, and that never reached her. He was a little Cockney who had somehow become an American citizen and always exclaimed, "Oh, my aching back!" when given the mildest order. He was also a rotten little thing and I should never have trusted him with that letter.

I was a good shot with a rifle, and the only trainee to earn an "Expert Rifle" badge. The rest of our small group of Americans and Europeans were poor shots, duly awarded a "Marksman" badge. In this way the GIs in Britain came to be festooned with ribbons and badges, to the scorn of our underpaid and increasingly envious British comrades-in-arms. Money didn't just talk in the Britain of 1943. It screamed in every face and at every street corner, and legions of British girls screamed with it.

Sadly, so many of these girls became angry rivals. They nursed desperate hopes after brief encounters with GIs who offered little more to reward their fervent expectations than a condom-protected fuck, and a nostalgic smile about home in Tennessee. Their fever would abate only when the war was over and we'd all gone home.

Two weeks after I began training at 10th Replacement, a great friend turned up in the dashing but improbable person of Raimund von Hoffmannstal. After Alice divorced him, he had married Diana Cooper's niece, Lady Elizabeth Paget, one of the great English beauties of her day. Raimund's charm and verve and long rolling Rs were undiminished when we talked wistfully (over sausages and mash at the British canteen down the road) of long-ago suppers at the Savoy Grill in London, and of summers at Schloss Kammer before the War.

Eleven weeks later I was finally "shipped out" to London, where I joined the U.S. Army Special Coverage Unit (SHAEF). In Piccadilly, wearing the uniform of members of SHAEF soon to be sent to the departure dock at Southampton, I ran into Evelyn Waugh. "Off to the beachhead?" he inquired with arched eyebrows and a note of envy.

"Yes. How about you, Evelyn?"

"No. I'm off to White's."

And with a bitter smile he headed for St. James's Street and his favorite club.

That night Cyril Connolly told me that Evelyn had dirtied his copybook so often as an officer in the Marines, that they were giving him very little to do.

Two days later our unit received orders to be ready to ship out to Southampton at once. The night before, a platonically beloved childhood love told me that she had asked her husband (whom I knew well) for permission to spend the night with me, as she feared she might never see me again. Surprisingly, he had given his consent. And so for the first and last time in our long lives we held each other close, and more. Early next morning, a beautiful June day, I was in a truck on the road to Southampton. I felt at one with my cousin and the world, united with her laughter and all our memories; and I also felt, after that night, whatever happened to me now wouldn't really matter.

At first I had little to do with the forty-year-old commander of our outfit, the well-known Hollywood director, George Stevens. But I had got to know another of its members, Irwin Shaw, at thirty-two already famous for his short stories. We became hostile friends. He was dressed in canvas leggings like the rest of us, and our first exchange occurred when I told Irwin that he had the short-legged swagger of a Japanese bullfighter.

Irwin laughed his loud, bitter laugh. "The army's going to do you good, Moffat. It'll toughen you up."

"Toughen me to a pulp," I said, and Irwin laughed again. I had first heard that laugh one night at the Gargoyle Club, when I introduced him to Phillip Toynbee, a longtime carousing friend destined to remain on the edge of literary fame. Irwin and Phillip had been enjoying each other and talking close. Suddenly Phillip said, "Excuse me a moment, will you?" and vomited to the floor. "Now that's carrying good manners a bit too far," Irwin said, and gave his laugh.

William Saroyan was another member of our unit. We had become good friends, and as he and Dylan wanted to meet each other, I arranged it at 12:30 a.m. in the back bar of the Café Royal. Dylan was cherubic and mildly inebriated. He listened with silent yet aggressive shyness while Saroyan talked and joked in a merry, show-off mood. Finally, as if feeling left alone on the stage, Bill started to vocalize. "She rides my limousine," he sang, "I buy the gasoline!"

Dylan spoke for the first time. "That song's no bloody good, there's only one good song!" And he proceeded to sing, "Old Mother Carey, Queen of All the Fairies, did a double somersault and landed on her twat."

I don't think they met again.

A week after D-Day we assembled on the dock at Southampton with packs and carbines, token low-caliber weapons whose ejection mechanism worked by a spring, and a far cry from the M-1 rifles we trained with at the Depot. We watched as a crane clumsily hoisted one of our jeeps on board the ship, causing it to smack into the wood-and-canvas latrine slung over the port-side rail. This left us only the starboard latrine to squat over, regardless of the wind's direction or its force.

I went below to inspect our sleeping quarters, tiers of narrow bunks, four deep. No way I was going to lie down there in the dark. I determined to stay on the promenade deck even if I had to stand on my feet all night; but in fact I was able to lie down on blankets, and nobody bothered me.

In the morning I saw the coast of France for the first time in five years. Utah Beach, as it came to be known. Irwin came up beside me and gazed at it.

"A lot of men died there," he said.

Our truck was supposed to be able to drive from the shallows onto the beach, but the engine choked up, front wheels on the shoreline, rear ones in the surf. I could hear guns in the far distance. Smoking a Camel while I waited, I thought how much I was enjoying my first cigarette on French soil, or rather on French sand. George Stevens, with a camera crew, group of assistants and fellow officers, had filmed the actual D-Day landing from a warship, and it was hours before we caught up with his outfit in a Normandy pasture a few miles from a town called Carentan.

We dug our foxholes there. It was soft and quiet under the thick branches of trees in our bivouac area, we walked on a carpet of pine needles and grass. Later, I sat on the front seat of an empty army truck, reading *All Quiet on the Western Front*. Gunfire sounded a little nearer than before, the wind blew quite strongly around the truck, and I felt safe, alone and comfortable inside it.

I had read *All Quiet* years earlier, but felt it was the right time to read it again. The phrase "the Western Front" had always cast a spell over me, half romantic and half fearful. There was something haunting and eternal about it, implying the existence of some permanent divide, not in the sense of Germany and France, but in the very nature of history and time and ourselves; and *All Quiet on the Western Front* has a shivery resonance for me to this day.

We ate our K-rations and slept under the stars. In the morning, loudspeakers mounted on trees above the encampment informed us of the widening beachhead in Normandy. As we drove through the countryside, I saw a fantastic, unimaginable amount of war materiel. It streamed along the narrow roads in an unending profusion of variety and weight: no greater mass of tanks, bulldozers, prime movers, four-

and six-wheel trucks, jeeps and ammunition carriers had ever been crammed into such a space, anywhere before in the world.

Obviously this would prove to be the overwhelming factor on the Allied side. Forget elite corps, I thought to myself, forget individual acts of gallantry, forget skill and experience in battle, forget the superiority of German infantry and generalship, in the scales of war all those things will count for little against the concentrated industrial power of the United States, projected across the Atlantic in a logistical feat of extraordinary complexity and magnitude.

And none of this, I also thought, would have been possible without almost total superiority in the air.

Although it was still spring, roads and hedgerows everywhere were covered in dust. Wires dangled from telephone poles. Bloated cattle lay stinking in the meadows. In the middle of a small village, an upturned umbrella floated rigidly on a pool of dust. Trucks packed with U.S. infantry poured eastward toward the unyielding German defenses around Caen and St. Lo.

My close companion all this time had been Leicester Hemingway. He was determinedly and absurdly gung-ho about everything. He wanted action for action's sake, as he mistakenly believed that his brother would. He poured a shot of Calvados into his canteen cup and raised it in salute "to some good casualties among our officers."

Leicester despised the officers' unwillingness to move closer to the front line, and so did I, but in deluded imitation of his brother as a man of action, he overdid it a bit. Even in London I had nicknamed Leicester "the preposterous Hemingstooge," and it had stuck. Still, I liked him. In his big, lumbering, shortsighted way he reminded me of Pierre in *War and Peace*.

Colonel Stevens and I stood by the roadside near the cheese-making town of Ysigny, watching the constant procession of vehicles of war. "Jesus," he said. "I'd love to take a few reels of that, just for future record."

"Why don't you, Colonel?"

"And ship them back to the War Department? They'd think I'd gone nuts!"

Despite our differences in age and rank, Stevens and I had begun to develop an affinity, strong enough to make me feel that his intelligence was in need of more variety than the company of his fellow officers could provide. They consisted of assistant directors, cinematographers and film editors. Only one of the editors, Major Calhoun, had an independent, sophisticated mind, and was by far the most popular of the group among us enlisted men.

My first clash with Stevens took place in a stationary jeep, when I realized there was a slightly paranoid side to this talented man. I was the only person in the outfit who could speak a word of any foreign language, being reasonably fluent in French and German. But when I struck up a conversation in French, or asked the way to a town, there were raised eyebrows, smirks and knowing glances from almost all the officers.

Stevens listened as I translated, but I realized that his sense of "authority" and his need to control were being challenged.

"Private Moffat, you're forbidden to talk French from now on."

I had no intention of obeying such an absurd order, and wrote a satirical poem to make the point. Its last lines were, "Feel yourself no longer free / To speak in the tongue that first spoke liberty." Pretty feeble stuff, but Stevens overheard me reciting it.

He laughed. "Okay, Private Moffat. Order temporarily rescinded."

From then on, in spite of differences and occasional hostile moments, we became friends.

In July our unit of eight reached the town of Coutances, recently liberated by Patton's 3rd Army. A vindictive ritual was taking place in the main square. Beside the 1914–1918 war memorial, decorated with with a fluttering tricolor, two gray-haired women in their sixties were chained together. Two men were clumsily shaving their heads with what looked like sheep shears. The heads of both women were bleeding, as the blades kept piercing their skin.

I asked someone in the crowd of jeering onlookers what the women had done.

"Collaborated with the Boches."

"What sort of collaboration?"

Nobody seemed to know. One man volunteered that the women

had probably been selling vegetables and other produce to the Germans, something that patriotic citizens would never have done.

As I glanced at the tricolor, which seemed to flutter somewhat equivocally above the scene, a blond American army captain appeared. He looked overwrought and waved a revolver.

"Stop it!" he shouted in bad French. "This is not the way to start building democracy!"

I admired that. The two shearers began arguing with the captain, who wore an armband with some kind of official insignia. He argued back, increasingly angry, until they started to unchain the women. The captain holstered his revolver, got into a jeep and drove away.

Prematurely, as it turned out. Almost at once a small convoy of ambulances drew up, with a smartly uniformed American woman in the driver's seat of each vehicle. The leader of the pack, a Park Avenue type in her late forties, powder-blue hair and red fingernails, leaned out from her window and addressed the crowd in broadly American French.

"*Continuez! C'est pas son affaire! Continuez!*"

As the shearers eagerly began chaining the women together again, I shouted back at the Park Avenue type: "*Et c'est pas votre affaire non plus!*"

She glared at me. "Who the hell are you?"

At that moment the captain returned in his jeep, accompanied by a Frenchman in a dapper double-breasted suit. The leader of the ambulance pack waved an arm in a forward gesture, slammed down her window, and the convoy moved off. The shearers were clearly unnerved by the Frenchman's presence. Anticipating his orders, they quickly unchained the women again.

Ernest Hemingway joined our unit at Mont St. Michel, a small cluster of houses below a tall medieval church, perched on a small rocky island near the border of Normandy and Brittany. Irwin had taken me to meet Hemingway in his suite at the Dorchester Hotel in London, where he had shown off his collection of shotguns and rifles, pre-invasion rows of boots, and a portable canvas device that would enable him to cross rivers.

I had wondered why he needed all that stuff as a war reporter for *Colliers,* but was either too awed or too polite to ask. A few weeks later

I had met Hemingway again at the beachhead. He wore a Wehrmacht belt and told me, "I got it off a dead Kraut." This time I wondered, again without asking, why he bothered to explain.

At Mont St. Michel a woman ran out from an inn to greet Hemingway, and he lifted her up in his arms as she laughed and kissed him and called him Papa. Then, at the inn, he toasted Irwin and Stevens with wine and Calvados, and we ate delicious omelettes, the first good meal any of our outfit had tasted since London.

As it grew dark, brilliant artillery flashes lit up the sky, not very far away toward the east. They grew even more dazzling as the sound of gunfire grew louder. An American colonel joined us and said there was a heavy German counterattack from Mortaing, aimed at splitting our army in two. By then we were all a bit high, and enjoying a sense of vicarious participation in an event that was exciting but not in the least threatening.

In the morning Hemingway and I climbed the steep narrow steps to the church, then up to the church roof, where we scraped our initials on one of the slate tiles, and Hemingway grinned like a kid.

The roads to Paris were lined with thin but cheering, flag-waving crowds. In one small town a boy ran out in front of our jeep, and our driver carried his dead body into his parents' house. Deep sorrow for such a tragic accident, but not much time to express it.

Early that evening, in beautiful late-summer weather, we reached the outskirts of Rambouillet. Wasps alighted restlessly on our food, some of them faltering in the marmalade and crushed by our spoons. We drove on to a designated bivouac, and on the way our driver told how he'd thrown pebbles at a young girl's bedroom window one night. She climbed out, and they headed for a nearby meadow.

"And then," he said, "the cocksucker rained!"

I found this an odd phrase. "Did he mean the weather was a cocksucker?" I asked Stevens. "Or fate? Or even the powers that be?"

Stevens laughed. "No," he said. "But in our Puritan way of thinking, a purely sexual act has to bring trouble. It's that way in Hollywood. In this case, all the sonofabitch did was bring rain."

And at this culminating moment of the campaign, I gained new respect for our colonel's judgment.

Next morning Stevens secured written permission from a French colonel for our Special Coverage Unit to join up with the French 2nd Armored Division as it entered Paris, even though General de Gaulle had insisted that a French division should have exclusive film rights.

It was August 25. The previous day there had been an uprising in the city, aided by detachments of the Paris police. Under clear skies and a brilliant sun, armored columns were advancing via the Porte d'Orléans to the Avenue Aristide Briand. The first armored column was already in the center of Paris, but the line we joined was not continuous. Bursts of machine-gun fire came from the side streets as our jeeps and trucks moved between cheering crowds that dispersed every time the gunfire started, running for cover behind trees or lying prone on the sidewalk.

The atmosphere of excitement, danger and anticipation intensified as the rifle-fire from snipers became more persistent. I was in one jeep with a friend, Dick Kent, and Stevens was in front of us with four others. He halted the jeep as the firing sounded louder and closer, and the driver ran for cover behind a tree. Stevens took the wheel, drove his jeep off the middle of the avenue and parked it beneath sidewalk trees. A gendarme held up his hands to stop our jeep, and explained to me (as the lone French speaker) that there were snipers in a side street to our right, members of the notorious pro-German French militia known as the Milice.

I told the gendarme we had orders to proceed to the center of Paris, and it wasn't our job to deal with snipers. To clinch the point, I nodded my head at several members of the Forces Françaises de l'Intérieur (FFI) who were hanging around armed with rifles and wearing khaki armbands. Why weren't *they* going off to the side streets?

The gendarme motioned us forward, but three or four blocks farther on we were stopped again. This time a very serious gendarme explained that there was a little square just ahead, and if we looked up, we would see a sniper at the third-floor window of an apartment building.

You must deal with him, the gendarme said.

"*Bien*," I said, unslinging my carbine and injecting a 22-caliber bullet into the breech. It seemed absurd that I should be assigned to the job simply because I was the only one of our group who spoke French. I glanced again at the FFI members and wondered what the hell *they* were supposed to be doing. Later I realized that danger and farce are equal partners in war, and only boredom is more potent than either.

I rounded the corner, ducked behind a municipal sandbox that the gendarme had pointed out, and gingerly raised my helmeted head. Across from me was the apartment building, and on the third floor an open window framed with curtains that billowed in a light breeze.

No sniper in view, however. I leveled my carbine at the window, figuring that if there *had* been a sniper there, I would surely have been shot by now. But I thought it best to do something, because the crowd at a safe remove behind me was watching expectantly. I aimed at the window and pulled the trigger. Click! Furious, I ejected the bullet and another fell in place. Another click! and a murmur from the crowd. The first American soldier they'd seen in action was in effect forgetting his lines. I realized that dust from the roads had penetrated the cheap spring mechanism of my carbine, and this time I rammed the bolt home as hard as I could.

Crack! My shot sent a tiny cloud of cement dust through the side of the window. A moment later, the façade of the building started to disintegrate. I stared in shock, then looked back. A French truck had driven up behind me and its machine guns were firing at the frontage they had seen me shoot at.

I stood up. The crowd behind me surged forward, and I was raised high in triumph on thin shoulders. Hero of the moment, I was carried to my jeep; and although flushed with exhilaration as we drove on, reminded myself that I had done precisely nothing.

It falls to relatively few soldiers to witness the end of one epoch and the start of another. As we approached the center of Paris, and laughing, roaring, caressing crowds of men and women pressed around us, I supposed that the French must have felt this way in 1789. Tossed bouquets of flowers, kisses and embraces, and the even more beautiful sight of Paris itself, combined with an awareness that we were celebrating a great moment in history, made me realize that no future event in my life could possibly equal the sensation of victory, glory and ecstatic delirium that gripped me then and has remained with me forever.

We entered the Place de Rennes and drove up the ramp to the Boulevard Montparnasse. Here, in the station, General LeClerc was to receive the formal surrender of the commander of the German forces in Paris.

Stevens was there, of course. He seemed flushed and his normally lumbering gait was unsteady. Pistol in hand, he fired a couple of rounds toward nearby rooftops, as if answering the sounds of rifle fire that echoed and reechoed from every direction.

And now, in an open command vehicle driven by French soldiers, the German general arrived. His staff accompanied him in a cavalcade of vehicles. The general got out first, a man of medium height, gold braid of his epaulets gleaming in the sunlight, red collar tabs above his gray tunic matching the color of his face. He stood there as if he expected to be stared at and reviled, but his bearing was dignified and even had a touch of defiance. The picture, in fact, of what one would have imagined a German general to look like under the circumstances.

For a few moments he appeared to survey all of us in the same way as we were observing him. Then he turned and entered the Gare Montparnasse to meet LeClerc.

We regarded him as a villain, of course, but on August 25, 1944, we had no idea that he had defied Hitler's orders to destroy the Louvre, Les Invalides and all the Seine bridges.

His staff of officers followed the general into the station. Their faces had a curious greenish-white look, as if they hadn't been in the open air for months. One of the FFI officers kicked the boot of an officer as he walked past, and I disliked the commonness of the gesture.

When our unit entered the station, the general's staff was standing in stoic line opposite a throng of eyeballing Americans and French. Stevens, I saw now, was tight. "C'est la guerre," he said to one officer, who neither looked at him or responded.

"C'est la guerre, goddammit!" This time Stevens raised his voice, and I wished he'd shut up. But then, as if realizing that he lacked an audience, he fell silent and after a moment ambled away.

Outside the Hotel Scribe, where our unit and the press corps were billeted, there were more cheering crowds, sometimes cowering for shelter when shots cracked out from rooftops. I found myself in the middle of an admiring cluster of men and women, talking and being talked at. An entrancingly attractive girl stood close to me. She had slightly olive skin, hazel eyes and a French movie-star face. We both suddenly felt the kind of attraction that moments of drama, glory and tension can create.

I wanted to be with her, never to lose sight of her. She was more perfect at that moment than all the girls I had known in the first pulse of encounter. We embraced, regardless of everyone, everything, except ourselves.

Then a U.S. Army sedan drove up and an officer called out: "Hey, soldier!"

"Sir?"

"I have to drive out to Le Bourget to send off these reels of film, and I need you around to help."

"Sir, I'm with this girl and we're in the middle of . . . getting together, sir."

"Sorry, soldier, but I've got to get these reels to the airport and there's still a war on, you know."

I looked at Giselle. "Get in the car!" I said, and she did, and we embraced with a sweet passion I still remember.

"For Christ's sake, soldier!" the officer said.

Giselle got out. So did I, and held her, and she slid her hand into my open shirt and said: "*Restez intact.*" Then she disappeared into the crowd.

When I got back from Le Bourget, there was still a crowd outside the Hotel Scribe. I searched every face, but never found Giselle. The crowd roared into the night, and finally dreams took over.

In the morning I went to the Ritz Bar with Ernest Hemingway. We drank champagne, then went to the manager's office together. I had been asked by American relatives to look up my great-uncle Andy Graves if I ever got to Paris. He had been stranded there by the War, and was well known at the Ritz.

"Ah, poor Andy!" the manager said. He dialed a number on the phone, listened, and passed me the receiver.

A harsh American voice answered. "Curtis?"

"No, Uncle Andy. His son, Ivan."

"By God! I told them last night at the club that a member of my family was bound to be in the vanguard."

My great-uncle was an old Wall Street warhorse, who had played football for Yale, and way back in the 1880s his pet bulldog had become the Yale mascot. He asked me to dinner that night at his apartment off the Bois de Boulogne, and later I wished I hadn't accepted.

After dinner with fierce old Andy, there was a vicious German air raid on the center of Paris. As I was driven back to the Hotel Scribe, a French armored car careened into the rear of the jeep, and smash! I was tangled up on the rear seat with a bone sticking through my trousers and my right foot in serious trouble.

When an ambulance arrived, a nurse gave me a shot of morphine; and on the way to the hospital I was surprised and bewildered to find a girl sitting beside me in the ambulance. After a moment I recognized her as one of the little crowd of sympathizers that had gathered around the scene of the accident.

She was a not unattractive girl in her twenties, with very full lips. But what on earth was she doing at my side?

I woke up some time after dawn, lying on my back on the floor of a hospital corridor, and had hardly recovered consciousness when I saw the same full-lipped face hovering above my own. She leaned her mouth to mine and kissed me, and I vomited over her blouse. Presumably I passed out after that, because I woke up in the hospital ward, with a wounded man in the next bed.

Through him I learned a curious and (I believe) little-known fact. He had been shot in the lung while fighting on a rooftop, but the man who shot him was neither a German nor a member of Milice, but a Japanese art student. According to my hospital friend, a number of Japanese art students in Paris had decided, after Pearl Harbor, to drop their paintbrushes and take up arms on behalf of their faraway emperor as soon as the opportunity arose.

It arose, of course, when American soldiers arrived in Paris. Opposite my companion, visible through a semitransparent glass screen, were three more members of the FFI who had also been wounded by Japanese art students. We all waved to each other like comrades in arms.

Meanwhile a wire cage had been placed over my legs to protect the casts. A nurse entered the ward to inform us there was no food in the hospital, and virtually none in all Paris, but champagne would arrive shortly. It did, bottles and bottles of it.

When the full-lipped one returned, she sat close by me on the bed and uttered a few words of sympathy. Then she ran her hand beneath the sheets, and proceeded to make love in the only way possible. The man on my left had his face to the wall, the wire cage over my legs gave us some protection from the eyes of the three FFI members behind the glass screen, and no nurses were around.

Among other sensations when it was over, I had to admire the full-lipped one's boldness. Before she left, I asked her to go to the Hotel Scribe and make contact with anyone there from the Special Coverage Unit. She told me that she came from Bordeaux, and it explained her accent when she asked if I felt better: *"Cha va miex?"*

I told her I did. She promised to come back tomorrow and was as good as her word. When she ran her hand beneath the sheets again, I wondered if it was (among other things) a form of therapy, as I'd heard they set hospital patients to weaving baskets and similar things. In any case, this was better, although only up to a point, of course, and fortunately that point had been reached well before I was transferred to the American hospital, then flown to England.

Before I left, Irwin Shaw paid a visit, bringing K-rations and cigarettes. The head nurse was with him and gave me a look of commiseration. *"Le pauvre,"* she said. *"Il est si jeune."*

Irwin gave his harsh laugh and said I wasn't all that young, it was my profession to be young.

Back in England, it seemed like a miracle when I learned that I was to be transferred to a hospital only a few miles from my beloved cousin Virginia's house at East Knoyle in Wiltshire. I asked one of the officer-nurses to telephone her.

Nothing doing. It was forbidden, pending notification of my father in the USA that I'd been wounded.

He had already been notified, I said.

"We have no confirmation of that."

"Dammit, nurse, what sort of confirmation do you expect to have?"

She went off in a huff. The padre with his unctuous, soothing voice was no help either. But the window above my bed was open. I scribbled a brief letter, placed a pound note inside the fold, called to one of the electricians who was repairing an exterior fuse box, and threw the note out the window.

Virginia and her husband David Tennant arrived next afternoon, both so good-looking and elegantly dressed that an army doctor and two nurses gave them an effusive welcome as they entered the ward. At the end of that week Natalie Newhouse arrived, hobbling on a cane. She had broken her thigh in a fall and spent several weeks in hospital. She wore her familiar emerald-green coat and skirt and smiled her half shy, half roguish smile. She told me that she was now living with Robert Newton, the famous and equally roguish actor. I was delighted, like the British press, when they got married a few weeks later.

A letter from Leicester Hemingway informed me that our unit was now in Belgium, the weather was cold, tempers short and morale low. I wondered how it got past the censor, and felt glad to be in a warm, safe, comfortable, boring English hospital. Not long afterward came the news that I had been awarded the Purple Heart, and it made me wonder again: What on earth for?

More important than any of this, the army offered me a choice. I could be sent back to the States with an honorable discharge, or volunteer for "limited service," which would exempt me from a few disagreeable tasks, notably having to march while I shouldered a pack.

Back at the 10th Replacement Depot, the news of the day was that British and American troops were fighting the Communist partisans in Greece, and proposing to restore the Greek monarchy. As the partisans had been a major force in resisting the German invasion of Greece, I realized that the aim of American and British policy was to limit the effect of the Soviet Union's advance in Eastern Europe. And at morning parade I persuaded our company to shout, "Down with the fascist king of Greece!"

The officer in charge didn't know what we were shouting about, and nor did most of the company. But it gave my passionate if superficial left-wing enthusiasm (which I never renounced) a sense that the morning had not been entirely wasted.

Before going back to France, and rejoining SHAEF, I was given two days' leave in London. I spent one evening at the Gargoyle with Virginia, and as so often, we reminisced about our youth.

"Do you remember," she asked, "how our parents would say *every* morning that last night at the theater, or last weekend in Paris, had been absolute heaven?"

I remembered all too well. "Even a dull evening in the country was absolute heaven when they got back."

"That was the whole idea of our lives," Virginia said. "The idea that absolutely *everything* was absolute heaven. But it wasn't really like that at all. Was it?"

"I'm not so sure now," I said. "Maybe it *was*, a bit."

Virginia looked thoughtful. "And you think it still is, in a way?"

"At moments."

"Surely you can't say that about the army?"

"I can, actually."

"Then perhaps the whole thing," she said, "all the awful things as well, perhaps *everything* has been, in a way, sort of, absolute heaven?"

"Perhaps," I said.

A hellish midnight walk with a bad left leg, and a bruised, bloody right foot, took me from the port of Le Havre to a camp nine miles uphill. If I'd fallen out, I'd have been hospitalized, then shipped back to the USA, so I plodded on, reaching the camp in late morning, and a sympathetic medic bandaged my foot.

That evening we were packed into closed cattle cars with the famous stickers, *Chevaux 8, Hommes 40* (Horses 8, Men 40). At 1 a.m. the train stopped at a junction far outside Paris, my cattle car's doors were rolled open, and about eight of our group jumped out.

I asked a sergeant where they were going. "Tear off a piece of ass, I guess," he said.

"At one in the morning on a February night, at some godforsaken railroad junction?"

"I guess."

GIs from other cattle cars had started to jump out, many of them carrying flashlights. I saw French girls appearing out of the dark, heard laughter and the clink of bottles before they and the GIs went off into the night.

"How the hell did they *know?*" I wondered. With even the strongest sexual instinct in the world, how could even one GI have divined this forlorn spot to be a kind of Sargasso Sea of mating?

But when we reached Paris, the delirium of last August was over. A winter's familiarity had dulled that early luster, and GIs were just GIs, in Milwaukee or Montmartre.

Leicester Hemingway, forever bullish, told me about a wonderful girl nicknamed "Sarbakhane." He said that he wasn't getting involved with her because he'd decided to quit our outfit and join the infantry, where he'd finally get to see some action. But he took me to meet her in Ernest's suite at the Ritz.

Several girls were present, but I knew "Sarbakhane" the moment I saw her. Thick, blondish-red hair worn in shoulder-length pageboy style, serious gray-blue eyes and a voice that reminded me of Angelica's, soft like the wind. Natalie Sorokin was a White Russian. "Sarbakhane" had been conferred on her by Simone de Beauvoir and Sartre, as they told me later. The name was exotic and they found Natalie exotic. Also, they said, eccentric and odd, or perhaps a mixture of all three, and of course beautiful as well. With a touch, Sartre added, of "something beyond that."

"Something beyond that," unfortunately, was prophetic. But I couldn't know it at the time. All I knew was that Natalie, or Natasha as most people called her, was handmaiden and sometime lover to de Beauvoir, and general dogsbody to Sartre. He was less enamored of her than de Beauvoir. Her sullen lapses and challenging moods irritated him, although he admired her beauty and was sometimes amused by her unpredictable rebellious outbursts.

George Stevens's Special Coverage Unit of the U.S. Army Signal Corps, shooting footage at Dachau, later used at the Nuremberg Trials

The three of them lived at the Hotel de la Louisiane on the Left Bank; and it was there, on our second night together, that I surprised Natasha (and myself) by asking her to marry me. I'd had many involvements, of course, and it seems to me now that I suddenly wanted to cut through the whole business of starting an affair, then explaining my way *out* of getting married, and untangling, sometimes painfully, a host of accumulated feelings.

There were palpable things I could offer Natasha, not least the opportunity to go to America. But instead of answering my proposal, she claimed to notice a flea on my chest and slapped it.

Next morning she answered me in a very long letter, written in multicolored inks, that amounted to "Yes." And early the following morning my outfit was due to start for Germany. To see Germany, and see it in the company of George Stevens, was the main reason I'd reenlisted. Natasha set the alarm clock for 5 a.m., and while I put on my uniform, she made coffee at her little gas ring in the bathroom. On our way to the Metro she danced in front of me, still in her nightgown, barefoot and smiling.

It was early March, dark and cold. At the Metro we embraced, and she pressed something warm into my hand. It was the last of ten precious eggs I had scrounged from a farmer in exchange for two boxes of matches. I thought we had already eaten the last of them, and it was Natasha's parting surprise.

In Germany, of course, all of us expected shocks; and there were plenty when I entered Dachau concentration camp with Stevens and his film crew on April 7, 1945. The name Dachau had been synonymous with the kind of infamy associated with the Nazi regime soon after it came to power. Although it had never been an extermination camp, in the final weeks of the War the Germans began evacuating prisoners from camps further east, and brought in two thousand or more Jews, some on foot and some in the notorious cattle cars.

Those cars were now open, and piled with hundreds of half-frozen corpses. Some bore traces of sporadic acts of cannibalism, a gnawed arm here, a gouged leg there. In the central compound and square, which our unit filmed and photographed, lay hundreds more of the dead. There were entire rooms filled with corpses, and more corpses stacked on the ground, naked buttocks of one body up against staring eyes and gaping mouths of the face of another. A number of SS men had been shot by American soldiers after surrendering, and their bodies lay on the ground as well.

Around thirty-five thousand prisoners had survived, some barely staggering on their feet, others dying as we watched, in their striped cotton rags of uniforms. The majority were in poor but not totally drastic shape, although cholera, typhus and dysentery were still taking their daily toll. In the barracks washrooms, they brushed their teeth at chromium-fitted sinks, gingerly stepping around the bodies of prisoners who had died during the night; and it was strange to think that Dachau had been considered a "model" camp, turning out porcelain figurines, growing herbs and tea in the garden plots.

Alexander Rosner was a boy of perhaps fourteen, with rosy chubby cheeks and sleek hair that made him seem positively flourishing. I asked, in German, if I had anything with me that he might need.

"Yes," he said. But I didn't understand the German word that followed.

By way of explanation, Alexander stroked his fingers through his hair. I gave him my comb, and he went straight to a nearby window, using it as a mirror while he lovingly combed his hair.

The camp had a very crude hospital nearby, no more than a wooden hut with tiered bunks, where the sick and the soon-to-die huddled in blankets. The first inmate I talked to, a Belgian youth of twenty-one called Langenakens, asked me to write his family in Brussels to tell them he was well and would be joining them soon. He had a feverish high color on the otherwise death-white skin of his face. He talked volubly, as if he needed desperately to do so, and spoke good English. I wrote his parents next day, but their sorrowful answer, with a hint of reproach, only reached me months after the War ended.

They had never seen him again.

Another man I spoke to was also Belgian, in his mid-forties and formerly a civil servant in his country's War Office. All things considered, he looked reasonably well. I asked him what he thought of the Germans, and he answered in French: "Monsieur, I have been through two German invasions of my country, in 1914 and 1940. This camp was a place of hell. You could bring twelve German children and shoot them in front of my eyes, and I wouldn't blink. But having said that, I must tell you the Germans were like angels compared to the Poles."

"The Poles?"

"Yes, the Polish prisoners put in charge of us by the Germans. Prisoners in charge of working battalions of other prisoners were called Kapos, and the Polish Kapos did far more than the Germans to make us suffer."

Next day this man suddenly died. But before I left him in the hospital, he told me that hundreds of those working battalions had labored long hours underground. When I went to see the place he'd described, I found myself in a gigantic system of tunnels that the Nazis had dug into the Harz Mountains. It led, deep in the center, to a factory they constructed for producing the V-1 and V-2 rockets that had bombarded England.

I spent nine days and nights talking with prisoners and making notes. One of them was a German Communist of the old school. He had been appointed by the SS, as part of their system of checks and balances, to run the internal administration of the camp. The Jewish chaplain of the 10th Corps had proposed to hold a service for the surviving Jewish prisoners, some of them women, and the German Communist thought it "not such a good idea."

"Why not?"

"It's a bit sectarian."

This was an old Party word meaning "divisive."

I pointed out that the Poles had held their own celebration a day earlier, and nobody called it "sectarian."

That was different, the German said. The celebration was to mark Poland's Independence Day.

"But this will be the first time a Jewish service has been held in Germany for years," I said, growing impatient. And I added that we would definitely allow it to take place.

The majority of the prisoners here won't welcome a Jewish service, the German Communist warned, and as camp administrator he would take no responsibility for anything that might happen. In particular, he said, the Poles would be angry, and the Poles numbered more than half the prisoners.

I suddenly felt sick. When Dachau concentration camp, the symbol of Nazi bigotry and persecution, proved itself a hotbed of anti-Semitism, it seemed to turn my oversimplified world inside out.

Pointing to the flag flying over the camp, I said that wherever the Stars and Stripes flew, a Jewish or any other kind of service would be held if someone wished it. Then I stomped off.

The service was duly held in the great central square; but nobody, not even the Jewish survivors, attended. Much later I told this story to Irwin Shaw, who wrote an inaccurate version of it in his novel *The Young Lions.*

• • •

Our movie unit had been filming in Dachau for nine days when the German army unconditionally surrendered on May 7. Many of the prisoners were still dying, and the rest were barred from release by the U.S. Army. Day and night the striped ones with shaven heads crowded around us, begging, plucking at our sleeves. At first we had given freely, but after a few days we were surprised to find our patience and charity used up.

The days had become soft with spring, and the smell of death everywhere. Groups of striped men sat around small smoky fires, cooking. Some used corpses for cushions. Bundles of discarded clothing lay around like the dead, and the dead lay around like discarded clothing.

On the morning that the 45th Division newspaper announced WAR ENDS, a dozen or so members of our unit left in our jeeps for Austria. On the first evening we camped by a small Bavarian lake, the Kochelsee, with a mountain range looming above it. As we unpacked and built a fire, six boys from the nearby village, evacuees from bombed and devastated towns in the north, came to inspect us.

At first they were cautious and kept their distance. But curiosity and the smell of bacon and the sight of bread soon drew them close. Their ages ranged from ten to fourteen, so-called "typical" Aryan boys with fair hair, wearing leather shorts. Everything about us enthralled them—our equipment, our weapons and cameras, the fact that we came from unbelievably strong and faraway America.

We gave them food, they ate and smiled and talked, they washed our pots and pans in the lake. Most of them spoke a little English, and I spoke enough German to make up the rest. We answered their questions about New York and cowboys and California. As darkness fell, two of the boys played harmonicas and sang by the fire.

We still hadn't figured out what attitude we should take. It was difficult to hate them or accuse them, they were very young and seemed very innocent. But why did they smile at us, and adhere so quickly to us, the enemy? We speculated that because everything around them lay in ruins, ideas as well as buildings, we represented the advance guard of the future, and their loyalty went to the future.

Ivan on his way to Austria after the end of World War II

Until—

They came back before breakfast, while we were packing up our things, and they helped us. They said they were sad to see us go. Then we noticed, approaching from the foothills, a detachment of Wehrmacht mountain troops in green uniforms and peaked caps. They had mules and a small howitzer. Like the boys, we watched them come closer, then stop. Their sergeant came up to us. He smelled of sweat and leather, the smell of the German army. When he glanced at the boys, they looked away.

The sergeant asked where he and his men should go to surrender. We told him there was a Military Police post in the village at the end of the lake. He thanked us, saluted, and without looking at the boys again, started to lead his troop along the shore. After a long moment of silence, we finished our packing, and there was no more laughter or talking from the boys. But as we got into our jeeps, they lined up in order of height to say a formal goodbye.

Ernst, the fourteen-year-old, was at one end of the line, and ten-year-old Max at the other.

"We want to thank you for being such good comrades to us," said Ernst, and the boy next to him added: "Such good comrades we never have had."

Little Max flushed with anger. *"Nein, das kannst du nichtsagen!"* he told the others. ("That you *cannot* say!") Then he turned away and pointed to the distant group of Wehrmacht mountain troops as they headed for the village. *"They* were our true comrades!"

As Max gazed after them, his eyes filled with tears. The others avoided our eyes and remained standing in line, half at attention, while we drove off.

Going east again, we arrived at Buchenwald concentration camp. I talked to many prisoners there, and listened to many disturbing stories. One of them concerned a detachment of Hungarian Jews who believed they were to be part of an official labor battalion, and sang as they marched into the camp. Then the gates closed behind them, and they saw hundreds of desperate emaciated men in striped uniforms, staring at them. The Hungarians stopped singing, and after a brief interval of total silence, the crowd of longtime prisoners burst into loud, derisive laughter.

By this time I had started a new process of thinking about Nazi Germany and the whole Nazi phenomenon. The process intensified as we moved deeper into Germany, and I was able to reflect on the way the Nazis had conquered almost all of Europe, with so many non-Germans eager to do their bidding.

The Germans we encountered were often sullen and hostile, yet anxious to comply with rules and regulations. Their compliance stemmed from more than habit and a traditional way of life. In view of the chaos all around them, they longed to be part of a working mechanism. At the same time, some remained bitterly resentful, like ten-year-old Max at the lake, because the working mechanism was also an agent of chaos.

"Alles kaput!" was their doleful comment, not only on the terrible physical destruction but the collapse of a cherished ideology. Even in a small town whose infrastructure was undamaged, *"Alles kaput!"* was the somber verdict pronounced on loss of belief.

Driving along deserted roads at night, especially through forests, we were in constant fear of being attacked by the much-vaunted Werewolves, the alleged fanatics that Goebbels had ordered to rise up across Germany. But we eventually realized there was no such spirit left in the German people, whether hostile or not, and the Werewolves remained a dream.

I found this strange in view of the fanaticism of the SS that persisted right to the end. There was a grisly and haunting example of it in the Leipzig town hall, a building that had been fiercely defended and was now littered with scores of SS corpses. Upstairs there was a windowless chamber, lit by a single dangling electric bulb. In the center, several half-empty bottles of beer stood on a long wooden table, and around the table sat six tall high-ranking officers frozen in attitudes of death. One sprawled back in his chair. Another clasped a Schweissen hand machine gun. At any moment, I felt, the tableau might unfreeze and these powerful-looking men would kill us. They seemed so intent on death, ours or their own.

While Winston Churchill, Joseph Stalin and the less imposing figure of Harry S Truman attended the Potsdam Conference, a few miles away the Berlin black market was at its height. American colonels, majors, captains and (it was whispered) generals all took advantage of it, feverishly converting their so-called "Occupation Marks" into dollar postal orders.

The sums involved became so enormous that the army decreed all such transactions must cease immediately. There was universal dismay, a few days later the order was rescinded, and once again we were selling cartons of cigarettes, faster than we could buy them at our well-stocked PXs, to Russian soldiers for $100 each.

One farsighted member of our outfit had noted that Russian soldiers paid the highest prices for Mickey Mouse watches. Somehow he managed to cable his parents in Cleveland to send him a batch of a hundred, and sold them all at $100 apiece in three days. This whole black market operation was said to have cost the U.S. Treasury millions of dollars, because it had to honor not only the American-issued Occupation Marks, but the Marks issued to the Russians, which they gave us in exchange for our cigarettes, watches, perfume, soaps and bottles of liquor.

Meanwhile the Potsdam Conference had been suspended to await the outcome of the British General Election. I bet George Stevens that Clement Attlee (leader of the British Labour Party) and not Churchill would be returning to the Conference. He scoffed at the idea, and took my bet two to one—a hundred bucks if I won, fifty to him if I lost.

Two years earlier I had been in an English country pub. A news broadcast was coming in on the radio, and we heard Churchill in the middle of a speech. "And by the terms of our long-standing treaty with the ancient Kingdom of Portugal," he was saying, then the publican exclaimed, "Aw, shut up!" and switched him off.

I won my bet.

In September, to my gratitude and surprise, I was granted leave to fly back to Paris and Natalie. But the owner of the Hotel de la Louisiane shrugged when I asked where she was. *"Elle est rigolote, vous savez."*

Although I knew that meant, "She's a strange one," I didn't know why he said it. But I hung around the lobby anyway, and finally Natalie arrived, all smiles, saying I looked too tanned for her taste.

We had often written to each other, and because of all her letters during a long absence, I supposed that I had got to know her better. Three weeks later, when our outfit was shipped from Le Havre to Boston, I wasn't so sure. As a White Russian, Natalie had no papers when we first met, and the mayor of the sixth *arrondissement* demanded a carton of Chesterfields before he would marry us. But as a GI bride, she would soon be able to join me in America, and I supposed I would get to know her better there. In any case, another urgent question preoccupied me. Like a couple of million other GIs, I had begun to wonder what to do after being discharged from the army.

Meanwhile, Boston was close enough to Martha's Vineyard to allow me to visit my father, who had been living there for several years. When he drove me to his house, I was touched to see that he had placed a star in one of the windows. It meant that you had a son in the army.

Fond of Curtis as I was, he had always tended to be a coldish father, although unfailingly kind, and an artist of original, impetuous fantasy. But there was nothing cold about the Moët & Chandon 1936 except the temperature; and we ate hot toast with the last of the pâté de foie gras, now precious and hard to come by. I spent two lovely days with him, his wife, Kathleen, and my seven-year-old sister, Penelope. Alas, it was the last time I would see Curtis before his suicide four years later.

At Martha's Vineyard, and on the bus back to our camp near Boston, I was conscious of a new mood in the USA, a sense of rising confidence and a hopeful kind of strength. A new teenaged world was being born; teenagers were no longer kids, but people in their own right. The autumn of 1945 was a warm, safe, gently forward-looking time. Fifty-five autumns later, the mood was far from safe or gentle, and I looked back on it as the best of all American times.

When I enlisted in England, I gave Iris Tree's home in Ojai, California, as my address in the USA. I did this in case I decided to go there after the War ended and, in fact, six years of separation had made me eager to see my mother again.

Ivan and Natasha just after getting married in Paris, September 1945

The journey from Boston to California in a long army train took four days, and on the last lap cowboys rode close to the tracks and saluted us. I had my mother's phone number in Santa Monica (wherever that might be), and we arranged to meet at her apartment there.

She was now living part of the time in a spacious apartment above the famous carousel on Santa Monica pier. Perhaps on purpose—because she had an instinct for drama, and of course the apartment and its ocean view setting were dramatic—her back was turned toward me as I came through the door. And when she turned to face me, again a little theatrically, we embraced. Soon afterward she said, "We're going to Salka Viertel's tonight," as if the name was a household word. It meant nothing to me, but I soon learned that Salka Viertel had been an actress in Europe, became a friend of Greta Garbo's in Hollywood, worked on the screenplays of several of her films, and established a famous salon for European expatriates and Hollywood cosmopolitans.

There were a lot of people that night at Salka's house in nearby Santa Monica Canyon. Charlie Chaplin was instantly and easily recognized, like Garbo with the smile I'd seen so often in movies, and the uptilted face that seemed to imply a secret sorrow. Aldous Huxley I had known well in England, Bertolt Brecht I recognized from photographs. In a buttoned-up shirt with no tie, his hair cropped short, I thought for a moment, he looked like an inmate of Dachau. Christopher Isherwood I also recognized from photographs on book jackets. Thomas Mann, a commanding figure, bowed rather stiffly when my mother introduced us. George Cukor, of course, I knew by name, and Igor Stravinsky looked shriveled beside his majestic wife. Max Reinhardt's son Gottfried, first met at Schloss Kammer, was a familiar face, laughing as usual, and like me still in GI uniform.

Of the rest, some were famous and some unknown to me. It was strange, on my second night in California, to be precipitated straight from war-weary Europe into a world I had heard about from books, films and legends, and to find my mother very much part of that world assembled in Salka's modest living room.

An elderly lady in an armchair beckoned me, with a slightly flirtatious look, to sit beside her on the arm. She glanced approvingly at the ribbons on my uniform, then asked in German: "Are you garrisoned here in Hollywood?" I couldn't believe it, not only because she was the first person at that party to speak to me, and she spoke in German. The question, coquettishly asked, came from another, older world; and in the extraordinary new world that I had just entered, it sounded almost grotesque.

Ojai, where my mother had an apricot ranch, was adobe-quaint, perfumed with eucalyptus, orange blossom and dust. (Absolute heaven.) Suddenly, my first thoughts were of Natalie. A letter had already arrived, and I had two undeveloped rolls of Leica film of her, which I'd dropped off in Ventura on the drive to the ranch. She wouldn't arrive here until February 1946, on a ship for war brides, but I'd left money for her with Uncle Andy: money I'd obtained partly by buying a first-class English shotgun in London, and selling it at a huge profit to a Frenchman in Paris. Like all Frenchmen during the Occupation, he'd been obliged to surrender all his guns to the Germans, and was still waiting to get them back.

At another party I met Clifton Fadiman, a former book editor and writer for *The New Yorker*. He was now head of the script department at MGM, and offered me a job as a "junior writer," a category that ceased to exist many years ago. I thanked him and accepted gladly, knowing that my modest credits in documentary films would hardly be adequate recommendation in a new and tougher world.

I was now twenty-seven, and Irwin Shaw's laughing comment in that Paris hospital came back to me: "He's not so young. It's his profession to be young."

A talent scout from 20th Century-Fox had come to a play that my mother produced and acted in at a little theater in Hollywood. He approached me in the lobby and said he wanted to take me to meet Ernst Lubitsch.

"What for?" I asked.

"He's looking for a guy like you, English accent, good-looking, on the classy side, you know what I mean."

"I'm not planning to be an actor," I said.

"But what the hell can you lose by meeting Lubitsch, for God's sake?"

I met with Lubitsch, the talent scout standing at my side. Lubitsch had a dark reddish complexion, looked almost saturnine and had, of course, instant presence. In this instant, a kind of hostile charm. The part he had in mind was for a movie called *Cluny Brown* (and was eventually played by Peter Lawford).

When I said that I didn't really fancy becoming an actor, Lubitsch turned a deeper red. "So what the hell did you bring him here for?" he asked the talent scout.

"Well, sir," the talent scout began, "I— I—"

To save him embarrassment, I interrupted. "Mr. Lubitsch," I said. "I'd like to be a film director. I've done a bit of directing in England and—"

It was now my turn to be interrupted. "You want to be a film director? Okay! Go and be a film director, but don't waste my time!"

A few days later the phone rang at my mother's house. "Is that Eyevan?"

Ivan and Natasha in California, 1946

I recognized the voice at once. George Stevens always pronounced my name that way.

"How are you, Colonel?"

"Well, it's good to be back here, I'll say that. What are you doing, partner? How about some lunch one of these days?"

We had lunch at Romanoff's in Beverly Hills. Both Stevens and I were still in uniform. He was at his most relaxed, with the deceptively "howdy-doody" ambling manner that disguised an incisive and somewhat subversive view of the accepted order.

Alfred Hitchcock was at the next table. After wiping his chin with the napkin tucked beneath it, he gave Stevens a ceremonious but at the same time negligent little bow. We ordered Bloody Marys, and a large man in a dark suit passed our table with a broad smile.

"Well, George, welcome home! When are you going to take that suit off?"

Stevens glowered mildly. "When are you going to put yours on?"

Another man passed our table. "Hi, George!"

"Well, say! . . ."

Then another. "Hi, Mr. Stevens, remember me?"

"Well, how you doing, partner?"

And so on through another round of Bloody Marys.

Toward the end of that round, Stevens told me he was about to form a company, Liberty Films, with Frank Capra and William Wyler. They would each produce and direct three films, he began to explain, then broke off as Jean Arthur came up. Stevens got to his feet, they embraced warmly and kissed. They hadn't seen each other since 1943, when he directed her in *The More the Merrier*. He gave her a quizzical look and said he hadn't realized that Romanoff's was one of her stomping grounds. Jean laughed and said it wasn't, but her agent was taking her to lunch.

"And I think he needs to be seen," she added.

Then Mike Romanoff himself came over to welcome Stevens. He had a very mobile, expressive mouth under a thin mustache, and a deep voice that he used to express himself in very precise, punctilious turns of phrase. Everyone knew, of course, that Mike wasn't a Romanoff, in spite of the crowns and imperial monograms on every book of matches

in the restaurant. His real name was Harry Gerguson, and he was a wiz-
ard at croquet, which he often played with Darryl Zanuck, who had a
passion for the game. Mike was also a first-rate chess player, a game that
was hardly anyone's passion in the movie business, except for Gottfried
Reinhardt, soon to resume his job as a contract producer at MGM.

After Mike left us, Stevens suggested that I consider joining Liberty Films, and I asked in what capacity.

"Well, let's say you'd be working with me as an Associate Producer."

I didn't know enough about Hollywood to have any idea what an
Associate Producer did, but it sounded rather grand.

"Don't make up your mind right away," Stevens said. "Take your
time and think it over. But it might amuse you to find out some of Hollywood's secrets." He grinned. "Although, on second thought, it probably wouldn't. Because, you see, there really aren't any."

When I went to Fort MacArthur for my discharge from the army, they
looked at my file.

"Enlisted in the UK, right?"

"Right, Sergeant."

"Then you're supposed to get your fare back to your place of enlist-
ment. How much d'you reckon that'd be?"

"From here in California, Sergeant, I reckon about eight hundred
dollars."

They fussed for a while, then consulted an officer, and gave me the
money. Eight hundred dollars was a fair sum in those immediate post-
war years, and combined with my black market earnings, it bought me
a bright red 1938 Packard convertible at a used car lot. I didn't have a
driving license and was unable to put the engine in reverse, but figured
if I just drove west, straight ahead to Ojai, I'd be all right. After a couple
of hours I was, more or less.

Every letter from Natalie was precious, but the latest one informed
me she was pregnant. Although she always had some vaguely "existen-
tial" idea that she didn't need or want children, she now changed her
mind.

The bonds of domesticity had not been uppermost in my mind on
the night I cavalierly proposed marriage, and I didn't believe it had been

on Natalie's mind when she wrote that ten-page letter of acceptance. So I wrote back that I thought it too soon to have a baby, and counseled an abortion.

Nothing doing. Baby or no baby, I was longing to see her; and meanwhile there was canned orange juice, powdered milk, chocolate and vitamin supplements to be packed in cartons and mailed to Paris. Meanwhile, too, there were all my photographs of Natalie to look at, some with much love and admiration, others with considerably less of either. Although I recognized it was not the way I should be looking at them, I couldn't stop myself differentiating between the Natalie of one photograph and the Natalie of another.

The pictures were all correctly lit and focused, but in some of them I saw a face that didn't fit my most cherished memories, a face that suddenly replaced tenderness and charm with hostility and a kind of anger. Over the years, it would be the second face that I saw too often.

By the time Natalie arrived, I had accepted Stevens's offer to work with him at Liberty Films, which occupied a bungalow on the RKO lot in Hollywood. I was to be paid $125 a week, far from a high salary by the

Ivan with Irene Dunne and Rudy Vallee on the set of I Remember Mama, *his first assignment as associate producer with George Stevens's Liberty Films*

standards of the time. But it didn't bother me. In spite of an occasional stab of anxiety about my domestic future, I was in high spirits.

The main text of Absolute Heaven *ends here. But Ivan wrote a few additional sections that he planned to incorporate in earlier or later parts of his autobiography. They begin in 1932, with an account of his schooling at Dartington Hall, where his parents decided to send him instead of Stowe, and end in London during World War II.*

Dartington Hall

Dartington Hall was the brainchild of an idealistic couple, Dorothy and Leonard Elmhirst. Dorothy was a Whitney heiress, and in 1925 her money enabled them to buy a fifteenth-century manor house, with extensive gardens, farmland and orchards. Its hillside estate, overlooking the river Dart in Devon, had been neglected for years, and the manor house itself was a rats' playground. But they immediately set about converting farm buildings and stables into schoolhouses, and restoring Dartington's great banqueting hall, medieval kitchen, and courtyard with the crest of King Richard II (half-brother of the original owner) above the porch tower entrance.

The school, which opened in September 1926, was extremely revolutionary, first of all as the only genuinely coeducational school in England. Boys and girls had their rooms next to each other, as in a hotel, instead of being housed in separate buildings like all the other so-called coeducational schools. "It is to the man of imagination," the original brochure stated, "that we owe all that is greatest in human enterprise and discovery"—and for the Elmhirsts enterprise and discovery covered a wide field of human activity, from the arts to agronomy, a textile mill, pottery and furniture workshops, a cider press.

Some people thought it a very wicked place, especially when people like Bertrand Russell, H. G. Wells and George Bernard Shaw came to lecture, and the local clergyman said that the devil had transferred his headquarters from Moscow to Dartington Hall. When we heard that, we relished it. It made us aware of being in a marvelous place, a place where we felt free. There were no punishments, except being forbidden to attend class, which some students thought a great idea at first, but after three days out of the classroom, they couldn't wait to get back.

There were sons and daughters of famously "enlightened" parents at Dartington. Bertrand Russell sent his son and daughter there. Aldous and Maria Huxley sent their son Matthew there, but with less happy results. It worried them that after two years his fascination with woodwork classes had made him neglect what they considered more important aspects of education, and they transferred him to another school.

The restored Grand Hall at Dartington Hall, Devon, where Ivan went to school from 1932–35

Michael Straight, Dorothy's son by her first husband, was at Dartington during my first year. He went on to Cambridge, where he was persuaded by Anthony Blunt to join a Communist cell, but soon thought better of it. Sigmund Freud's grandsons, Clement and Lucian, were three or four years younger than me, but we overlapped briefly, and Lucian's eyes made an immediate impression, very pale blue and, I thought, somehow shrill.

Raimund von Hofmannstal

Gliding across Lake Attersee, on a summer night two years before the outbreak of World War II, was the barge with red sails that belonged to Schloss Kammer, Eleonora von Mendelssohn's castle.

Our host, Raimund—my mother's friend, and the friend of women in general—had said this would be our last summer in Europe. The idea of power and Empire still shimmered then: India, the Grand Fleet, the horizon-blue army of France.

The lake was slender and long. There was no moon, but the outlines of the mountains on either shore lay clear against the stars. The engines stopped and we drifted, the warm air holding such stillness that our drifting seemed softer than the silence.

"Listen!" said Diana Cooper.

"Listen to the lapping," said my mother.

"Not to the lapping. To the silence."

We listened.

Raimund turned toward the stern and raised his glass as a signal to three musicians there. The horn player stood up, facing the nearest mountain, lifted his horn and played the opening bar of Archduke Johann's Hunting Song. He stopped just as the echo of his first note sounded back from the mountain. As it died, violin and harmonica joined as if in salutation. Melody and refrain, horn, harmonica and violin, echoed and reechoed across the lake.

"Look!"

Heads turned.

Something flaming was afloat, a quarter of a mile ahead in the black middle of the lake.

"It's a birthday cake!" said Diana.

Elizabeth Paget turned to Raimund. "Come on! What is it?"

Raimund was separated from his first wife, Alice Astor, and not yet married to Liz Paget. She was twenty, dark-haired with silvery skin, and said by many to be the most beautiful girl in England, just as her aunt Diana was said to be the most beautiful woman.

Raimund signaled to the man at the engine, the barge moved on again and the music played on.

When we came closer, we could see that the lights were eight flaming torches, placed on the castle's bathing raft. It had been towed, complete with dining table, to the middle of the lake at dusk.

In the pink light reflected from the surrounding water, two footmen were standing on one side of the raft; and they made sure that no one lost his balance stepping from barge to raft to dining table, formally set but casually strewn with flowers.

Angelica Weldon sat next to me. Her eyes were gray-blue, sometimes green-blue, and she wore a diamond star at her throat. She was American and beautiful, with a slowly widening smile.

Beyond the circle of light came sounds, the dry bumping of oars as a boat set out from the shore to watch us. Visible soon were curious, unsmiling faces, mustachioed men wearing open shirts, and their wives.

My mother threw a flower as far as she could. Friedrich, her tall Austrian lover, put a gentle hand on her arm. A peasant woman, still unsmiling, reached into the water and picked up the flower.

"*Guten Abend!*" Raimund called quietly, but his "Good evening!" was not answered.

Watched in silence from the boat, we all fell silent. Then Raimund clapped his hands. "*Musik!*"

From the darkness a hundred yards away, a second barge lit up, and a brass band began to play a waltz. Above the music, Raimund called again: "*Feuerwerk!*"

From a third barge six rockets rose and burst softly into stars.

Champagne and vodka were drunk with the meal, poured again and again from buckets of ice. We sat and drank, some holding hands, eyes gleaming in the flares.

Raimund saw that the eyes of the girl next to him were wet, and when she turned her face away, he put his arms around her. "One must never be ashamed to show tears, you know." Then, as if mocking himself: "As long as they don't mean one's taking one's own pleasures too seriously."

Toward the far end of the lake, a small fire seemed to be breaking out on a hillside. It grew into four hooked arms of flame. A huge swastika had been lit in the darkness.

The band played quietly while the rowboats drifted beyond our circle of light.

"*Raimund, has du gesehen?*" said Friedrich.

"Yes, I saw it. That's why I said earlier, this will be our last summer in Austria."

On a rainy afternoon in the autumn of 1943, I was sitting on the barracks floor of the U.S. Army 10th Replacement Depot at Litchfield, where a sergeant from Kansas was demonstrating how to assemble and disassemble an M-1 rifle. There were twenty-five or thirty of us, all more or less misfits, American nationals who had enlisted in England.

From somewhere behind me, I heard an unexpected voice, rich with softly exultant rolling *R*s, calling my name.

Raimund stood laughing, handsomely dressed in green denims and wearing one of those hats with a floppy brim that completed the inelegant uniform known as "fatigues." On him, partly because he wore a cashmere scarf around his neck, they looked as well cut as the vicuna suits I used to admire in Austria.

"I had absolutely no idea, you know!" he said.

The sergeant gave him an angry look. "You there! Quiet!" Then, staring at Raimund: "What's your name?"

"Von Hofmannstal."

"Where's your rifle?"

Raimund hesitated.

The sergeant raised his voice. "Didn't they issue you a rifle?"

"Certainly. Yes."

"Then where the hell is it? In the guardroom?"

"I think so. Yes. Certainly it must be in the guardroom."

"Then go fetch it!"

Raimund started to walk along the narrow row of bunks leading to the door.

"At the double!"

As Raimund made his way past the bunks, a staff sergeant entered the room and glanced at the rest of Raimund's newly issued clothes on his bunk.

"That your bunk?"

"Yes. Certainly."

"Don't you know that blanket's supposed to be blossed down so tight you can bounce a dime off the middle of it?"

"No, I had no idea."

"Then go ahead and bloss it down!"

Raimund had never heard the army slang word "bloss" before, but rightly supposed he had been ordered to smooth down and tuck in the blanket as tightly as possible.

The staff sergeant watched him scornfully for a moment, then jostled past him.

"You don't have to brrrush past me so rrrough, you know!" Raimund called.

The sergeant turned back. "What did you say?"

"I said, you don't need to brrrush past me like that. Just because we are fighting Hitler doesn't mean you have to be so rrrude!"

The sergeant stared at him. "I *know* Hitler, you know," Raimund added for good measure. "And I prrromise you, you are not going to win this war *one single second earlier* by brrrushing past me so rrrough."

Silence followed, broken by the sergeant-instructor's voice. "Hofmannstal, go fetch that rifle on the double! And pull two nights KP!"

But Private Hofmannstal did not do as others did. Although he fetched the rifle, he never pulled a single night at Kitchen Police. The following weeks of infantry training were hard, and the long route marches with field pack and rifle took their toll on him. At forty, he was by far the oldest among us, and had been a favored customer of the best London and New York restaurants.

Still, he was adaptable, naturally strong, and above all ardent. While some of the younger soldiers usually lay by the roadside during the brief rest periods, panting or even vomiting with exhaustion, Raimund merely showed by standing uncharacteristically silent, with bowed head, that the exercise had taxed him to the limit.

At night we would sometimes walk the cold and windy mile-and-a-half to the British canteen, which was officially within limits, for a late meal of bacon and eggs and tea. At neighboring tables, gray-looking and high-ranking British sergeants appeared remarkably old to our eyes, and sat darning socks. They seemed to dwell in a private backwater of their own, very remote from the garish competitive bustle of the American camp. To Raimund this enclave of aged sergeants became England, and because he enjoyed fantasy, he likened our late feasts there to long-ago suppers at the Savoy Grill in London.

We talked with love of times past and built future castles in the air; at one with each other and the world, we believed its hopes were ours. On one occasion Raimund returned from spending Christmas leave at the country house of the Countess of Dudley (who in her youth had learned to pilot a plane and even loop the loop). As he described the impact of that house party on his luxury-starved senses, his barracks-room audience listened with wonder. Even the staff sergeants paid attention, envy overcoming doubt.

"What is so fantastic, you know," said Raimund, singling out the sergeant-instructor, "is that whole extrrraordinary world of women."

The sergeant shifted his chewing gum from one cheek to the other.

"Yeah? What's so extraordinary about it?"

"Well, on one hand, you know, they have this exquisite sense of fantasy, this instinct for beauty and also this sense of *arrrangement*. Their idea of the prrractical is so much better and simpler than ours. In the midst of the beauty they love, they can even take the kind of ugliness you and I have."

The sergeant shifted his gum again.

"I don't mean that personally, you know. I mean, they accept far uglier men than even you or me. And they not only ignore it, they actually *love* us! My wife is the most beautiful girl in England, and yet she loves me!"

His audience looked more doubtful now.

"And the *chandeliers!*" said Raimund. "The white shoulders!" He sighed, turned to his bunk and said softly, for my benefit alone: "*Ach, Gott!*" Then he picked up a Bible and lay down. "I have never actually read this, you know." He laughed quietly to himself. "I mean, from cover to cover, as they say."

And over the following weeks he started to read it, beginning at page one.

When I was ordered to "ship out," as they always called it, I said goodbye to Raimund, who had another two weeks of training. I said that I hoped we would soon meet again in London. But he doubted it. He was destined for some mysterious duty, possibly in civilian clothes, and could not tell me its nature or whereabouts. It seemed clear that an important assignment awaited him, which probably explained why he had enlisted in the first place.

Soon afterward, when I arrived in London, my principal military duty was to lay coal fires in the grates of the two upper floors of what was then known as "Thirty-seven Grosvenor," a building that occupied part of the site of today's American Embassy. It had five floors and steep staircases. There was plenty of coal in its dark, freezing basement, but kindling was difficult. In late January, the lazy but tolerant officers on the two upper floors would stand around in their overcoats until the rooms warmed up. Sometimes this took all day, even though I was required to lay and light the fires long before they arrived each morning at nine.

To ease my task, I made a secret cache of kindling in one of the farthest corners of the basement. Fumbling for it in the darkness early one morning, with the help of matches, I heard someone stumble among the coal heaps. Then a voice called out, as incongruous, welcome and familiar as it had sounded in the barracks room at 10th Replacement Depot. I lit another match and saw Raimund. He was dressed in fatigues, coal bucket in hand. It took a few moments before he started to laugh. But he never explained why he was there.

First Love
(What I could make of it . . .)

I was in love with Angelica Weldon, and she knew that. In New York, in the winter of 1937, I was nineteen and she was twenty-one; but she was fond of me. I loved it when she would smile, with her wide wayward smile, at something I said. Sometimes she laughed at something I said, and I loved her all the more then, but couldn't tell her. I couldn't tell her my instinctive reaction when she confided that she always bought a carnation from the man selling flowers outside the Colony restaurant, who said to her after several months: "I love you but it doesn't concern you."

I felt sure that such a man would never have said such a thing. But I understood why Angelica was so kind in her telling. Although I didn't believe her story, I guessed she was telling how she felt about me, and also that she knew how I felt. And when she said, "Honey, you know how I love you," I sensed exactly what she meant. She loved me less than the older married man we both knew.

But I was nineteen and there was no belief then that either of us would ever be loved, in the end, by anyone we loved.

Before I left New York, Angelica gave me a copy of *Man's Hope* by André Malraux, and a tiny glass plate of a color photo of herself (sapphire eyes, matching turban around her head) that had recently appeared in *Vogue*. On the third day of 1938, which was also my third day on the liner bound for Southampton, the ship's newspaper had a series of bold headlines: "Germans Enter Austria!" "Hitler declares an 'Anschluss!' " "Crowds in Vienna Welcome Troops!"

When the steward came into my cabin to make up the bed, he told me: "Lord Beaverbrook takes a very serious view of the situation, sir."

Beaverbrook, of course, was widely known in England as the owner of three newspapers, including the *Daily Express,* that propagated his imperialist views.

"He's a passenger on board?" I asked the steward.

"Oh, very much so, sir."

How ridiculous, I thought. When Beaverbrook's dead, will anyone take him as seriously as this steward is taking him now?

And then, suddenly, I'm thinking of the summer at Schloss Kammer only a few months earlier, when I first met Angelica. My mother and Friedrich, Eleonora, Raimund and Alice, Gottfried Reinhardt—are all there. Angelica wears a different dirndl every morning, and one morning I tell her that I'm trying to get a message to a newspaper, because I want to be a spy and work for the Republicans in Spain.

"What newspaper?" she asks.

I tell her that Max Reinhardt's assistant, Rudolf Kommer, knows the editor of *Die Salzburger Volksblatt.*

"They wouldn't send you to Spain, not for the side you're on." Then she pressed my arm. "Honey, for my sake, don't try and go to Spain. I want you intact." She smiles. "I'm selfish and I want to keep you close for a long, long time."

I wonder intensely if this is true; and if true, how true, and in what way?

Angelica is older, cleverer and infinitely more sophisticated than me. I smell her perfume, which she tells me is called "Rumeur." Then she says, in her soft self-mocking way: "Besides, honey, you're too pretty for me to let you go off and get killed. Do you want me to spend the rest of my life in mourning? Always wearing black?"

At dusk it started to rain. I walked along the corridor to my mother's room. She was sitting up in bed, wearing a yellow nightgown and smoking a cigarette. Angelica lay at the end of the bed, knees raised. This was interesting, but I didn't care. I wanted most of all to reunite with Angelica, so I settled on the bed between the two of them.

September 7, 1940

Nobody knew, of course, early on in that late summer evening of 1940, that one of the turning points of World War II was about to occur. By the time I got to the roof of my father's apartment at 4 Fitzroy Square, the warning sirens had died away and all seemed quiet. For most of the summer the sirens had died away, and all had seemed quiet. But this time, gradually, a new sound began. It was different from any sound we'd heard before, a low, purposeful, pervasive giant-beehive humming that came from everywhere, and yet in that soft evening sky, showed no sign of coming from anywhere.

Then it grew in volume, reverberating so massively that it had to be the sound of planes, hundreds of them. But *where?*

And then, far up above, far higher than my eyes had focused, a prick of red light, and smoke puffs—and suddenly I saw them, formation after formation after formation, hundreds of tiny silver flies, so tiny as to be nearly invisible in the pale September light. Little bursts of smoke opened up below them, and a sound shook the roof, shockingly close, while the silver specks cruised steadily, unharmed and apparently harmless—until huge, thick, black and gray towers of smoke began to climb above the burning docks of the East End.

This was how the Blitz came to London on Saturday, September 7, 1940. The fires in the East End raged all through the night, and the bombers returned to intensify them. The year had begun (before France surrendered) with relative complacency, but now Britain was alone in the War, facing a triumphant enemy in command of more than half the rest of Europe.

And nobody knew, of course, that within a few months the RAF would have destroyed so many Luftwaffe planes that the city was able to enjoy a reprieve until the V-1 and V-2 rockets renewed the attack three years later. At the time I shared the general sense of foreboding, which was secretly shared by powerful figures in Britain's corridors of power. It was even felt, momentarily at least, by Prime Minister Churchill himself. Although he always adopted a mask of Britain's invincibility, soon after that first night of the Blitz, Churchill confided his foreboding to his Minister of Information and close friend, Duff Cooper.

His wife, Lady Diana Cooper, told me this in confidence a few years before her death in 1986. She said (and understandably, I remember her words very well), that Duff had come home late to their house on Gower Street looking "very green under the gills. I said to him, 'What on earth is the matter?' And he said, 'I've just been with Winston. I asked him what he thought was going to happen now, and he said, "I'm afraid we shall go down, but we shall go down gloriously." ' "

Duff Cooper had been dead for many years when Diana told me this story. She hadn't told it to anybody else, she said; and I, in turn, was not to tell it until after her own death.

Gargoyle Times

One thing may be said for certain about the Gargoyle Club. There was nothing serious about it. It was designed as a place of entertainment for bon vivants of both (or all) sexes, and the business of being not too serious—while trying to avoid the taint of outright frivolity—became a tightrope along which the club and its members walked, and sometimes teetered.

The need to escape relevance to the times we were living in, especially during the drab years of wartime London, was something which David Tennant, the Gargoyle's founder, could well understand. Born to wealth and the "best" country house society, he had almost no formal education until (coached by a series of tutors) he was accepted by Trinity College, Cambridge; and toward much of the world David always had the eye of an untrained, restless and intelligent human colt. Despite a streak of coldness, he veered with a smile between the superlative and the excessive, relishing either mode; and either way, he was half cockeyed and half brilliant.

Although my father had known David well, I owed my friendship with him to his second wife, my cousin Virginia Parsons. (His first wife was the actress Hermione Baddeley.) Virginia and David made a romantic and beautiful couple. With her screen of golden hair often partly hiding her heart-shaped face, Virginia seemed to be hiding behind David as well. The gesture tended to conceal more than just her physical presence. It disguised a strong underlying personality and will.

David was physically very strong, "about the strongest member of the upper classes," as one of his friends rather enigmatically said. For exercise he chopped trees. His jaws were taut and dark, and he habitually clenched them, perhaps because, for all his charm, his air of confidence, and an imagination capable of transforming an unremarkable, neglected Victorian building into a sophisticated and cosmopolitan private playground for some of the most talented and notorious figures of the time, he was basically shy.

In the autumn of 1940 a Gargoyle familiar, Brian Howard, was sitting at the club's high bar, alone and proud. Behind and below him, five young army officers sat drinking and eating from a plate of cold chicken. Since the British Army's heroic retreat from Dunkirk after France had surrendered to the Nazis in June, Britain had also been alone and proud in its way. Night after night the population of London sat in their bomb shelters singing "There'll Always Be an England" and "Roll Out the Barrel, Let's All Have a Barrel of Fun."

And at the Gargoyle that night, Brian turned to stare at the group of cheerful young officers. "Hmmm, my dears!" he said.

He didn't catch their attention the first time. But at the second, louder "Hmmm, my dears!" they looked up and saw Brian swaying cobra-like above them. He waved a brown velvet cuff, and his voice sounded as if made of the same material.

"Members of a rather unsuccessful *profession*! Members of His Majesty's *forces*!" Brian shook a bejeweled and reproachful forefinger from side to side. "Dunkirkie-wirkie, my dears, Dunkirkie-wirkie!"

Natalie Newhouse was sitting beside me at a nearby table. For the next five seconds, she took my hand in a rare moment of trepidation. Brian exhaled a puff of laughter and turned back to survey the array of bottles behind the bar. The moment passed, and I marveled that in

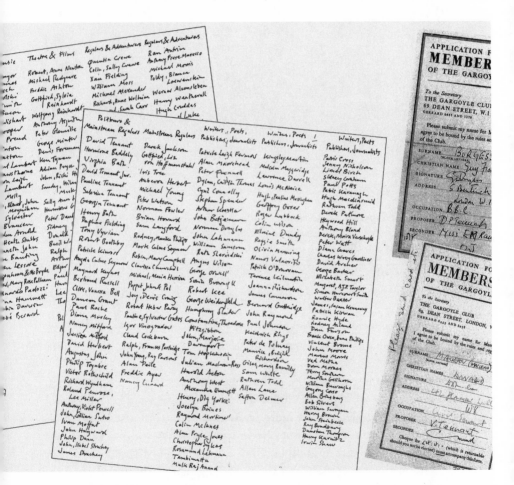

A list of the distinguished members of the Gargoyle Club, with Ivan Moffat in the far left column, fifth from the end

Caxton Hall, London, November 1938: High Bohemia in formal attire at the wedding (a civil ceremony) of David Tennant and Virginia Parsons. Left to right, front row: David Tree (actor son of Viola Tree), Ivan, Lady Felicity Cory-Wright (Ivan's aunt), Iris Tree, Lady Elizabeth Glenconner (David Tennant's sister, married to Lord Glenconner), Curtis Moffat. Back row, on step: Agnes Beerbohm (sister of Max Beerbohm), unidentified man, Courtney Merrill (behind Curtis), manager of the Gargoyle Club

no other country of the world—and perhaps nowhere except at the Gargoyle—could such behavior, at such a time, have escaped serious retribution.

I glanced at the officers as they tolerantly resumed picking at their chicken legs and drinking. Could such men win the war? Perhaps not, I thought, but they were no more likely to lose it. And just as surely as there would (somehow) always be an England, there would always be a Gargoyle of one sort or another.

In fact, as far as the Gargoyle was concerned, there would not—for a while, at least. The decision to close, after three months of the Blitz, was made partly because David was about to join the army, and partly

ABSOLUTE HEAVEN   193

because the club had become almost as deserted as the streets of Soho. Some of the regulars had taken to leaving London before nightfall, and taxis were very scarce during the nightly air-raid alerts.

On a late yellowish afternoon in December of that 1940–1941 winter, David and I performed the simple ceremony of drinking the remaining opened bottles of the bar. After he polished off the Poire, and I the Slivovitz, David drained what was left of the Fernet Branca. Then he announced that somewhere in the bar there was a bottle of "Strongwater," as he called it, a drink allegedly much favored in the eighteenth century to induce vomiting. Unable to find it, he produced instead a bottle labeled Alcool de Montpelier. One sip was enough to tell us that it was the next best thing.

As night fell, and we also polished off the Grand Marnier, the Cointreau, and the Crème de Menthe, and German bombers could be heard droning above the clouds, David started trying to define what the Gargoyle had stood for. "The thing is," he said, "it's been a *very* long time since it stood for anything I wanted it to stand for. Except, of course, for one's own *terribly* begrudging hospitality."

He said this without smiling, and I realized the night had entered a darker phase for David. Usually he found many things to be amused by during an evening at the club, although at other times he would sit alone at the bar, avoiding everyone's eyes, and take a lonely, frowning nightcap. When Virginia was there he might seek her out, but more often than not he would spend a dark hour alone.

On this night, however, David decided on a brisk walk as far as Oxford Street. It was on my way home to Fitzroy Square, and I accompanied him. "To think we shall never be laughing in the Gargoyle again!" he said as we both started to walk a little unsteadily. The thought seemed to give him a moment of grim satisfaction. "But it might be the best possible thing for all of us," he went on. "In short, a blessing in so thin a disguise that even Doctor Watson could see through it."

By the time we reached Oxford Street, totally deserted and still, the clouds had parted to reveal a small bright moon. Far away over the suburbs, a single plane could be heard droning, and we could see tiny red specks of anti-aircraft shells as they burst in the sky. It seemed as if just one gun and one plane were involved, and when I remarked on this, David nodded and said: "Curious to think that one plane and a single gun are probably all that keeps the war going in the whole of Europe. Well, goodnight!"

He often terminated an evening in that brisk manner, but I found it surprising on that particular evening, which must have meant the ending of so many things for him.

The last great air raid on London occurred on May 10, 1941. Soho and Bloomsbury were especially hard hit with incendiary bombs, and the streets and squares had flared brilliantly in a magnesium light before fires took over, orange and red. By this time, David, on the verge of a nervous breakdown, had been declared "temperamentally unfit" for military service and invalided out of the army. When he reopened the Gargoyle six weeks later, a new, vigorous and more raffish phase of the club's existence began.

Among the most raffish newcomers were the painter Francis Bacon, and the actor Robert Newton, who first met Natalie Newhouse there. Guy Burgess recruited a fellow drinker and secret KGB agent, Donald Maclean, as well as Gerald Hamilton, the model for Christopher Isherwood's Mr. Norris of the *Berlin Stories*. Americans started to appear, notably three writers, Harry Brown, William Saroyan and Irwin Shaw, all in GI uniform. So was I, after my return from training camp, when the ballroom band, to my great embarrassment, struck up "Over There." Among the familiar regulars were Cyril Connolly and Peter Quennell (with their respective, colorful and frequently changing wives or girlfriends); also Brian Howard, Augustus John, Dylan Thomas and Philip Toynbee, drinkers almost as profound as Newton.

Formality, of which there had never been a great deal, all but vanished. Laughter and tears alternated more readily. Fistfights and love affairs broke out, often between the same couples, who sometimes threw bottles at each other, and at lunchtime the following day, members discussed them as eagerly as the brightening prospects of the war.

But it was Natalie, although not a newcomer, who embodied the new spirit of the Gargoyle: a spirit of gaiety and abandon with an underlying acrid taste. Gregarious or seated alone with a scowl, she seemed to know by instinct everything that a much longer experience of life might have untaught her. Unique and self-made, too true to herself, perhaps, to live long in the hard world she bravely and beguilingly confronted, Natalie seemed to arrive from heaven or hell, depending on her mood and the hour of day or night. She died unexpectedly in the mid-1950s, and was greatly mourned.

The last time I entered the Gargoyle (for ten years, anyway) was in September 1945, on four days' leave from France. Once again the place had changed. The War had ended, but the relief of victory was already giving way to feelings of deprivation and discontent. They were soon aggravated, as I learned from letters I received in California, by the stresses and shortages of the bleak cold winter that followed.

In this atmosphere of diminished expectancy the Gargoyle entered its period of final decline; although I doubt the decline was much noticed, amidst the restless laughter and quarrels of its members, until the party was all but over.

The Last of Iris

London, April 1968. "There are few things so sad," she said, "as the clothes of a dead dandy. Or harder to describe."

Half beauty, half broken doll, knight-errant gypsy, hair-helmet turning slowly through red, gold, to faded yellow, while her eyes—once lighthouses—became the sockets of dreams; striped skirts, champagne shirts, gold and silver sequins, parti-colored stockings, and in 1925 the first of faded jeans, then a plum-colored cloak, then a black, now a nightdress transparent over dying limbs.

Her gift was words.

"Iris," I said at last, at half past six, "would you now like anything to drink?"

"I think, maybe—yes—I think I would like . . ."

"Yes, yes—what?"

"All right, then—a little vodka, perhaps, to keep me quiet."

LETTERS

Although Ivan was not a prolific letter writer, the best of the few that survive provide valuable glimpses of his life in Europe and California between 1945 and 2000.

Julien Langenakens was the young Belgian POW whom Ivan met in the "very crude hospital" near Dachau, and who asked him to let his family know that he was alive.

TO M. LEON LANGENAKENS

Ptc. Ivan R. Moffat, 10601486
Special Motion Picture Unit
SHAEF PRD
APO 757
U.S. Army, Germany
April 15, 1945

Dear M. Langenakens,

I have great pleasure in being able to inform you that your brother Julien is safe and well in American hands. As you know he has been a prisoner of the Germans for some twenty-two months, but it will not be long before he is enabled to rejoin you once more. But a little time will be necessary for the organization of transport etc, for the large number of prisoners and workers who are daily being liberated by our troops.

I have had a long talk with your brother today during which he spoke of the many adventures he has had in German hands, but for obvious reasons I leave it to him on his return to give you the details you so urgently wish to know.

I hope, sir, that you and your brother may be most speedily reunited. Should you desire further information, you may reach me care of the above U.S. Army Post Office.

Yours faithfully,

Ivan Moffat

P.S. I would like to make it clear to you that I am in no way connected with the organization dealing with released prisoners or displaced persons, and that the initiative I have taken in this matter is entirely unofficial.

TO FAMILY LANGENAKENS

Box 90. Route 1
Ojai, California, USA
November 7, 1945

Dear Family Langenakens,

First I must apologize for the terrible time it has taken me to receive and reply to your sad letter concerning Julien, dated May 28. Your letter had apparently followed me through different army addresses, and in the meanwhile, I was returned to America at the end of the summer.

I will try and give you, my unknown friends, as clear a picture as I can of the circumstances under which I encountered and last saw Julien. He had been transferred from the terrible camp at Nordhausen (a kind of temporary prison settlement run by the Nazis) to the "hospital" of a V-2 factory camp at Dachau.

It was through the open windows of this wooden hospital that I caught sight of Julien when we were inspecting the place for photography. Now, I have seen many faces of prisoners before and since I saw Julien, and believe me they are not always a very inspiring sight. But Julien was an exception. He was lying on an upper bunk in the "hospital" ward, and thus had a clear view overlooking the outside space behind his head.

I was immediately struck by his clear, pale skin, his piercing eyes of a deep, almost violet blue, and the unusual intensity of his gaze. He looked pale and thin, but in full command of his mental faculties and his limbs. I immediately understood that I was in the presence of no ordinary person, and started to talk to him, give him cigarettes and such small amounts of food as I had on me. His somewhat fierce, almost angry facial expression softened at this gesture, and he smiled and seemed to be somewhat comforted.

It was while we were speaking together at the window that a photograph of us was taken by one of my fellow cameramen (but I will speak of this later). I then proceeded inside the building, where I interviewed Julien's neighbor in the next bed, Hubert Erdmann of Brussels, whose widow lives there and with whom I have had a similarly sad correspondence. This Hubert Erdmann had been with Julien throughout most of his period of captivity.

The tale he told was a long one—it was really the history of their constant movement from camp to camp, under slowly worsening conditions. It was a story of undernourishment and occasional brutality. I should guess from Julien's appearance that he had developed some form of tuberculosis—his eyes were so preternaturally brilliant, his skin so transparently clear and pale, his face so thin. In spite of this, I should judge him to have once been a very handsome boy.

During our conversation I realized that Julien was now, at least, happy and full of the feeling of freedom. There was no question in his mind but that he would make a speedy recovery, and that he would soon be able to see you. I must say I thought the same thing—he seemed so full of an inner vitality that should have assured his life. But I suppose the prolonged malnutrition had done its fatal work.

He was eating well while I spoke to him, and the impression I received that morning was of a young idealist of the best possible type— the type about whom books are written and films of the Resistance are made. This is not always the impression one receives from those who have been subjected to long periods of degradation, but Julien had survived, spiritually, all the horrors of his confinement.

We shook hands when I left, and I promised to write to you and say that he was well—that was what he made me promise to say. I am sorry for the pain I may have caused you. I had no intention of doing harm.

The photograph: it was taken through the window by a cameraman called either Richard Hoare or Kenneth Markey. They belonged to the Special Motion Picture Unit, PRD SHAEF. The date was two or three days (approximately) before the date of my first letter. It must be somewhere in the archives of the U.S. Army Signal Corps, Washington, D.C. The camera was a "speed-graphic." Don't forget to mention the window, the face of a young man in hospital, if you should ever apply for it. My advice is, do not. It may shock you. But if you do, please do not mention my name.

If I can be of any further service, don't hesitate to ask it of me.

Yours,

Ivan Moffat

TO KATHLEEN MOFFAT

400 South Barrington Avenue
Los Angeles 49, Calif.
December 6, 1949

Dearest Kathleen,

I'm glad you're back in this country again, and of course I envy you being in New York. One has to concentrate hard nowadays to remember what it's like living in a highly civilized part of the world. I most assuredly do wish I was there, or could see a chance of getting there in the near future. But it now looks as if we shall go straight into another production [*Shane*] almost before this one [*A Place in the Sun*] has been finally cleaned up and shown. It will be a very good film, I think, but sad.

As Natalie spends most of her day at the University [teaching Russian at UCLA], and I never come home before eight in the evening, Lorna is down at Ojai with Iris for the time being. We are paying for the support and wages of two Polish refugees who help Iris with the house and farm, and Lorna absolutely adores it down there. Iris is really extraordinarily good with her—and all children—and is able to devote most of her time to Lorna. Also, she has the freedom of the farm and its animals, and I am very pleased with the arrangement. We ourselves go down as often as we can, and are of course spending Christmas there.

Love,
Ivan

Ivan, Natasha, and Lorna in California

TO KATHLEEN AND PENELOPE MOFFAT

Hotel Boston
Via Lombardia, Rome
March 25, 1953

Darling Kathleen and Penelope:
    Rome is so much more beautiful, even, than I had imagined. Its richness makes it seem like the world's most enormous city, with the extra

dimensions of Time everywhere manifest, so that the places never look the same twice—there is always a new vision to catch the eye, a new color, a richness hidden heretofore by different lights and shadows. Paris has a formal beauty of course that is unequalled anywhere else, but Rome has this profusion, this generosity, handed down through history, of styles and streets and buildings from all its previous ages, still glowing in the sunset colors of ochre, red and saffron, and all in use, all lived-in and living. It is almost as ghosts of the twentieth century that we move unbelievingly among these buildings from the past—the Age is their Age, one feels, not ours.

I told Penelope that I would probably be here until July, and I hope this turns out to be so, as I do love it here. Officially our work [on a movie for Paramount, never produced] ceases on the first day of May, but they tell us we are very likely to be here until late in the summer. I move into a very comfortable, rather richly gloomy apartment next week on the Via Gregoriana, in the heart of old Rome, above the Spanish Steps, and I do hope that the season will see you both here.

There are lots of English people here from the old days, and all *sorts* of gossip, most of it, of course, unrepeatable. One amazing thing: David Tennant and Virginia are getting divorced—she is going to marry the Earl of Bath, who is very nice but sort of fast in an intelligent kind of way, and charming, while David is going to marry, of all improbable people, the rather frightening little girl I had a great deal to do with, Natalie, who finally married Robert Newton and is now divorced from him. I really call that making ends meet! [But Natalie died the following year, David settled in Torremolinos with a very young wife, Shelagh Rainey, and opened Shelagh's Bar, which became fashionable for a while.]

However, I think Virginia at least will be very happy with Bath, who used to be [Viscount] Weymouth, rather sort of scandalously married in those days to Daphne whatever-her-name-was [daughter of Lord and Lady Vivian, later Daphne Fielding]—you and Curtis must have known them.

Much love,

Ivan

TO GEORGE STEVENS

Columbia Pictures Corporation
1438 Gower Street
Hollywood 28, California
July 1, 1958

Dear George:

I do know how busy you are trying to keep the boys and girls happy [while filming *The Diary of Anne Frank* for 20th Century-Fox], but all the same I wish you'd find a couple of hours on a Saturday or Sunday to see the French movie [by André Cayatte] *We Are All Murderers* at the Beverly Canon. In effect, it's a plea against capital punishment, and much of it takes place in the condemned cells of La Santé prison, Paris. It also deals to some extent with Paris under the Germans.

Interestingly, the way it sets up the drab mechanics of execution procedures reminds me of *A Place in the Sun,* although of course in this case the film has much more to do with that. The detail and the use made of it is terrific. Despite the over-convenience of the characterization of the leading figure, I think you will really find this a worthwhile film.

See you soon, I hope.

Yours ever,

Ivan

TO LORNA MOFFAT

12101 Mulholland Drive
Beverly Hills, California 90210
[undated]

Darling Lorna,

You will already have had your happy Christmas, so it's too late to wish you one, but I do wish you all the success in your good work [for environmental groups] for next year and time to come.

Remember that lovely poem by Yeats which ended: "And pluck till time and times are done / The silver apples of the moon / The golden apples of the sun"? Go pluck 'em, kid!

Love,

Papa

Soon after Kate divorced him, Ivan had a "walk-out" with Laura Canfield, who had become Laura, Duchess of Westminster as a result of her brief (third) marriage to the 10th Duke. Their mutual friend, American producer Kenneth Hyman, was domiciled in England at the time, but had contracted to produce a film for United Artists in Hollywood. He signed Ivan to write the screenplay, and facilitated his return to Los Angeles by loaning him his "rather grand" house in Bel Air.

TO LAURA, DUCHESS OF WESTMINSTER

351 Delfern Drive

L.A., Calif. 90024

[1974]

Darling Laura,

Many thanks for your sweet letter, with its bitter enclosures about England. I still miss it, and OF COURSE I miss YOU, very much. What I'm up to here is not so much having a good time (although that happens now and then) as making it possible to revisit England under better circumstances than before. I'm not even here for tax-avoiding purposes, but simply to make enough money to pay taxes here or anywhere else!

In other words, now that I'm here gives me the chance to re-establish myself in the international film world. I have been given that chance, am working on a "big" movie for Ken Hyman, and I've got to go through with it.

I shall try and come to England for a few weeks in the early autumn, and maybe spend Christmas there after that. Meanwhile when the money comes in I can start to pay off some debts and overdrafts and feel something like a carefree man again, after some years of worry and gloom.

Everyone here talks about England, mostly with sympathetic pessimism. The last of the film Americans from London—[writer-producer] Carl Foreman and [producer] Irving Allen—have come back here, pretty much to stay. But American visitors return from London with ecstatic accounts of Annabel's [disco] and how lovely it all is.

Marguerite and Mark Littman are here and being much feted. Mark predicts a two-dollar pound. (You lent me not a few pounds at 2.35, which I hope to start repaying at that rate!)

Lots and lots of love,

Ivan

TO LAURA, DUCHESS OF WESTMINSTER

12101 Mulholland Drive
Beverly Hills, California 90210
(213) 278-7065
Sept 28th [1974]

Darling Laura,

It seems such ages since we spoke or wrote to each other. I think of you often and wonder how you are, and hope that you're well, and have often wondered about the drought [in England] and the lawn at Gallibrands [her country house], to say nothing of the trees and flowers and shrubs. Here the insipid Beverly Hills autumn—which never becomes winter—is drifting onwards.

I've rented a pretty little shack in the sky, high up overlooking the city, with a nice pool and masses of plumbago in permanent blossom, very private and what's called "in its own grounds" of about three and four acres. Often I don't go into the town for days, but stay up here and type. Things are still going well [on the screenplay], touch wood. It's such an incredible feeling just to know what the next few months will be like and to have anxiety of that sort all melted away from one's life, anyway for the time being. And thank you again for your sweet generous help while I was in London. I am herewith sending you some of what you kindly lent.

Anyway, let me have a word. Lots of loving thoughts. Darling Laura. I miss you.

Ivan

FOR GEORGINA [MOFFAT], ON HER CHRISTENING, 1989

Though you'll see summers far away
And bathe in next century's sun
There'll be time I hope for us to play
And for me to share some fun.
In an age I can but dream about
You'll answer questions I cannot frame
Of how the world was born, no doubt,
And whence it came.
You will win games not yet invented
Ride great trains on air suspended
Smell new smells as yet unscented
Tread old roads still not yet ended.
But into that time, to me so far,
I hope you'll take a part of me
And say you knew your grandpapa—
Ivan—of a family called Tree.

TO PATRICK LEIGH FERMOR

249 S. Spaulding Drive
Beverly Hills, California 90212
August 10, 2000

My dear Paddy,

Though I'm usually breakfasted by eight, I'm ashamed to say that when you called yesterday, I was still awash in the surf of those very light dreams which come with sound slumber.

I so deeply regret not being able to go to the dinner. What is honestly remarkable to me—though by no means a consolation—is the fact that I'm still sufficiently around to be able to miss anything at all.

Today is the 60th anniversary of the German invasion of France, and somewhere in the background of that memory I recall trying on your Irish Guards cap and shuddering at the mirrored image.

My fondest wishes to you on your 85th.

Your friend,

Ivan

TO LUCY LANE [GODDAUGHTER]

249 S. Spaulding Drive
Beverly Hills, CA 90212
June 6, 2002

Darling Lucy,

Here's a little something in the way of saying I hope you have fun on your birthday.

Today is D-Day—fifty-eight years after it happened, but I remember it every June 6th, and often on other days as well—which is as dull a bit of information as I ever hope to impart to you on your birthday.

Love always,

Ivan

VOICE PRINTS

During the California years, Ivan gave a great many interviews, many of them preserved on tape. Subjects included his World War II experiences; working with George Stevens on A Place in the Sun, Shane, *and* Giant; *movie and literary personalities in Los Angeles; Iris Tree's role in* La Dolce Vita; *a comment on reaching the age of* 83; *and his memories of Caroline Blackwood, privately taped for her daughter, Evgenia (Citkowitz) Sands.*

The Liberation of Paris

One knew at the time it was going to be the most exhilarating day [August 25, 1944] of one's life. I mean, it couldn't help but be, particularly as we thought that the War was pretty much over and the Germans were in headlong retreat. That proved, tragically, not to be the case. But the atmosphere was absolutely extraordinary, as I said, intoxicating, exhilarating, with these thousands and thousands of people embracing us, embracing each other under an absolutely brilliant sky, Paris looking absolutely marvelous, not at all shabby, the women beautifully dressed, an atmosphere almost like a bullfight, with undertones of a sort of vindictiveness and vengeance against those who had occupied the city. Acts of spite and vengeance, quite understandable, against the occupying Germans whenever they appeared.

But, above all, this roaring welcome and this extraordinary sense of not liberating Paris, but our being liberated *by* Paris. Our spirits absolutely opened, you know, like balloons shooting up into the sky. And this marvelous embrace, this totally genuine love affair which took place between the people of Paris and all the Allied soldiers who arrived during the first two or three days, and you knew it was a love affair that couldn't possibly last, but whilst it did it had this incredible intensity.

A Meeting on the Elbe

It must have been late April [1945] and we were driving along these narrow roads towards the town of Torgau on the Elbe, which is an old fortress town occupying principally the eastern bank of the river. We knew that we going to meet the Russians, and this was tremendously exciting and we suddenly felt, "Well, when we meet them, theoretically we can just drive on to Vladivostok, and there's not an enemy in between, and then, bar the Japanese, you could take a ship across the Pacific."

It was a sense of the whole world being encircled once more. Navigable, as it were. Anyway, there were lots of German prisoners on either side of this road, very passive, sitting on the ground and watching us, and then you came into this steep town, Torgau, and exchanged sights—the usual tangled wires, tangled telegraph wires falling on the ground. That was always the thing in the War, broken telegraph wires, white dust. And down this steep street, two GIs—only two GIs visible, both drunk—one pounding on the doors of each house as he passed it with the butt of his rifle, and wearing nothing on his head, the other

George Stevens with two Russian soldiers. This became a publicity stunt: in April 1945 U.S. troops link up with Soviet troops on the River Elbe.

Ivan at the Truman Bridge on the Elbe with photographer Dick Hoar, left

wearing a black top hat and carrying a fiddle, staggering down the street to no apparent purpose. Strange spectacle.

And then we came down to the river's edge. The bridge had been blown up so there was a ferry which could take people across, backwards and forwards, and there were the usual crowds of people making their way home—east to Russian-occupied Poland or west from that part of Germany to France, to Italy, wherever they had to go. That was, by the way, one of the most extraordinary features of that marvelous spring when the War was coming to an end and one sensed that everybody was going home. All the men who had been either in the army, or imprisoned, or in forced labor, making their way back, mostly on foot, down those dusty roads—Italians, you know, going south, Norwegians going north, French going west, Poles and Russians going east, Greeks going to the Balkans, everybody passing and passing and passing. Survivors.

The first Russian I saw—I think we took a photograph of him—was a bald-headed private. They had some quite old privates in the Russian army, sort of bald-headed hoary old fellows with gold teeth and shaven heads, and this private was unspooling some signal wire. He had a big spool of wire on his back and he came up to me—this sounds very improbable but it's true—came up to me and grinned. "*Capitaliste!*" he said to me, then he pointed to himself and said, "*Communiste!*" And grinned again.

Then George [Stevens] and I went over to the east bank on the ferry, and as we were going up the grassy bank on the far side, one of the Russian soldiers who'd been sleeping out—he was tight and sleeping it off, and was cradling a submachine gun—one of his comrades came by and gave him a violent kick on the shin, and the soldier woke up and started firing his machine gun at the one who'd kicked him. And everybody lay flat, you know, we didn't want to die, and then a Russian officer ran up the bank to the soldier who was still shooting at the other to no purpose, and he took the gun away from and wagged his finger at him, and that seemed to be the end of that.

Later the Russian general invited us over to where there was a great vat of fried eggs, which was nice because eggs were scarce then, and he gave us wine as well, and a lot of them started dancing, Russian women soldiers, men doing that dance on their haunches, you know, which was great fun. Then we looked at each other's equipment, saw their cameras and machine guns, and I remember so well from seeing that old Russian film, the Eisenstein film *October*, where they had those strange old-fashioned machine guns like old World War I machine guns on wheels—and here they were again, the same things.

George Stevens and World War II

I think that seeing the extent to which the prisoners at Dachau had been reduced to fear had a tremendous effect on George. The obvious terror with which they looked at us, even though we were liberators.

George had sometimes felt humiliated as a child by the pomposity of his father [Lander Stevens], a rhetorical actor with elaborate gestures and a sententious, superior way of speaking. The theme of humiliation goes through so many of his films. *Gunga Din* is ultimately a humiliating story of somebody who isn't really a soldier but pathetically trying to be, and [is] put down by the others for trying. In *Alice Adams* the heroine and her small-town family are put down for being socially inferior. *A Place in the Sun* is basically the story of somebody from a humble branch of the family who comes into contact with the richer, more powerful branch, and given a job that puts him in an inferior position.

Shane had the theme of the underdog homesteaders being trodden down, unable to withstand the onslaught of the ranchers. And when the Southerner played by Elisha Cook, Jr., is shot by the hired gunman, he's only killed after he's been insulted and humiliated. James Dean in *Giant* was an underdog like Monty Clift in *A Place in the Sun*, but a supreme underdog who came up and made it. The Mexicans in that film also endure humiliation when they're not allowed in the diner and the hairdressing salon. *Diary of Anne Frank* (which I didn't work on) has a fundamental situation where people, because of their race, have to wear the Star of David and hide ignominiously in an attic for years.

Humiliation on a small scale is comedy, but humiliation on a larger scale, which George was in a position to observe in Europe at the end of World War II, is no longer comic and becomes a tragedy. I don't think that in all his earlier light treatments in comedies like *Alice Adams* it ever occurred to George that this kind of thing could be practiced on such an extraordinary scale of cruelty.

When I first met him, George didn't like *Citizen Kane*. He said it was just tricks of depth of focus and other effects which we'd all known about. And then, by the end of the War, he'd reconsidered all that, and thought how serious and marvelous it was, one of the best films he'd ever seen.

About books he also became much more serious, and much more tolerant of intellectual thought. He had been somewhat of a philistine

Ivan in the secret underground passage at Goering's house, which led to many rooms, including a projection room where George Stevens checked the movie log to see if any of his films had been shown

in his outlook before then, and rather boohooed anything that smacked too much of intellectuality.

George had beautiful manners, and he understood what manners were for, what they were about. But underneath this Howdy Doody–like manner, and golf playing and fishing in the mountains, was a somewhat rebellious character in his attitude to society and established government—increasingly so after the War, as his films show.

At Berchtesgaden, by the way, we went into Goering's house, and there was an underground passage that led into a network of underground passages. In one room there was a movie projector and a list of films shown there. I remember George looking at the list to see if any of his own movies were on the list.

George Stevens as Director

One of the things that made George a good director was his way of organizing a scene on several levels of comprehension; and giving the actors a good deal of freedom to make use of their talents, while he himself knew how he thought the scene would shape up but didn't tell anybody.

He liked everything to be unexpected. He liked an audience to be able to follow the story totally, but not to know where it was going next. And he recognized that human beings are really awkward in their dealings with each other—it was another theme that ran through many of his films—and he would put a cushion or some obstacle between two people who were seated on a sofa, to make their approach to each other more difficult.

He always had most of the walls on the set [built] "wild"—so they could move, and the actors never quite knew from what angle the scene was going to be shot. And then he would tell the actors, in a very easy-going sort of way, "Let's see how this scene works, how you feel with it," and they would try it out. But like all people, you know, actors have self-doubt, and at the end of the rehearsal they would often feel ready to be helped. So George would smile and say, "Well, that's very nice, but how about if you sit there, and suppose we put a cushion between you and her?" And he'd shape the scene and give the actors, as it were, moral stepping stones to overcome any difficulties they'd felt at the first rehearsal—which, of course, George had noticed at the time.

So, suddenly, the actors were braced with new ideas, new suggestions of movement, as to how to use the furniture and the props on the set. George was very good at doing that, enhancing the actors' naturalness, giving their movements more realistic shape. And then they would feel they were in confident but not dominating hands.

George spent about twice as long in the cutting room as any other director I knew or knew about. Morning, noon and night, Saturdays, sometimes even Sundays, sometimes by himself with a cutter, sometimes with others, running and re-running and squeezing different meanings, different nuances into the scenes. And sometimes changing the whole concept of a scene in the re-cutting.

He was a thorough man in another sense, too, a curious sense. He would never go about anything very directly. His was always the sense of indirection. If there was something to be seen that a crowd was looking at, he would always look at the crowd looking at the scene. He was never so interested in the thing the crowd was looking at, as in the nature of the crowd looking at it.

In the same way, he would never sit in a given position [on the set]. He would always be moving around, looking at something from every conceivable angle, not only to look at it, but to get people off the idea that he had a viewpoint and the scene was going to be done from that viewpoint. He didn't want people to know where they were supposed to look, or how they had to orientate themselves, or react.

A lot of discussion went on about the vital question as to how exactly to shoot the scene of the drowning of Alice in *A Place in the Sun*. At the end of the movie, the priest says to George Eastman in the condemned cell, "Then in your heart was murder, George." But as the drowning scene was edited, it could be seen as an accident, an ambiguous combination of physical missteps and wrought-up feelings. In *An American Tragedy*, Dreiser presented it as an intentional act, as it was in the original 1900 murder case on which he based his novel. But all of us involved wanted the act itself to appear ambiguous. In taking Alice out on the lake, George's motive was murder, but when it came to the point he had second thoughts. The scene was therefore shot and edited with that in mind—morally guilty, but in a narrow technical sense, innocent.

George was a very volatile, unpredictable man. He was capable of tremendous laughter as well as a good deal of anger, and could be very sentimental at times. After all, you couldn't get more saccharine than parts of *I Remember Mama*. He was also very courageous sometimes. During the anti-Red scare in Hollywood, one of his friends was a very left-wing lawyer, who had defended several so-called Reds. George invited him to the studio for lunch in the commissary, where a lot of people wouldn't have been seen dead with the guy.

Incidentally, George was a quarter or an eighth Comanche Indian, and very proud of it. He had a jeep that he named Toluca, after the lake near his house in the San Fernando Valley. "Toluca" was an Indian word for good luck.

("The Liberation of Paris," "A Meeting on the Elbe," "George Stevens and World War II," and "George Stevens as Director" from a 1965 interview conducted by George Stevens, Jr., in the George Stevens Special Collection at the Margaret Herrick Library of the Academy of Motion Picture Arts and Sciences)

George Stevens as Humorist

Aside from his many famous accomplishments, George Stevens had a marvelously antic sense of humor. We were up in the Sierras, above Lake Tahoe, scouting locations for the drowning scene in *A Place in the*

Sun, and he liked a retinue, quite a big one, so we had a cavalcade of three black Cadillacs provided by the studio. We bumped over a series of narrow rocky roads and finally came to the edge of this totally remote and deserted lake.

Quite a few people—the art director, the cameraman, the lighting people, myself and various others—gathered on this secluded lakeshore while George inspected it. When he decided that it wasn't really quite right, he said: "Everybody get back in the cars." But then he lingered for a moment, and raised his viewfinder once more for another look, and a woodsman or hunter—wearing a jacket with a check pattern and a duck hunter's cap—emerged from the woods and came over to see what we were doing.

Although George was still staring through the viewfinder, he was aware of this man out of the corner of his eye. "Pretty nice lake, eh?" the man said. And George said, still staring through the viewfinder, "Yes, sir, pretty goddamn nice lake. If you had a girl and she was pregnant and you had to drown her, you couldn't find a better lake to do it in."

With that he put the viewfinder away, and hardly glancing at the man, got back into his Cadillac.

Billy Wilder

When Mike Todd was killed in a plane crash, he had a man called Art Cohn with him, who was writing—with Todd's approval, of course—a biography of him.

Now Art Cohn had been a screenwriter of no great distinction, with a few credits for "Additional Dialogue" on a few films. We don't have that credit anymore, as the Writers' Guild has disallowed it.

The day after the plane crash in which Art Cohn as well as Mike Todd died, I was having dinner at Charlie Feldman's house. There were quite a lot of people there, and they were discussing the crash, and a nice woman (I forget her name) said: "What an awful thing for Art Cohn's widow, that almost every account of the crash in the press hardly mentioned his name."

And Billy Wilder said, "Yes, at least they should have given him credit for Additional Dying."

An Evening with Marion Davies (1)

Marion Davies was the mistress of William Randolph Hearst, who was lying upstairs, moribund, when I accepted her invitation to dinner for a reason that I won't go into now. [See "An Evening with Marion Davies (2)"]. She lived in Hearst's huge house on North Beverly Drive, and you didn't enter through the front door, which was locked. You went through a side entrance where there were all these teleprinter machines and other devices connecting the house to all the Hearst newspapers throughout the USA.

It was an extraordinarily disorganized evening. Marion, who was a great admirer of General MacArthur, was wearing a cap with gold braid atilt on her blond hair, and singing "Old Soldiers Never Die." Somebody was accompanying her on the piano, and among the strangely ill-assorted collection of people there was Clare Boothe Luce, with a fashionable Catholic priest in tow, and Marion's nephew Arthur Lake, who played Dagwood Bumstead in that innumerable series of *Blondie* films.

At dinner, which was served quite remarkably late, Marion had a sort of auxiliary woman in nurse's uniform who sat beside her, or sometimes just behind her, and poured drink into Marion's glass. It was almost like she was administering a medicinal dose, but not in small quantities. She filled the glass to almost the maximum, and then— because Marion's hand would be unsteady by that time—helped her raise it to her lips.

Marion Davies "reviews the troops" in a musical number from Cain and Mabel, *1936*

After dinner, Marion would "review the troops," as she called it. They consisted of about twelve guards, who first of all guarded the house, and secondly, helped man the enormous number of teleprinter machines. She would select a guest, in this case me, because I was a newcomer, and these guards in gray uniforms and peaked caps would line up, standing at attention, while I was obliged to march past with Marion as she reviewed them. Part of the evening's ceremonial, you see.

Marion was a well-wisher, sweet and generous and kind, and also wonderfully insolent. Clare Boothe Luce was an extremely strong Catholic convert, of course, and her priest was a well-known figure in Hollywood's Catholic circles. He was also quite good-looking, and he pressed Marion's hand rather warmly as he was leaving. "You know," he said, "we're very, very fond of you, Marion." Presumably "we" meant the Church, although he didn't say so.

"Yes, well," Marion said, "I want to see the last of you, because otherwise I'm going to find you in my bed when I wake up."

She was very cracky, very funny, Marion Davies.

("George Stevens as Humorist," "Billy Wilder," and "An Evening with Marion Davies (1)"
from a 1965 interview with Gary Conklin)

An Evening with Marion Davies (2)

In the spring of 1951, shortly before *A Place in the Sun* was due to be released, we were very concerned that the press would start Red-baiting it—I think Michael Wilson, one of its scriptwriters, was about to be summoned to testify before the House Un-American Activities Committee. And given the nature of the film, and the people involved in it, we thought that perhaps we'd be attacked on the communist issue.

To forestall this, I proposed to George [Stevens] that we show it to Marion Davies. I didn't know her personally, but my parents had known her, and she had once or twice called me to go to her house. I thought, well, let's be a bit corrupt about this, and blunt the weapons which are going to be used against us. So I went to dinner at Marion Davies's house one night, and I said, "We have this film I'd like to show you." She liked looking at films—although she was never alone, she lived a very isolated sort of life, not too many people were showing her old movies anymore, but she ran them all the time in that strange projection theater of hers.

She said she'd be delighted to see the film, which really was a gesture of kindness, as I think she was accustomed to putting up with a lot of bad movies in which relatives and friends had some special interest.

Paramount didn't like the idea of showing prints of unreleased movies outside regular channels. For one thing, Louella Parsons, who wrote for the Hearst newspapers, hadn't seen it. Anyway, I took the reels up there, and by the time it got shown it was awfully late, around 10:45. Marion usually drank a lot, and she certainly did that night, with her white-coated auxiliary person behind her to serve her drinks—the arms came around her from behind her to pour each brimful. Thus, she was four-armed.

The projection theater was enormous and very elaborate, with chased leather walls. The projection lamps weren't arcs, they were electric bulbs, so that the screen was yellowish, and Marion liked that because it equated all the new films with her old films. That night she sat down pretty tight, and had a good deal to drink during the performance. After a minute or so she whispered to me, "Good photography!" And then she became rather involved with the film, and to sense that her hospitality wasn't really being abused by having to watch it. At the end she got up and said, "It's tremendous." Then she said, "We must review the troops!"

So I had to review the "troops" with her, which meant marching past the guards she'd lined up. Twelve of them were always on hand to keep watch on the house and the ticker-tape-and-telegraph room. Then Marion called her male secretary—a thin, tall young man in a dark double-breasted suit, with a face the color of paraffin. "Who's on the paper tonight?" she said. "Mr. Henderson," the secretary said, meaning the night editor of the *Los Angeles Examiner,* and Marion said, "Get Henderson!"

So we sat in this outer office, half police station and half communication center, with the ticker tapes ticking and a painting of William Randolph Hearst in Cuba during the 1898 Spanish-American War. He was on horseback, wearing a Panama hat and a red tie, watching American troops as they went through the jungle. When the secretary said on the phone, "Henderson, hold on," and handed it to Marion, she didn't need to say, "This is Miss Davies," or anything by way of introduction. "Henderson, I want all the publicity in the world, do you understand, for *A Place*—" she simply said, then broke off. "What is it?" she asked me, and I said, "*A Place in the Sun,*" and Marion said to

Henderson, "Mr. Moffat is the direct—" and I said, "No, that's not it." So Marion said on the phone, "Well, hold on, Henderson, and I'll get Mr. Hearst."

Then she turned to me and winked, because of course Mr. Hearst was moribund upstairs, and would be dead within a few months. "Mr. Hearst has just seen the film," she told Henderson, "and he thinks it's the best film to come out of Hollywood in fifteen years!"

Next morning, wondering whether all this was a fantasy or not, whether or not this was some mad empress maneuvering armies that didn't exist, I got to the studio around 9:30, feeling pretty tired. Not more than ten minutes later, after I'd described the events of the previous evening to George, the head of Paramount publicity called up and said: "What the hell's going on? We've had calls from the *New York Journal*, all the Hearst newspapers in Chicago, Houston, San Francisco, and the *American Weekly* is going to devote an entire issue to *A Place in the Sun*. And that's not all. Every Hearst paper has to mention the film at least once a day between now and its release. I don't know what to do, because it's too soon, it's starting too early." But after a moment he added, "You couldn't get this sort of publicity short of three million bucks."

So there we were, and the film was never attacked on a political basis. None of the other newspapers ever took it on in that respect. But in the year of 1951, the sort of times we made the film in, it undoubtedly would have been attacked without that absurd piece of nonsense.

(From the American Film Institute seminar with Ivan Moffat, "Producing the Film" class, May 13, 1975)

Dylan Thomas in Hollywood

Dylan turned up in Hollywood in 1950, when we hadn't seen each other for about five years. He took one look at me and said, "God, you look old."

I suppose I did. He didn't. He looked very cherubic, as always, very flushed and happy. I took him to lunch at Paramount Studios, where Henry Ginsberg was head of production. At the time I think he was having some problem with the company people in New York, bankers and such, who had come out here on a visit.

I didn't know they served beer in the Paramount commissary. Nobody ever drank anything alcoholic at midday. But Dylan found out they had some, and ordered two bottles brought to the table. He stretched out his legs, drank both bottles, ordered another, and started to talk extremely loudly.

Meanwhile Henry Ginsberg was seated at the next table with two bankers on either side. He wasn't the most prepossessing man, by the way, and looked a little bit like the *Punch* cartoon character in England. Finally, Dylan was talking so loudly that I said something I should have known better than to say: "Dylan, don't for God's sake talk quite so loudly. That's the head of the studio at the next table, looking right at you because you're making an awful lot of noise."

Dylan turned to look at Ginsberg, and after staring at him for a while, he said as loudly as ever [imitating Dylan's voice]: "That's the head of this studio? But I've never seen such a terrifying face!"

Well, of course, the bankers on either side of Henry Ginsberg—and poor Henry himself—registered this remark. I don't think it helped to suggest that Paramount was in the best of hands.

Charlie Chaplin

That night [after the Paramount lunch] I took Dylan to Preston Sturges's club, The Players, and invited Shelley Winters to join us. Dylan, who was much intrigued with Shelley, poked his finger at her bosom and said, "Are those real?" I thought the move a little bit out of tune, but Shelley seemed to like it.

After dinner the three of us went up to Charlie Chaplin's house. By that time Dylan had had a good deal to drink, of course; and Chaplin, being an extremely decorous kind of host, became almost like a sort of English colonel in his attitude to the correct way everything should go. Not that Oona cared; she was very tolerant, but Chaplin liked everything to be very proper, and he didn't like "bad" language or swear words of any kind.

We began talking about the press being hostile to Chaplin at that time—for political and supposedly moral reasons—and Chaplin asked Dylan: "What would you say to them?"

And Dylan said, "Well, there's only one thing you *could* say. Tell them to go fuck their bloody eyelids."

Oona went on peacefully knitting, but Chaplin was horrified. He turned around to see if any of the other guests—Christopher Isherwood among them—had heard this remark, and obviously hoped they hadn't.

Mr. and Mrs. Chaplin at Manoir le Ban, Vevey, Switzerland, c. 1960

Although Chaplin had heard about Dylan, and admired what he'd heard, I don't think he admired what he'd read, because I don't suppose he'd actually read any of Dylan's poetry. But when Dylan said what a hero Chaplin was to his own family in Wales, Chaplin very kindly put through a telephone call to them. He had a long talk with them, and Dylan was very pleased.

The next day Chaplin discovered that someone had peed on his living room sofa. Later, in various published accounts, he was reported as attributing this to Isherwood, who in that sort of regard was punctilious and disciplined, as Dylan was not. So I think that Charlie, as he often did, got it a bit wrong. He vowed that Christopher would never come to his house again, when he should have made that vow about Dylan.

Charlie had this elaborate idea of a host's role, which I think he'd learned from movies, or perhaps from playing a superb headwaiter in one of his own movies. Anyway, he would usher you into your chair with a sweep of his hand, like a very graceful maitre d', and say: "Would you care for something on ice?"

He was tremendously welcoming, but he didn't always get it right. Once he took Oona, my mother and myself to dinner at Chasen's. At the end of the evening, the bill came and Charlie signed it. The headwaiter said, "Thank you, Mr. Chaplin," but looked a little bit at sea, and so did the maitre d' who came by a moment later. Chaplin realized the problem, of course, and said, "Excuse me, so sorry," reached into his pocket and produced a fifty-cent piece. The headwaiter didn't react too well, and Chaplin said, "Excuse me, I'm so stupid," reached into his pocket and produced a twenty-five-cent piece.

I think the headwaiter and the maitre d' were used to this, they said, "Thank you, Mr. Chaplin," and so on, but Charlie had no idea, you see, exactly what behavior involved. He'd never been taught that. In a sense, he'd always been isolated in the actual world. As he said to me on another evening, he'd never known happiness until he married Oona.

"But surely your success, and all that?" I said.

"Success was wonderful and all-important in my life," Charlie said. "But I never felt the audience loved me. They only loved the Little Tramp. When I went to London in 1929 and they mobbed me, the police had to keep them back. But it wasn't *me,* and if they'd known what I was, they wouldn't have liked me at all. Although they loved the Little Tramp, I had no personal relationship with the audience to make me happy, unlike many star actors who were personally loved by their public. I never had that, and although success was wonderful, it didn't in itself gratify or please me, or make me feel more at ease with the world."

Preston Sturges

As I often went to have dinner at The Players Club I got to know Preston Sturges fairly well, and later I got to know him really well. But from the start, he was fascinating. He liked to think of himself as a sort of Renaissance figure, a man of many spheres and deeds and creative disciplines.

He had a slightly sententious way of talking. He was French-educated and larded his conversation with French phrases. He would refer to someone whose career he considered a little bit on the downward path as *faisandé,* then explain that it referred to game that had been hung too long and was starting to smell high.

His last days in Hollywood, when I saw a great deal of him, were rather extraordinary and sad. Around 1952 I was working at Paramount at the same time William Wyler was preparing *Roman Holiday* with Audrey Hepburn. But poor Preston was really at his wit's end, out of work and out of money, and United States marshals were constantly visiting him at The Players with writs and horrible things like that. One day he happened to be lunching in the Paramount commissary, where a few short years before he'd been the great man, the writer-director of *The Lady Eve* and *Sullivan's Travels* and *The Palm Beach Story,* followed by an entourage of twenty or thirty people. Now he was without anybody, except his little wife, whom he called Sniper. And when Willie

Preston Sturges in costume as himself in Paramount's all-star Star Spangled Rhythm (*1942*)

Wyler, who was a bit vague in some ways, saw Preston there, he didn't realize the state he was in, or the fact that he hadn't worked in movies for three or four years.

"Oh, Preston, are you doing anything right now?" he asked.

Preston said, "No." And Willie said, "Well, we need a rewrite on the film I'm doing, *Roman Holiday.*"

Of course Preston was overjoyed at the prospect of resuming work and getting some money at last. But the idea didn't sit very well with the new head of the studio, Y. Frank Freeman, whom George Stevens used to refer to as "Why Frank Freeman?" He made a rather bad deal whereby Preston would write the first forty pages, and if the studio liked them, they would engage him for more money to complete the script. And if they didn't like them, Preston told me, Y. Frank Freeman would pay him $2,500 and that would be the end of it.

But it was all Preston could get. He took the deal, and was given an office on the fourth floor at Paramount, where all the writers worked, and there was a shower room and a coffee room with a telephone exchange and telephone lady. And he and his wife took up residence there, they literally lived there for the ten or twelve days that Preston was writing the first forty pages of *Roman Holiday.*

When all the writers came to work in the morning, Preston would already be there in the coffee room, receiving us, and he'd say, "Gentlemen, twenty-four pages completed in one night, I think that's not a bad achievement, in fact it's a considerable one." When he'd done about thirty pages, he wanted me to read them, and I could tell he was proud of them. In fact they were pretty good except for one absolutely hateful thing. He'd taken eight whole pages of Byron's poem "Childe Harold," which contains the line, "butchered for a Roman Holiday," and put them in the script—in stanza form, as they were written.

I knew the front office would loathe that, and I said, "Preston, for God's sake, take those lines out."

"Well, I think Byron was a somewhat better writer than the present occupants of this floor, don't you?" he said.

"Of course, but that's not the point," I said. "They're not employing Byron, they're employing you to write that script, and if they see eight pages of Byron's poetry—you know what they're like, they're philistines and they'll hate it."

But Preston was adamant, and of course it took the front office one day to read those forty pages, and he was out, finished. On his last day at the studio he asked me to stay after everybody had gone and talk things over with him and his wife.

"I'm waiting for a telephone call," he said. By this time it was around six-thirty, and Preston was waiting to see if Y. Frank Freeman would honor his promise. Around six-forty-five the telephone switchboard started to light up, but the telephone lady had left, and there were a lot of plugs and of course we didn't know which ones to plug in. Miraculously we managed to connect, and it was Y. Frank Freeman's office calling.

Preston asked me to stay and wait, which I did, and about twenty minutes later he came back with a check for $2,500 as promised, and was pretty happy about it. Then he and his wife left the room, and I never saw him again. But when I went back to the studio next morning, I realized they must have stayed the night. Inside the door of both the toilet cubicles in the men's washroom was pasted an exquisitely written instruction, in almost Elizabethan English, on the proper use of sanitized seat covers, the things used by people who prefer not to sit directly on the toilet seat.

Some writers, apparently, had been thrusting these seat covers down into the toilet bowl, and that night the cleaning woman had obviously told Preston of the trouble they caused. So he'd written this wonderful treatise, which was quite long, typed it up and attached a copy to the door of each cubicle. I took care to cover both copies with cellophane and scotch tape, to preserve them for posterity, and I've no idea if they're still there, but I hope so.

(From the interview with Gary Conklin)

David Selznick and the Golden Age

I adored David, as many people did. He was enormously charming and loved to laugh. Even in those days there weren't so many producers who loved to laugh so much. But David was full of joy and delighted in life. He had a curious way of talking (which he also loved), a sort of offhand regal way. He'd say things like, "By the way, I'm going to remake *Anna Karenina*. That's confidential." It was slightly ridiculous, it was not confidential, and it wasn't even going to happen. But he was lovely and he had a sweet, generous side—though I must say, his quality of generosity was somewhat strained, in the Shakespearean sense, because he loved to give but sometimes didn't want to give.

One Christmastime we were in Austria together, working [on *Tender Is the Night*], and decided to take ten days off for a holiday. My mother happened to be around then, and I went back to California to bring my daughter Lorna over. David was giving a dinner for five or six of us, including his wife Jennifer [Jones], and he was looking at the restaurant menu. He wore those very thick glasses, but he'd take them off to scrutinize the menu, very close, up and down, up and down, until he finally turned to Jennifer and said, again in his offhand parenthetical manner, "Jennifer, you don't want caviar, do you?" Well, of course none of us expected David to offer caviar, and we dutifully recognized his note of caution. Jennifer said, "No," and so did my mother, though she longed for caviar. Lorna, who was thirteen, was about to say yes, so I gave her a nudge, and she said, "No thank you, David," and so did I. "Hmmm," said David. "I think I'll have some."

I always laugh when I tell that story, because it's so typical of David; and I laughed at the time, which was forgivable, because it was so ludicrous, asking everybody in a tone that meant, "You don't want it, do you, please?"

His famous memoranda, of which I was the recipient of a great many on *Tender Is the Night,* made him known as a perfectionist, but didn't really serve much of a purpose, because he used to write them out higgledy-piggledy, you see. There was no sort of real order, no structure, so that the order in which you read them had no bearing on the order of their importance. He used to pile these things on the director's desk, or at the start of shooting, on his chair. When he was making *Stazione Termini* (AKA *Indiscretions of an American Wife*] in Rome, with De Sica directing, the poor director would receive these sheafs and sheafs and sheafs of memoranda in English, which had to be translated by a batch of lawyers who understood or spoke it. They had to be sure, you see, that nothing was going on that De Sica didn't know about.

David was the kind of producer that doesn't exist anymore. He made sure each film was as much a David Selznick production as he could legitimately make it. He had three directors on *Gone with the Wind,* so it became more a David O. Selznick picture than a George Cukor or Victor Fleming or Sam Wood picture. Today you don't see a producer's name so prominently on the credits, partly because there are multiple producers, six or seven of them, to say nothing of associate producers, executive producers and the like.

I didn't get to Hollywood until the autumn of 1945, and at that time we thought its so-called golden age was the late 1920s and the 1930s.

Now I suppose the 1950s and 1960s have also become the golden age, and perhaps the 1990s will eventually be considered part of the golden age, you never know. In any case the golden age becomes longer and longer, but it always has to be at least ten years ago. But in the 1950s we didn't think of it as a golden age at all. We used to rather hate and despise the studio heads, not realizing that we would lament their absence later, the Selznicks, the Goldwyns and the Zanucks, who were certainly very good fellows compared to what you usually meet nowadays.

(From The Looseleaf Report, *August 4, 1992)*

Aldous Huxley

I had known Aldous Huxley before World War II, because I and his son Matthew went to the same school, Dartington Hall, and I occasionally visited Aldous and his Belgian wife Maria when they were in London. But I renewed the acquaintance in a much deeper way in Los Angeles.

In the old days Aldous never suffered fools very gladly, and had been rather ironical and sometimes even harsh. Since then he'd not only become partially blind, but extraordinarily gentle, mellow, luminous—and rather wonderful. I hate to use the word "spirituality," but it seemed to apply. He really glowed with kindness and seemed equally interested in everybody. In the old days he tended to disregard some people in the room, but now it didn't matter who was speaking—the youngest or the least significant—he'd be equally interested in and fascinated by them.

He still liked to impart slightly mischievous revelations [imitating Huxley's voice], "Oh, they say he's got the longest testicles in the world," or to announce some fairly unlikely scientific discovery [imitating again], "Oh, they found out yesterday that the Chinese had developed offset lithography four thousand years ago." One didn't have to believe any of this, but it was entertaining, as Aldous intended.

The first time he took me to lunch at the Farmers Market in Hollywood, an open-air market where you chose your food at one of the stalls, he put his chosen plate on the table and went to fetch his salad. He looked very birdlike with his huge glasses, you know, and [his] rather long face—and as he brought his salad over, a crow swooped down and carried off the meat from his plate.

Aldous didn't bother to get any more. With a sort of cheerful interest, and only faint disappointment, he accepted it as fate. I offered him my plate, but he wouldn't have it.

His first wife, Maria (who died tragically of cancer in 1955), was very much Aldous's curator. He was prone to bronchial infections, and if you asked how he was feeling, she would say: "Aldous is very well today. He was just as good yesterday." Although he was perfectly capable of answering for himself, Maria would always intercede and tell you the state of affairs, as if it were her official business to disclose Aldous, bit by bit. But you never got the full view.

(From the interview with Gary Conklin)

Hollywood and the English

When I first came to Hollywood, the English formed a small, aging group, the social leaders of which were a retired diplomat, Sir Charles Mendl, and his wife, the former interior decorator Elsie de Wolfe. The rest were mainly actors: Ronald Colman, Herbert Marshall, C. Aubrey

Smith, Brian Aherne, Nigel Bruce and such. There were other British actors, of course, like Charles Laughton and Elsa Lanchester, and Gladys Cooper, but they never became part of that group—which was, as has often been suggested, rather colonial-like, with a don't-let-the-side-down attitude. In those days there was an English side not to let down. There isn't anymore.

That group behaved in a certain way, a kind of polite English way, rather as I imagined British people in high positions in India behaved in the old days. You certainly didn't make fun of the local princes. You knew which side your bread was buttered on. I remember very well when I first went to lunch at the Mendls'—I was never part of their group, by the way—I remember making some slightly derogatory remarks about Louis B. Mayer and William Randolph Hearst. "Oh, don't say anything unpleasant about Mr. Mayer," several of them said. "He's been very nice to us, you don't do that here."

It was always *Mr.* Mayer, which surprised me. There was always a great deal of respect for the local nabobs. These English were gentlemen. They were acting, they were gentleman actors, they were acting as gentlemen. That was their status and their way of behavior, they played cricket and wore blazers and scarves, and there was an atmosphere of mustaches and that sort of thing.

They all melted away in the 1950s. There were still plenty of English people remaining here, but they were not a particular center of attention. Although there were still famous British actors in Hollywood—Deborah Kerr, David Niven, Merle Oberon—and they all knew each other, they were not a tight social group like the earlier cricket-and-blazer set. Attention shifted away from the Ronald Colmans to literary people like Aldous Huxley, Christopher Isherwood, Gerald Heard. But they weren't much publicized as a center of English life, and in the 1960s the attention switched to music, the Beatles and Rolling Stones, and the predominant English aspect was no longer upper class.

It's an interesting fact that the hundreds of people with so-called regional accents who have migrated here from England, Cockneys and northerners for instance, they seem to have assimilated an American accent more readily than those who speak the so-called King's or

Queen's English. They seem to place a canopy of American language over their own, and overlay it with much more readiness than their predecessors. Perhaps it's because, even if there were a side to let down, they wouldn't be interested.

In any case things have really changed since the days of Sir Charles Mendl and C. Aubrey Smith, and if you're looking for English life in California now, you should go to Santa Monica by the sea. Go to the pubs, which are crowded with English people. They're not movie people, they work in insurance, the space industry, factories, and they go to a store called The Tudor House to buy tea, to buy crumpets and Cornish pasties and that sort of thing. And they go to these pubs. And when events of international importance that concern Britain, like the Falkland Islands war, are discussed on television, it's to the pubs that the newscasters go for the English viewpoint, not to the homes of any remaining "distinguished" English people.

(From a 1982 interview with Patrice Chaplin)

New York Memories

For an English schoolboy, New York in those days—1926—was absolutely magical. Electrically quick. Everything snappy and razor sharp. "Taxi?" "Yes, sirree!" "Thank you for calling!" "Yes, indeedy!"

On Long Island I had a great-uncle, Robert Graves, with a huge house on Huntington Bay, and an enormous yacht and a four- or five-car garage. And on Long Island there were wonderfully colored birds, and turtles crossing the road, which I'm sure is not true any longer. But from a young boy's point of view it was an absolute paradise.

This great-uncle was on Wall Street. After the 1929 crash his fortune was reduced from, I believe, twenty to about six million, and he felt a failure. He had high blood pressure anyway. In 1933 he shot himself—the first shot went through his ear, the second shot killed him.

New York was still razor sharp, and not at all dangerous in the winter of 1937–38. Practically every night one went out in white tie, to the opera or something. I had a girlfriend down in Greenwich Village, but I was living on Park Avenue with my aunt, and I'd walk from my girlfriend's place on 12th Street to Park Avenue and 60th in the early morning in top hat, opera coat and white tie. It must have looked ridiculous, but nobody cared.

You couldn't do that today, of course. First of all, you'd be laughed at. Secondly, you'd be killed.

(From an interview by Michael and Randalyn Foster, May 20, 1995)

Iris Tree and La Dolce Vita

My mother knew Fellini when she was living in Rome, and in 1959 he got her to appear as herself in *La Dolce Vita*. She was a great personality and she had this famous Belgian sheepdog called Aguri, which means "good wishes." Somebody told me that Aguri held seminars for other dogs, a class of about twenty who would listen while he held up his paws and told canine wisdom, all the wisdom of dogs. I don't think I believe this to be true, but he was an incredibly wise and intuitive dog, and Fellini put him in the film, too. They were in a party scene at the house of Marcello Mastroianni's intellectual friend, who later in the film commits suicide, and Fellini gave Iris a few ridiculous lines. "Listen, I don't want to say that," she told him, and he said, "Don't worry, it's not a take, I'm just checking the movements and the lighting."

So Iris said these lines that she didn't like at all, thinking it was just a rehearsal. But Fellini had tricked her, so she said them in the movie, and as she was playing herself, they were totally out of character. He gave her a glass of what looked like Scotch and she said, "I drink to my lovers and my whisky."

But Iris never talked about lovers, it wasn't her style, and she didn't like whisky. So every time I see that film I hate that moment, much as I love *La Dolce Vita* as a whole, and I feel embarrassed for my mother.

(*From* The Looseleaf Report, *December* 20, 2000)

Eisenhower vs. Stevenson

During the 1956 presidential campaign, when Eisenhower was running for reelection against Adlai Stevenson, he or one of his lieutenants said that they were going to launch "a Cromwellian crusade." And Stevenson wondered, in one of his campaign speeches, why the Republicans chose to associate themselves with Oliver Cromwell, a Puritan who launched several imperialist wars. One of those wars was against the Irish, he said, so naturally Cromwell was anathema to the Irish. But the real reason they approved of Cromwell, Stevenson went on, was surely that he was known never to have cracked a single joke.

Of course the audience absolutely adored that. What a difference to the USA if Stevenson had won. He was so wonderful. How well he would have coped with the Cold War, I don't know. But if he'd become president, we probably wouldn't have been in Vietnam.

(*From the interview with Michael and Randalyn Foster*)

The Media and the Gulf War

During the Persian Gulf war, Operation Desert Storm, a lot of the American public disliked it when the media showed or described anything that would put a damper, as it were, on the whole experience. The public got furious, there was quite an outcry, when they showed a lot of Iraqi dead, or a building in Baghdad that had been targeted by mistake. It was as if showing these things were a sort of bad sportsmanship, or not putting the American team in a good light.

By the time of the next Olympic Games, the media had learned their lesson. They would show the women gymnasts from the former Soviet Union winning, but you felt as if they were metaphorically biting their lip, and would rather be showing a winner whose hometown was in the Middle West. And if something goes *too* wrong—the *Cubans* winning too much—they'd cut to the Dream Team getting off a bus. Or something.

I'm not exaggerating, and it's not healthy.

(*From* The Looseleaf Report, *December* 20, 2000)

Bush vs. Gore

In the case of George W. Bush's so-called election, I thought the Florida Supreme Court was disgraceful. Not to mention all the hypocrisy from the Republicans. The judges could easily have extended the date for a vote recount to November 18th, but they insisted on the 12th. In other words, they insisted on stopping the damned election.

The whole thing was an outrage. I thought Justice Stevens was wonderful when he said that the victim of this affair was much more than Gore. The victim was the people's belief in the judiciary, and of course the judiciary itself was damaged by the decision.

A lot of black people, who would have benefited from a recount, have been demonstrating. And the prospect for the next four years has suddenly become, if not disastrous, at best dull. Colin Powell is intelligent but dull. The only hopeful sign is Condoleezza Rice. Okay, she's right wing, but at least she's intelligent and has a good grasp of international affairs and she's an extremely articulate person.

[Note: Ivan later admitted that he said this because he found her sexually attractive.]

As for Ralph Nader, what did he accomplish in his campaign? Absolutely nothing positive. He didn't even receive the five percent of the vote he set out to do, only three percent. And he remains totally unapologetic. On the *Larry King Show* he was asked if he felt guilty, or responsible for putting Bush in office. Of course he didn't. All he said was that he would try to get more votes in the next election, so he could do the same thing to the Democrats. He's got some very good ideas, which we all know and like, but he's an egotist. He's also got some ideas that were not included in his public platform, and there's one that many people won't like, which is to cut off all aid to Israel. I don't think it's such a bad idea, but coming from him it'll never work because he's a Lebanese Arab.

(*From* The Looseleaf Report, *December 16, 2000*)

On His Eighty-third Birthday

Some forty years ago, Winston Churchill was in his decline and had long ceased to be Prime Minister. But he was seated as an ornament on the platform of a Conservative Party conference in London, and the Party chairman, Lord Bossom, was making a speech. Churchill hardly knew him. However, the speech was long, Churchill was endeavoring to be patient, and he turned to his wife Clementine, who was sitting next to him. "That fellow who's talking, what's his name?" he said. "That's Lord Bossom," she said.

"Bossom?" said Churchill. "Bossom? Why, it's neither one thing or the other, is it?"

Well, that's pretty much what I feel about eighty-three. Nondescript. It's neither one thing or the other.

(From The Looseleaf Report, *February 18, 2001)*

Caroline Blackwood

The last time I talked to Caroline at any length was when she called me from her house in Sag Harbor, and talked mainly about a book that had just come out about Cyril Connolly, whom of course she had known well. She said how much she liked the book [Jeremy Lewis, *Cyril Connolly: A Life*], how well written it was—much better than she expected—and how well the author had captured Cyril. And there was a significant pause, and then she said: "I'd forgotten how awful Cyril was."

Of course, she had mixed feelings about Cyril. She had, as the years went by, increasingly mixed feelings, I think, about a lot of things and a lot of people, and the more strongly these feelings were mixed, the more she liked them. Had she been at her memorial service, or had she been able to observe it, I think her feelings about that, too, would have been somewhat mixed.

I first got to know Caroline in Rome in the late summer of 1956. I'd been in Greece, involved in the making of a movie [*Boy on a Dolphin*], and she was at my mother's for a drink, with several other people. And she sat there staring—morosely, I thought—and not saying too much. But she looked lovely in her special way, and the next day we had lunch and the following night dinner.

She was interested in California and Hollywood. I think very strongly that she was in need of an identity, of some kind of raison d'être in life, sort of an armor, because she was very noticeable, very much on view, even though she didn't particularly want to be, and she felt a need for self-explanation. She asked me what Hollywood was like, and I said rather lightly: "It's a lot of shacks."

We became friends, but we didn't get to become close. But a couple of weeks after I got back to Los Angeles—to the house in Santa Monica where I was living—I got a surprise telegram: "Coming to visit shacks September 7."

Well, that involved a pleasant idea, but a good deal of responsibility, because I knew she knew nobody here—only me—and she would be

Caroline Blackwood in California, photographed by Ivan

entirely in my hands and might feel an awkward dependence on me, which I was very keen to avoid her having to feel. I'd booked her into the Beverly Hills Hotel because I knew that would sound familiar and friendly and comfortable. And when she arrived, I met her at the airport, drove to the hotel, and later on in the day picked her up, and we had dinner, and went to my house on Adelaide Drive, overlooking Santa Monica Canyon.

There she made some phone calls to England and Ireland, spoke to her aunt Oonagh [her mother's sister, Lady Oranmore and Browne], who then spoke to me and said: "Will you please buy Caroline an overcoat? She doesn't have an overcoat."

Well, it was hot weather and I didn't really see the need for it, but I took her to Saks the next day and bought her an overcoat, which she wore a great deal, and took her around to friends' houses and such. We both consumed a certain amount of wine during that time. Caroline particularly liked German wine—a Berncastel, an exquisite dry white wine that was extremely expensive. When we very often had lunch together, and dinner every night, we'd always have one or two bottles of that wine. It pleased her. And it pleased me, too.

She was not very forthcoming among people. She had that rather hostile reserve. Not that she couldn't talk if she wished, but they were all strangers, and some of them she didn't particularly take to. So she often sat again in that somewhat morose silence, and it was difficult occasionally.

I began to see that she was interested in having an acting career, if it could be done, and I introduced her to one or two people who might have been of help. And indeed she did do a test, I think. There was an Italian producer who did not have a particularly strong position in Hollywood, and I think he was interested in giving her a test. In any case nothing much came of it.

Meanwhile our relationship flourished. We became lovers and I became extremely fond of her, of course, but as time went by her position as my guest became increasingly anomalous, especially when we appeared in the gossip columns. And the expense of the Beverly Hills Hotel began to bear on me a bit. So she moved to the fairly large house in Westwood of Alexander Mackendrick, the Anglo-American director (who had made *The Ladykillers* that year) and his wife, Hilary. And there she stayed for a while.

Finally she decided that she had to do something with her marital position. She was still married to Lucian [Freud], and decided to go back to England and get a divorce. But she only got as far as New York, and got embroiled there in the social or the artistic scene, or both, and as she put it, "things got very hectic." She was evasive as to exactly what the hectic qualities of her life consisted of, and I became rather uneasy, feeling I was stuck in Hollywood on a job [*They Came to Cordura*], while Caroline was mobile, but chose not to move.

Despite the fact that Caroline and I got on well enough to discuss our futures together, and she'd accepted with some pleasure a gold band that I'd had made for her, she'd not been really happy in Los Angeles. She still felt somewhat out of place, and was the object of a curiosity which she was no more willing to satisfy than she had been with people in Rome. She never felt at ease in California. She was morally speaking *en route* to something else, but didn't yet know what that something else was.

She was restless, and her absence in New York made me rather restless and uneasy. We used to speak on the telephone every so often, and once it became almost unbearable, her prolonged absence, or her prolonged inactivity. When I was supposed to be writing a scene for the movie [that was due] next day, before I got down to it, I had to get it off my chest—and I wrote a long letter, starting at about half past seven in the evening, and at three o'clock in the morning, I still hadn't finished it.

By the time the sun came up and started to illuminate the Pacific below my windows, it was just about finished. A long letter, what shall I say, self-serving and feeling sorry for myself. But I posted it anyway the next day, and apologized deeply to the producer that I hadn't been able to do the scene. Somehow it was all forgiven and forgotten, but it seemed like a worry at the time. Two or three days later Caroline called me. I asked, after a while, if she'd gotten the letter, and she said rather brusquely, "I think we'd better forget about that letter."

Of course I knew that she was right. It was not a letter to be well remembered.

Although, when she felt like it, Caroline in her intelligent way was highly talkative, affectionate, receptive, and loved to laugh, the prevailing mood was so often that of gloom that I'd once told her, when we were having dinner together and enjoying our white wine, that she looked like somebody staring out of a porthole of a sinking liner.

She liked that, and she said that she still had those gloomy moods, even in New York.

Finally, early the next spring, we decided to meet. She didn't want to come back to Los Angeles, so we met in Denver, Colorado. Slightly more than halfway from her point of view.

We spent two or three nights there, driving around, and she still wore her gray, warm overcoat, and it was a lovely time. But as far as I was concerned, not long enough. And I didn't see her again until the following summer.

I went to New York to see her, and she was staying at the apartment of her aunt Oonagh, who was then married to Miguel Ferreras, a Cuban dress designer, a marriage that didn't last very long. Caroline had one of her pouting moods when we went to a very nice, rather grand French restaurant. She enjoyed the meal, and when we left, she suddenly bolted.

Suddenly ran. Quick, spontaneous, off like a flash. I didn't catch up with her until we were at the front door of her aunt Oonagh's apartment. She was waiting there, and she said: "Sorry for the marathon."

She didn't explain it, though, and I didn't even pursue the matter. Caroline could do [things like] that. She could suddenly take to her heels. I spent several days in New York in July, and was there for her birthday; and the following September I joined her in Venice, where she was staying again at the palazzo her aunt Oonagh had rented.

We got on pretty well. I don't think there was any bolting there. We drove around, went to Vicenza, saw the neighboring towns, and by and large we had a lovely time. But she'd gone off for a day or two to make a film test in Milan, and back in Venice was anxiously waiting for the result. A telegram arrived as we were about to get into a gondola. It said, "*Madame, vous êtes trop mûre.*"

We didn't know what "*mûre*" meant, and we looked it up in a dictionary. It meant "ripe." Unfortunately, Caroline was "too ripe" for the part. She didn't quite know how to take that, but clearly it was a disappointment. And of course Caroline hid her disappointments. She was too proud to acknowledge the feeling of failure or anxiety.

Caroline was extremely attractive, of course, and her very intelligence and intensity made one want to know her more, to penetrate that almost hostile façade. She made one feel that there was a constant lingering inadequacy about oneself mirrored in herself.

She was such a contradiction. For all her sophistication, she could be very down-to-earth, so cozy, so friendly, so affectionate, so simple. She loved scrambled eggs on toast, simple meals and simple gestures of affection and love. And she loved to cook, especially fish, which she invariably cooked with fennel, which I didn't care for. It reminded me faintly of licorice, but I never said so, because like anybody with an accomplishment of which they were proud, she had a barrier against criticism.

But she was also very amenable to perceptions of her own character. Even when those perceptions were unfavorable, she enjoyed them if she felt them to be accurate. At the same time, in a curious way, there was a fear of discovery. She was such a many-faceted creature, and one never knew which facet was going to turn toward one.

Running away—the bolting, as I've described it—is one thing. The arms of affection, sweetness, kindness, generosity, was another. I had never in my life met, let alone loved, such a complex person; and it became an almost agonizing temptation to try, somehow, to penetrate what she really felt. But I always hesitated to question her directly, to try and probe her too obviously, because I knew that resistance was always there. That resistance to inquiry, that shield she put up temporarily against the hardening of a persona—like a carapace of a profession that she hadn't yet acquired.

In the late summer of 1958 Caroline did come back to California and stayed a few months. During that time I introduced her to a great friend [and, briefly, former girlfriend] of mine, a very lovely girl called Kay Scott, a pianist and composer of songs. They got on very well and became close friends. Close to the point, I sometimes suspected, of being collusive in their relations with me.

Kay was married to the composer Leonard Rosenman, who eventually introduced Caroline by telephone to the musician Israel Citkowitz, whom she later married in New York.

Caroline was still very much in search of herself, that identity-seeking nature which I described earlier. As part of that exploration, she was determined to meet somebody who had taken LSD. One day at the Fox commissary we had lunch with Cary Grant, who had undergone a course of LSD treatment and recommended the doctor who administered it. Very bravely she undertook a course of about twelve sessions, increasingly strong doses of LSD, psychologically very painful. It involved her lying down, being almost held down by this doctor after being given the dose. Music was played and she would tell him what she was undergoing mentally, what she was feeling and thinking.

Grotesque images—half dreams, half childhood memories—would come bubbling to the surface. When I picked her up at the doctor's office and took her out to dinner later, as I invariably did, she would tell me some of these dreams, and some were nightmarish, very, very bizarre. And she marveled over them.

When she finished the course, it certainly had a tremendous effect on Caroline. She suddenly became very much clearer in thought, clearer of purpose—and she started to write. I never had a hint before that she'd been capable of writing, although I believe she had written some articles for a London magazine [*Picture Post*]. But then Stephen Spender asked her to write some film criticism [for *Encounter,* the magazine he coedited] and it was excellent.

Israel thought that I'd had a hand in it—and vice versa. No, she'd done it entirely on her own, and thus her writing career began, because she was very encouraged by the reception, and she followed it with another piece for *Encounter* ["Portrait of a Beatnik," about the Southern California Beats].

But seeing Caroline at her London house in Redcliffe Square, after her literary life was launched in the late 1960s and early 1970s, was to see her change from a smiling, intelligent hostess to a figure of almost incandescent rage at one o'clock in the morning, squatting on the floor, pounding the carpet with her fists, talking in angry monologues, vilify-

Caroline with Robert Sheridan Lowell and Evgenia

ing various people in her life. What had cheated her? Who had cheated her? What made her such an engine of self-destructive anger? What, with all that beauty, had led to such disappointment in her life? I'll never know.

It was very sad to watch, and to be near. At one or two in the morning I would say, "Caroline, I'm sorry, I really will have to be going now." Her answer would be to refill her glass and make a show of trying to refill mine. She wouldn't even speak about my leaving or not leaving. She would just take it for granted I'd want to stay on.

Such a transformation from the earlier Caroline I knew is really a story of what I knew of her. It remains a series of unanswered questions, sorrowful, echoing, disappointing. Tragic, really, and yet there was so much beauty in Caroline's life, which she made herself.

The men in her novels were on the whole weak, rather despicable, selfish, for the most part rather cardboard-like figures. I don't think Israel was like that. I don't think Robert Lowell [her third husband] was like that. I don't know of any of the men who were in Caroline's life who could have been the models for those weak men in her books.

It's all a mysterious business. I'm just very glad I knew her. All of it.

That's all I have to say for now.

Well, it isn't quite all I have to say. To go on with what I was think-ing, I don't believe any of the men in Caroline's life really came up to her expectations in every respect. She liked one for some reasons, and another for another reason, and this one for that reason. But I don't think she liked any of them for all the reasons she'd have preferred to love somebody for. They all had disqualifying qualities—and I think, in the end, that added to her sense of entertainment. She became very critical of men as a race, as a whole. And going back to what I said about her novels, I think that's reflected in them. She never told me of a man that she really, without any reservation, loved or worshipped.

So I don't believe she ever really had a hero. And ever since I first knew her, she had a somewhat malign or skeptical view of her own des-tiny—that things were always going to happen for the worst. This doesn't mean that she didn't enjoy many things enormously. But although she had preferences and tastes and delights, there was always a shadow that seemed to be hanging over her, a sense of things more likely to go wrong than right. As if that was the proper way of things, the way the world was arranged. At least in Caroline's case.

(Ivan's memories of Caroline taped for Evgenia Sands)

THE MOVIE FILE

A Place in the Sun (*1951*)

Theodore Dreiser based his novel *An American Tragedy* on a 1900 murder case in which a man named Gilette—the poor relative of a rich family by that name—was convicted of drowning his pregnant, working-class girlfriend. Dreiser's theme was that the rich world represented by Sondra Finchley—our Angela Vickers—would never in fact have given his Clyde Griffiths—our George Eastman—real access to that world. George was, therefore, pursuing a capitalistic illusion called the American Dream.

The first screenwriter, Michael Wilson, wanted our version to follow Dreiser more faithfully in that respect. So did I, at the time. But Stevens was a romantic, so the bleak social picture painted by Dreiser took second place to the steamy love affair between George and Angela.

There was a further reason for the change of emphasis. The previous Paramount film version, *An American Tragedy,* directed by Josef von Sternberg, had cast Sylvia Sidney as the working-class girl, and she portrayed an immensely sympathetic victim, truer to Dreiser's intent, thereby making her lover seem weak, and finally villainous. The film was not a box-office success, so Paramount was resistant to what they thought would be mostly a remake, until Stevens persuaded them otherwise.

(From Ivan's Notebook #3, undated)

In Dreiser, the true love story was between the factory girl and the boy. The other [with Sondra] was not a love story, but a story of infatuation and ambition, tearing the love story apart. Capitalism destroys true feelings, etc. George [Stevens] rightly or wrongly didn't want that, he wanted the other as a love story, identifying, in short, the virtues of that world Dreiser objected to, identifying the virtues of love with that flamboyant rich world. He [Dreiser] went out of his way to show that those people were not worthy, they were idle and frivolous, and they would take a person up and then drop him without even noticing it. They would never buy Clyde Griffiths, they weren't ever going to buy him, they wouldn't ever allow him to marry Sondra. And such was the end of his book. The girl was never really in love, and I don't think she paid too much attention when the boy was executed.

At one time, in the original script, there was a scene or scenes that suggested the hopelessness of George's quest. And a scene or scenes (that we did shoot, as far as I remember) between Monty Clift and Shelley Winters to illustrate that they were more bound together than they were shown to be in the final cut. But they were dropped.

(From the American Film Institute seminar with Ivan Moffat, "Producing the Film" class, May 13, 1975)

Despite the fact that Sylvia Sidney had played a very sympathetic victim, which threw the whole emotional balance off and was probably responsible for the failure of *An American Tragedy* at the box office, it was decided that our working-class girl should be a vulnerable creature. And we had in mind Cathy O'Donnell, who had been in *The Best Years of Our Lives*. And then George surprised me by saying, how about Shelley Winters? I thought that a very odd choice, because Shelley was a kind of self-made glamour girl, a little bit like Madonna later on.

But George had the idea that that side could be peeled away, and underneath would be a more ordinary-looking and somewhat tougher Shelley, who was such a good actress that she could evoke necessary hard truths by raising her voice and so on, yet evoke sympathy when required. So there was a conflict, Shelley wanting to be truer to Dreiser's theme, George wanting her to come out as a less attractive figure than she wanted to paint herself. But he insisted, and it worked, Shelley was wonderful in the part, and got an Academy Award nomination. Now she's very proud of her performance and will be happy to tell you so.

I no longer remember why Monty Clift was chosen, but as soon as he came into the foreground for that part, he seemed the obvious choice for it. He had this Russian coach and confidante [Mira Rostova], who was always on the set, whispering after each scene. And George didn't like it at first, but having talked to Monty Clift about it, he welcomed her as an adjunct to his ability to play a scene, because she boosted his self-confidence. She was a highly intelligent woman, and although I think, whatever she whispered, Monty would have been very good anyway, he was always very good, especially in the courtroom scene.

It was designed in the script, as many courtroom scenes are, for suspense. Will George Eastman be proved guilty or found innocent? We thought it would hold as far as the audience was concerned, but it didn't work that way, we had a lot of witnesses and cross-examinations, it took a long time—in screen time, I mean. So it was decided after we got to the editing stage that it wasn't a question of suspense, that the audience would probably have made up its mind that he'd be proved guilty. Monty Clift's behavior in the witness stand, his reaching back with his head, his mumbled words against a tide of absolutely conclusive evidence hitting him, as it were, in the face—he seemed almost crucified—this helped us readjust the whole mood and purpose of that sequence in the editing.

George Stevens, as you probably know, devoted twice as much time to the cutting of his pictures as any other director (twice as much as the next chap, in those days probably William Wyler). So the trial scene became a succession of inevitable blows, and a foregone conclusion, particularly when the District Attorney started to cross-examine him. The very force of his accusations served to make Monty Clift seem like a victim rather than the perpetrator of the crime. It was too late to reshoot anything, but we discovered that he'd been shot in such a way that it served our purpose in changing the point of view of that trial.

So it was no longer a question of suspense, but of heavy stones being cast in that courtroom in the name of justice, and of Monty Clift reeling back against their impact. It had a drama of its own, and was a much shorter way of hitting the audience just as it hit Monty Clift, because as an actor he had behaved so beautifully and already elicited some sympathy.

Elizabeth Taylor wasn't a foregone conclusion for the part of Angela, first of all because she was strictly an MGM star and had never made a film for any other company. They were reluctant to let us borrow her, and it seemed strange to me at the time that they would finally release her for a film which had darker, social overtones to it, when in the late forties and early fifties everybody was waving the flag. But she was the right age, which had very little to do with it, and very beautiful, which had everything to do with it, and she loved the part, and saw its potentiality. Still, her performance was somewhat of a surprise: how natural she was, and how good her instincts were.

When she first came into the Paramount commissary before making a costume test, she was only seventeen, most people had never seen her in the flesh before, but she looked pretty smashing and people were subdued when they looked at her. She came over and sat in our section of the commissary, at the writers' table. Billy Wilder was there, and he cracked, "How the hell did *she* ever get into movies?" And Hal Kantor, a writer who was a wit, said: "She lied about her height."

She became very fond of Monty, that sort of carelessly retentive and involved side of him, which came out in the movie and in his private conduct. I think he was reluctant, for reasons we won't bother with now, to plunge into a love affair with anybody in particular. She knew all about that, and perhaps it added to his attraction. He was certainly somebody with whom she felt immensely at ease, for whom she had great sympathy. He liked and understood her too, they became great, great friends and his subsequent life was a matter of great concern to her.

(From Ivan's commentary on the DVD of A Place in the Sun*)*

The slow dissolves in *A Place in the Sun* (a title I dreamed up, by the way, the result of a dream about Kaiser Wilhelm saying Germany wanted its place in the sun) were Stevens's way of seeking to overlay present and future, one overshadowing the other. Like premonitions or even omens. Put another way, they gave a sense of the inevitability of the unfolding course of events, a feeling of destiny and things preordained.

(From Ivan's Notebook #3, undated)

This is a very American story. I feel therefore it is worth giving serious consideration to the whole question of the semi-classical, elaborately orchestrated and European-type musical score which is generally used as background to Hollywood pictures.

My proposal is that we commission a first-rate young jazz composer to write the score for this picture and to orchestrate it for a few instruments—saxophone, trombone, piano, etc. A score of this sort would be infinitely more effective in creating the moods we need in this story. With a few well-used instruments, sparingly and pointedly employed,

For the scene in A Place in the Sun *when Angela Vickers and George Eastman go to the movies, George Stevens created a joke poster, and seated himself, as a down-and-out, by the entrance to the theater.*

we could get ten times the results that we could from swirling massed violins, cellos and what-nots.

(From a memo to George Stevens, May 11, 1949)

In his original score playing under the opening titles, Franz Waxman composed a grandiose introduction perhaps better suited to the Battle of Gettysburg. Stevens didn't want any suggestion of grandiosity or tragedy, he wanted it *piano* (soft), so as to build tension and drama rather than anticipate it.

The first line of Dreiser's *An American Tragedy* was pretty quiet, too. "Dusk—of a summer night" was the way it began. The title music was rescored by the composer. Even so, British film critics complained about the movie's "bloated score."

(From Ivan's Notebook #3, undated)

Anything to do with abortion was out in those days, and we had a lot of trouble with that scene [between Alice Tripp and the doctor]. We weren't allowed to even seem to be conveying an abortion scene, and the way we did it was as far as you could possibly go in those days. Naive and inoffensive as it may look now, the audience was deathly still—they couldn't believe what they were seeing, you know. In 1951 there was no question of anyone getting an abortion without extreme difficulty, danger and at great cost.

Some people in the movie colony argued that "anyone can get an abortion these days, it's a simple matter and why all this fuss? She need only to have gone to another doctor." There had been no abortion scene in Michael Wilson's script [or the second script by Harry Brown], and as it fell to me to write one, I wondered about that at the time. When I put forward the objections those people made, the answer came back, "Well, you just try." And six months later I had unfortunately to try, and I assure you it was, even in Los Angeles, almost impossible. I think for that reason most of the audience realized the scene was true.

(From the American Film Institute Seminar with Ivan Moffat, "Producing the Film" class, May 13, 1975)

Alice (Shelley Winters) with the doctor, pleading her case for an abortion in A Place in the Sun

INT. DR. WYELAND'S OFFICE — (NIGHT)

ALICE [Shelley Winters] enters the painfully small con-
sulting room. Two chairs are dwarfed by a large, crowded
desk. Any visible medical apparatus should look menac-
ing. But the DOCTOR himself looks staid and reassuring.
He greets her warmly.

                    DOCTOR
      Sit down in that chair to the left, won't you,
                     Mrs.—?

                    ALICE
                   Hamilton.

As if in answer, the doctor starts to fill out the name
she has just given him on a form on his desk. Now he pro-
ceeds to question Alice in a brisk and businesslike tone.

                    DOCTOR
                  First name?

                    ALICE
                    Sarah.

                   DOCTOR
            Husband's first name?

                    ALICE
                    John.

                   DOCTOR
            Your age, Mrs. Hamilton?

                    ALICE
                 Twenty-two.

                   DOCTOR
             How long married?

                    ALICE
            (after slight hesitation)
               Three months.

Her hesitation has caught the doctor's eye. He looks
up at her, then puts the pen down and leans back in
his chair. His face takes on a more friendly, relaxed
quality.

                   DOCTOR
Well now, what seems to be the trouble, Mrs.
Hamilton? You needn't be afraid to tell me.
That's my business—listening to other people's
troubles.

                    ALICE
Well, it's like this, you see . . . my husband
hasn't much money, and I have to work to help
out with expenses.

                   DOCTOR
                (encouraging)
                   Yes . . .

                    ALICE
So when I found out I was going to have a baby,

we didn't see . . . we didn't know of any
doctors . . .

Alice dries up for a moment, uncertain of her approach.

> DOCTOR
> (trying to ease the situation)
> What business is your husband in, Mrs.
> Hamilton?

> ALICE
> (a growing sense of futility)
> He's an electrician.

> DOCTOR
> (cheerfully)
> Well, now—that's not such a bad business. At
> least they charge enough!

He chuckles encouragingly. Alice hardly bothers to pretend a smile.

> ALICE
> Well, neither of us makes much, and we can't
> afford to—

> DOCTOR
> There are free hospitals, you know.

Alice looks directly into the doctor's face. Her eyes do
not waver.

> ALICE
> I know that.
> (after a short pause)
> Free hospitals don't solve everything.

Doctor Wyeland studies Alice very carefully and soberly
for a moment.

> DOCTOR
> Tell me, how did you happen to come to me,
> anyhow?

                              ALICE
        I've heard people say you're a good doctor.

Doctor Wyeland seems relieved by this answer.

                             DOCTOR
                             I see.
He clasps his hands together and looks at the ceiling.

                         DOCTOR (cont'd)
        Mrs. Hamilton, when you went to the altar three
        months ago you must have realized that you might
        have to face a situation like this.

                             ALICE
                      (almost a whisper)
                             Yes.

                             DOCTOR
                 (in an almost fatherly tone)
        Well, once you make up your mind to face this
        bravely, you'll find all these problems have a
        way of sorting themselves out . . .
             (He rises and takes a pace or so toward the
                             window)
        . . . Medical bills, clothes—I know my wife and
        I worried at first, and now we look back . . .

Alice crosses to him and grabs him by the lapel of his
coat in a rush of desperation.

                             ALICE
        It isn't like that! I'm not married! I haven't
                     any husband at all!

Doctor Wyeland gently disengages himself, and helps her
back to her chair, where she sits, sobbing.

                         ALICE (cont'd)
        He's gone away. He's deserted me. Somebody's
                     got to help me!

Doctor Wyeland now eyes Alice a little more severely.
Evidently he would like the interview to come to an end—

one way or the other—as quickly as possible. Her sobbing
has almost ceased.

>DOCTOR
>Miss Hamilton, you have no money—
>(Alice shakes her head)
>no husband, and you don't dare tell your
>parents—perhaps—the truth?
>(Alice nods)
>Then in relation to your difficulties, I have but
>one duty—to see that you give birth to a healthy
>child. I also have a living to earn and a family
>to support, and it therefore boils down to this.
>If you have come here to place yourself under my
>professional care during your pregnancy, I will
>do everything to ensure your health and the
>health of your child. On the other hand, if you've
>just come for free advice on material and finan-
>cial problems with which I cannot help you, I must
>ask you to consider this interview at an end.

Alice sits looking at him. She is calm, but also in a
state of final bewilderment at the failure of her plans.

EXT. SUBURBAN STREET — NIGHT

The worried George [Montgomery Clift] is sitting waiting
in his car. Now he sees Alice in the distance as she
comes out of the doctor's house, walking slowly toward
him up the street. When she reaches the car, he gets out
and opens the door for her. She stands for a moment.

>ALICE
>(her voice leaves no doubt what has taken
>place)
>Now what?

George's hopefulness, if any, becomes hopelessness. They
get in the car for privacy and sit there. The two equal
the sum of exhaustion.

(A Place in the Sun)

Shane (1953)

When we first started we just thought it would be a tight, good action movie with a gentle version of the eternal triangle set in the West, but we had no conception, I don't think even in George Stevens's mind, that it would become an enduring Western classic.

One of the things that is unusual is that the central part of the action—the Starrett homestead—is seen throughout the film in the huge geographical context of the Teton mountains. You can see the whole realm around it. In other words, in so many Western movies, you just cut to the place where the action is taking place. You see people riding and you cut to the exterior or the interior of the house. But here you see exactly where [the homestead] is in relationship to the whole landscape.

And Shane himself is just passing through—that's the point. He's passing through and he's waylaid, as in many a myth and saga and adventure story. I'd like to say something about Alan Ladd here. Up through about a couple of weeks of shooting, up there in Wyoming, Alan was sitting back in his canvas-backed chair, being massaged and having his false hairdo attended to, very relaxed, very pleased. And I said, "How do you like working with George Stevens?" And he said, "I like it, he's a great director. He gives me time. I may not be the greatest actor in the world, but I'm great in my pauses."

We used to have endless script conferences at night after the shooting was over. They were very onerous and sometimes rather torturous. New scenes would be written and there'd be two or three stenographers working nights, and in the morning we'd take the changed scenes to Van Heflin, Jean Arthur and Alan Ladd, in the trailers right on the set out there.

*George Stevens with Alan Ladd
on the set of* Shane

I gave a couple of scenes, one to Jean Arthur and one to Van Heflin, and Alan poked his head out of his trailer and said, "Are there any changes for me?" Well, we didn't have Alan talk too much in the movie, but his line in that scene had originally been, "Aha!" And I said, "Yes, Alan, your 'Aha!' has been changed to 'Ah!' "

Stevens had considered Montgomery Clift, who was a great star after *A Place in the Sun,* for the part of Shane. And of course the whole tone of the film would have been entirely different had he played Shane instead of Alan Ladd—as indeed the rest of the cast would have been correspondingly changed. For instance, had Katharine Hepburn played Marian Starrett, as was also considered at the time.

Jean Arthur, who played the part, was in her fifties, I think, at that time, and she looks remarkably young. She had gray hair, short gray hair, you know, and without makeup, looked her age. But here she looks twenty years younger. She was a passionate animal lover, and she was concerned about the condition of the animals [in the movie], whether they were properly watered and so on at night. And she'd drive down there all by herself, to where these animals were caged. And if she thought they weren't being properly looked after, she'd wake up the animal trainers then and there, even if it was midnight. She was an eccentric, a sweet one, very passionate about everything, and she was wonderful in the part.

A. B. Guthrie, Jr., the screenwriter, was a novelist, not a [professional] screenwriter. When he came onto the production he asked to see what a screenplay looked like. He was handed a copy of some screenplay to study it, and he brought it back on a Monday morning, and he'd already written fifteen pages of the script of *Shane*. I think George Stevens or somebody said to him, "You'd better not tell the Writers Guild, if you've already joined it, that you came in on the very first day with fifteen pages of screenplay already written."

He was a wonderful guy, Guthrie. But he left about three-quarters of the way through shooting, before we left the Wyoming location. He left Jack Sher [credited for Additional Dialogue] and myself to touch up whatever else was needed.

Sometime after *Shane* was shot, Y. Frank Freeman [studio head] came over and sat with George and started complaining about the cost of the thing. He pointed to a huge poster of *Samson and Delilah,* with Victor Mature and Hedy Lamarr, hanging on the wall above us, and said to George by way of reproach, "George, that film is going to gross over $800,000 in India alone." And George said, "Jesus, Frank, the next time I'm in India I'd like to take a look at it."

And of course, Frank Freeman being rather humorless, didn't get the irony of what George had said. "No, George," he said, "you can see the same picture frame for frame right here."

(From Ivan's commentary on the DVD of Shane*)*

SHANE: NARRATION AND SCENE FOR OPENING PROLOGUE

(During the location shoot in Wyoming, Stevens asked Ivan to write a prologue and epilogue to establish the story from the point of view of Joey, the boy played by Brandon de Wilde. But he finally discarded the idea.)

We open on a long shot that includes the valley and the Starrett home. It is well developed, trees are taller than in the later body of the story. A look of neatness and fulfillment.

A boy of about fourteen is busy at some farmyard task. He wears long pants, a big hat, work-clothes. He is whistling a tune that we later identify with Shane. ("The Colorado Trail"?) Now he looks up at the distant hills, and his attention becomes caught by something. Far away, we discern a solitary rider. He comes down the same ravine or gully that Shane will use. The boy, straining to see, mechanically drops what he is doing.

Now we see that an older man, his father Joe Starrett [Van Heflin], has caught the intensity and direction of the boy's gaze and is following it. The mother [Jean Arthur] also follows her husband's glance. When the far-off figure is discernible, it's not the man they hope it will be. And then silently, as if this were an oft-repeated routine, they cease looking and go back to what they were doing before. But the boy's glance lingers longest on the figure.

CLOSE SHOT — THE BOY

His head is partly turned away from camera as he gazes into the distance. The VOICE of his MOTHER is heard OFFSCREEN.

                    MOTHER'S VOICE
              It's not him, Joey.

The boy's head does not move as he answers. There is so little apparent movement around his lips that we are not aware whether it's his actual words or his thoughts that we listen to.

>   BOY'S VOICE
>   (quietly)
>   I know.

But his head still stays gazing. After a moment, the same voice goes on speaking in the same quiet, reminiscent way.

>   BOY'S VOICE (CONT'D)
>   Several times a year we do that. We've been
>   doing it pretty close to four years now. Some-
>   times just me, sometimes mother or dad, some-
>   times all three of us.

Again we hear the mother's voice calling to him. But this time it's a fainter echo of the first—something that has come down from the memory of past occasions.

>   MOTHER'S VOICE
>   It's not him, Joey.

>   BOY'S VOICE
>   (soft)
>   I know . . . Sometimes in the night I hear a
>   rider coming and I wake up and it's not him.
>   Sometimes it's just a dream, a dream that's
>   four years old, that I guess'll go on forever.
>   Unless he comes riding down that trail again.
>   Sometimes I wonder if he'd recognize our place
>   anymore . . .

Camera pans around Starrett homestead, and slowly we dissolve to the more primitive place as it looks through-out the rest of the picture.

>   BOY'S VOICE (CONT'D)
>   Because there's been a lot done in those four
>   years.

Now the camera has established the change, and the boy,
now smaller, gazing outwards.

> BOY'S VOICE (CONT'D)
> He rode into our valley in the summer of '89. In
> the clear air I could see him plainly, though he
> was still several miles away. There seemed noth-
> ing remarkable about him—just another stray
> horseman riding toward the far-off cluster of
> frame houses that was our town. Then he came
> closer . . .

END OF NARRATION FOR PROLOGUE

NARRATION FOR EPILOGUE

From the end of Scene 146 [as Shane rides away], we start
slowly to dissolve to the older boy of the prologue. But
before dissolve begins—over the final shot of Shane as he
becomes invisible in the darkness—the boy's voice starts
speaking. It continues into reversion of original shot.

> BOY'S VOICE
> I guess that's all there is to tell. The folks
> in town and the kids at school like to talk
> about Shane and spin tales about him. I never
> did. There's some say he was a certain Shannon,
> famous gunfighter down in Arkansas and Texas who
> dropped out of sight, no one knew where or why.
> But to us he was the man who rode into our val-
> ley out of the great West, and when the work was
> done, rode back.

> FATHER'S VOICE
> It's not him, Joey.

> BOY'S VOICE
> I know . . . And that's all we care about. For
> whatever he was, he belongs to us, and his name
> is Shane.

As the boy answers his father, camera draws back from him.
He picks up what he was doing in the opening shot, starts
slowly to work again. The whole valley is before us.

(Shane)

Giant (1956)

Most of the writing was done at George's house on Riverside Drive. He
attended every story conference. He paid more attention [to the script]
than any other director I worked with. We [Ivan, George Stevens and
Fred Guiol, his longtime associate] spent a lot of time making tea in the
morning to avoid getting down to work. We took our time, started in
March 1954 and did not finish until December.

Almost without exception, the script was shot as written. And that
was not George Stevens's usual habit. His normal routine was to spend
a lot of time changing the script—working at night after a scene was
shot—and then reshooting it the next morning. But George knew I
would not be available on the Texas location, where much of the picture was shot, and he later wrote me a short letter saying, "Thank God
we worked as thoroughly as we did, because I wouldn't have had the
energy down in Marfa, Texas, to go through what we normally did."

Edna [Ferber] was with us some of the time. The basic story is
there in her novel, but there was a good deal of trial and error, structural
changes, scenes which worked and didn't work. When we started, we
didn't know who would be playing the leading parts. Originally George
Stevens wanted Alan Ladd for the part James Dean eventually got. And
he talked to Audrey Hepburn, Grace Kelly and Eva Marie Saint about
the part Elizabeth Taylor eventually played.

There are scenes that aren't in the book, for instance when Rock
Hudson [Bick Benedict] fights [the racist owner] in the diner while the

jukebox plays "The Yellow Rose of Texas." That was our invention. Also, the wake scene at the ranch that gets out of hand and turns into a Texas whoop-de-doo. Edna Ferber didn't like that. She said to me, "You're a bunch of necrophiliacs."

Several times Jack Warner [studio head] tried to have certain scenes modified. [*Giant* was a Warner Bros. production.] Notably the derogatory reference Elizabeth Taylor [Leslie Benedict] makes to the oil depletion allowance which favored oil companies: "How about an appreciation for first-class brains instead?" The oil interests put pressure on the studio, one banker threatened to transfer his account, and Jack Warner begged Stevens to take the line out. But he said, "No dice." He was very independent.

Edna Ferber, by the way, had been a guest of the Kleberg family at

Elizabeth Taylor and Rock Hudson near the end of a very long day during the shoot of Giant

their vast spread in Texas, the King ranch. Then she wrote a novel which was critical of them. After it came out, she tried to avoid the Kleberg family, and once hid her face behind a menu when a member of the family came into the Beverly Hills restaurant where she was sitting.

James Dean was rather quiet and somewhat kept to himself. I remember the way he kept practicing this rope trick for a scene, fiddling with the ropes exactly like a ranch hand might. He had this funny laugh, a slightly goat-like laugh, and a nice, sort of cheeky sense of humor.

I know that he and George had some run-ins, I heard about it but I wasn't there. George thought it bad manners and unprofessional to show up late for a scene, and it was. But Dean was extraordinary in the role of Jett Rink. I remember looking at some of the dailies. There was a scene where Jett Rink is with his lawyers, discussing the future of this small property he's been left in a will. Dean wasn't speaking much in the scene. But George said, I remember exactly, word for word, "He's like a magnet. You watch him. Even when he's not doing anything, you watch him and not the others."

(From an undated interview in American Legends*)*

Reading the novel, it's clear that Edna Ferber found it hard to write convincing dialogue to explain why the Benedicts decide to go to Jett Rink's party. Seeing the film, it's clear that we did, too. "We'll go and do it right," Bick says, which is pretty lame. And the audience doesn't give a damn, of course. They just want to see what happens at the party.

James Dean could be very creative. In his scene with Carroll Baker [as the Benedicts' elder daughter], he's had a few drinks and indirectly suggests marriage. She plays it coy. It was written that way, indecisive, partly improvised. Dean improvised it even more, he threw in more hesitation and pauses and laughs. The dialogue isn't in the book at all. The scene in the movie, which I think is one of the best, describes two people circling around each other. Both are playing a game. He never proposes directly because he doesn't want to be rejected. She's not sure what she wants.

(From Ivan's commentary on the DVD of Giant*)*

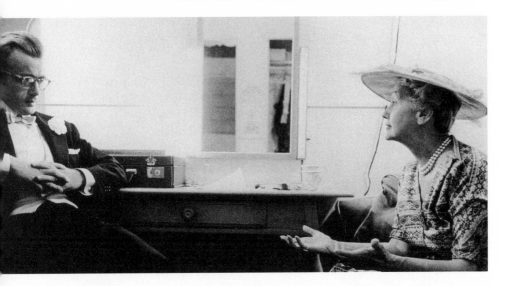

Hedda Hopper interviews a wary James Dean, made up for a scene in Giant *as the older Jett Rink, in his trailer.*

A few years ago the studio reissued *Giant* in a new format, on a big screen. They had this big opening in Dallas. Seeing the film again, I thought it had become a bit dated. The way Texans treated Mexicans was dealt with rather heavy-handedly. Today there are different social issues. But Carroll Baker played a 1950s teenager beautifully. The 1950s were rather priggish in terms of morals compared to the 1960s, or later. Back then, teenagers still pretended to learn something in school.

(*From* The Looseleaf Report, *May 4, 1992*)

(The credits of Giant *read "Screenplay by Ivan Moffat and Fred Guiol." But George Stevens, as Ivan explains, made an important contribution. He also asked Ivan to write, as guidelines for the actors, a series of "profiles" of the leading characters. By shedding more light on them than Ferber did in her own novel, the "profiles" became extremely helpful to Stevens as well.)*

BICK BENEDICT: A PROFILE

Bick before his marriage was a lonely man with only his
sister to keep him company on the ranch. It was like the
stale end of a marriage that is nothing more than a set
of patterns for avoiding inactivity in the presence of
the other: early morning coffee together, then Bick riding off to some distant part of his domain. Luz would
mostly stay behind to run the Main House—the servants,
the accounts, the ordering of the few necessities and
fewer luxuries which were bought on the outside.

"Luz runs the house," Bick was to explain later, and
ruefully add: "Some say she runs the ranch." And he felt
it was true. Most likely he was bored with his older
sister—her wasp-like restlessness, small dry hands and
tartly offending wit. But he could not turn from her in
the vast and lonely domain which he had inherited and
loved. It was a prison in which he was its captive, she
its jailer.

His escape, when it came, was accomplished by marriage. He cannot have been under any illusions as to how
Luz was going to feel about Leslie, or how Leslie would
react to Luz's wifelike shrewishness. When Luz got
killed (more than he had bargained for), Bick's sense of
guilt came welling forth. But we must acknowledge that a
great burden had been lifted from him. However, Leslie's
strength of will worked both ways, and Bick bore the
brunt of much of it. Although he had spoken of the freedom which Leslie would enjoy in Texas, he was not really
prepared for the fact that she would avail herself of it.
She took him at his word, and he discovered immediately
that it was not Luz alone whose ideas were in conflict
with his wife's.

True to human nature, Bick desired Leslie's original-
ity, but wished it to conform to his own conception of
how a wife should behave. He wanted an unusual sort of
girl but he wanted her to be unusual in a conventional
sort of way, that would not embarrass him with his Texas
friends. Perhaps deep down Bick had long known that some
of his views were wrong, and that Leslie was right in her
point of view, but he never admitted it. He indulged to
his own considerable satisfaction in unfavorable comments about the appearance of his half-Mexican grandson,

and relished doing so all the more because he had a
sneaking feeling that in actual truth the mixture of his
blood would 'be a pretty good one.

But Leslie's views, attitudes and behavior never
affected the tremendous admiration and feeling which
Bick had for her. She was, for him, a remarkable creature
whose vagaries and compassionate whims only served to
increase his almost mystified fascination. He relished
her wisdom while pretending to disdain it. He relished
also the posture of ignorance which he could adopt for
her. Right at the end, when Leslie was at last praising
him as her hero, and concluding that the family they had
made was a pretty good one, he pretended not to understand. "Leslie," he said, "I'll never understand a word
you're saying." But he understood well enough. And she
knew it. And he knew that she knew it, and he knew that
it pleased her.

JETT RINK: A PROFILE

Jett had many reasons, as a young man, to be angry.
First, he was a drifter in a world where he found himself
one of the few underprivileged and yet non-Mexican
employees of a young man of vast wealth. He had drifted
to the ranch, and now he was hung up there for some reason he did not fully know. Perhaps it was instinct, perhaps he knew his future was there.

He was angry because he was smart enough to appraise
the world in terms of its opportunities, and his limited
access to them, smart enough to perceive that the world
did indeed owe him a living, and that he could take from
it, if he was lucky, ten thousand times as much. Later he
was to be angry because Leslie, who owed him nothing, was
kinder, gentler and more understanding toward him than
the others, but still remained a Benedict—a figure to dominate and confuse the clear horizon of his bitterness.

Jett did not dislike the Mexicans. He knew, more than
most, they were getting a raw deal. But his only interest in life was to get into the same position as those
who were giving the Mexicans that same raw deal. The
world was a jungle, and if he sometimes felt that its

laws were outrageous, he proposed to avail himself of
them, not change them.

When Jett started telling Leslie about the conditions
of the Mexicans who worked for her husband, it was an
attempt to prick what he supposed was a complacent con-
science. Her reaction impressed him, and for the first time
he sensed, in a member of the dominant class, a genuine
note of compassion. He even felt that, in the well-
educated, unprejudiced person of Bick's wife, he had found
a kind of recognition of his sense of personal destiny.

On top of it all, Leslie was the absolute symbol,
morally and physically, of the unattainable feminine
goal. Unattainable, that is, in his present state. For the
future, he was ready to bide his time. And bide it he did.

As a product of Texas, Jett is an example of the phenomenon of someone who believes in a legend and is in the
rare position of making it seem to come true. But in his
heart of hearts, he knew that his struggle had little or
nothing to do with the self-congratulatory effusions of
those Texans who spoke of their state as being the very
cradle of opportunity and benevolence. It must have been
hard for Jett to look with any great pride upon the fact
that only accident had made him a native of Texas. And a
secret grudge grew up inside of him. All that his early
life had brought him in the way of loneliness, all that
his relationship to Bick had occasioned in the way of
envy and humiliation, he now blamed on Texas. All that he
had earned in the way of money and power, he felt he had
earned despite Texas, and he felt a vindictiveness
toward his Mother State which smoldered inside him and
finally erupted with violence.

Of all the people in our story, the only one who did
not grow up, or mature, or become reconciled to this
earth, was (in purely Texas terms) the most successful
one of all: Jett Rink himself.

LESLIE BENEDICT: A PROFILE

When Bick Benedict first met her, there was in Leslie the
elements of romantic rebellion against the mannered,

circumscribed and often petty qualities of the Virginia social world. She liked to dance at Washington parties, to ride and to hunt, to argue about affairs with the men and women around Government, but this was not what she sought from life or her own married future.

She had been led into a romanticization of the West, promising a kind of freedom and richness; and Bick, sensing it, had played upon this note in her. She was soon to discover that Texas was as different from what she had imagined as her own brand of nonconformity was different from what Bick had imagined. Each of them had been guilty of self-deception, and each was to be shocked and surprised at the consequences. At one time it almost cost them their marriage, and what saved it was not realistic appraisal, but love. Knowing this full well, Leslie even told Bick at the end of their separation: "I haven't changed. I'm just the same now as when I went away."

One of Leslie's problems was not that conditions in Texas were worse than in other places, but that Texans were exceptional in their unwillingness to admit that their state stood short of perfection. They were self-conscious and touchy about anyone, especially an outsider, saying derogatory things about them. This made Leslie's rather hopeless task all the more so, although she achieved much of her goal in a superficial but pleasing way. The big house was redecorated, books made their way onto the library shelves, delicacies appeared at mealtimes, and Bach sounded from one of the best phonographs in the state. But it was the same Bick Benedict, it was the same Texas, the poor remained poor and the rich remained rich.

It was in the aesthetic rather than in any other sense that Leslie's world and the world of Texas drew closer together. Her taste and flair was eagerly grasped and imitated by her friends, and the Reata house became a standard by which others were judged. Texan self-consciousness acted as a spur to this process, and unlike her social opinion, the seeds she cast in this regard fell upon fertile ground.

And slowly, Leslie, Bick and Texas matured and aged. The young girl full of vitality and zeal became a woman responsive to her surroundings, and in a way responsible for them as well. Feeling at home, rather than in a

strange country, Leslie was able to enjoy and cherish the
loyalty and strength of Bick; and today, when the hot
wind blows from the West, or the fresh cool wind blows
from the Gulf, or the north wind sings cold and dry in
the telegraph wires, they remind her that she is where
she wants to be, where she has chosen to be, and where
she will remain.

*(From the George Stevens Special Collection, Margaret Herrick Library, Academy of
Motion Picture Arts and Sciences)*

The Greatest Story Ever Told (1965)

I worked very briefly on *The Greatest Story Ever Told,* but I have a feeling that George started out being very brave in his approach, and in his
conception of what the story should be about. But the pressures of
church and society, and the establishment in all its forms, combined
with his own somewhat insecure theological assumptions and feelings,
made him withdraw and take a step or two backward, and perhaps
downwards. Finally, he was out of his depth.

The reason that he chose Carl Sandburg to work as story consultant
on the script was to put up a front. But as time went on he grew impatient with him. One afternoon Sandburg came into the office wearing a
cap and a slightly whimsical smile, and after he settled himself in a
chair, he said: "Somebody told me recently that the houses had no windows in those days, the days of Jesus." And George said with suppressed impatience, "That's right, Carl, they didn't have windows in
those days." And Sandburg nodded and went to sleep.

*(From an interview with Susan Marlow, the George Stevens Special Collection, Margaret
Herrick Library, Academy of Motion Picture Arts and Sciences)*

Bhowani Junction (1956)

(Changes imposed by the studio, and Sonya Levien's collaboration on the script, make it impossible to select any one scene as definitively Ivan's. But from Ivan's summary of his approach to the story for Cukor, which follows, and Cukor's later comments on the changes, it's clear that the result was as helpful as Ivan's "profiles" would be to Stevens on Giant.*)*

Victoria Jones [Ava Gardner] is a girl in search of her identity in a time of change, unrest and danger [in India]. It's a crossroads in time for all the characters. For the men it has the effect, at first, of confirming them in their original attitudes—Patrick [Bill Travers] becomes more aggressively, defensively Anglo-Indian; Ranjit [Francis Matthews] becomes increasingly the dedicated, religious and patriotic Indian; Savage [Stewart Granger] remains uncompromisingly British. Upon Victoria this moment has the effect of making her question her past values, and go out in search of a different self, a different future.

Victoria alone has seen and lived the most within the three worlds: the Anglo-Indian world of her upbringing, the free-moving world of the upper-class English in Delhi, the subjugation, passion and frequent torment of the Indians themselves. Vulnerable and lacking self-confidence, she makes a kind of Odyssey, journeying in turn with three different men, each in a way overlapping, yet each a world and an outlook which she cannot completely accept and which cannot completely accept her.

She tries first of all to embrace Ranjit's purely Indian world, and sees it now for the first time. She becomes intensely aware of the meaning and problem of India, she evaluates her surroundings as if they were novel instead of familiar. But the world of India, although it would take her to itself, will not accept her *as* herself. And she is too strong in her own individuality, and too weak in her new conviction, to bow to this. She runs from India, sinks gratefully into the physically passionate security of Savage's love. He will take her for what she is, will possess her physically in the way that Ranjit—the symbol of sacred as opposed to profane love—had refused to do.

But being taken for what she is by an Englishman presents a new problem; what of the fact that she is *not*, and can never become, English herself? Even if she wanted to be, would there not be the atavistic shadow of her dark Indian mother clouding her life in England? The betel nut, the rundown stockings, the prematurely ravaged beauty? Will her husband, in accepting her, be accepted himself? And does she want to turn her back forever on the country and the single man who needs her with a desperation unknown to the other men?

The fact that Patrick represents her first love is made even stronger by her woman's knowledge of the strength of his need. To some women, to be needed strongly is to love strongly. And Patrick has finally changed. The spectacle of his arrogance turning to despair and self-doubt moves Victoria. She can rescue him—and does so at the moment of greatest need. For she now has the confidence and the freedom to face the future with him.

(From Ivan Moffat, "Summary and Discussion of Theme," December 1, 1954, in the George Cukor Special Collection, Margaret Herrick Library, Academy of Motion Picture Arts and Sciences)

They Came to Cordura (*1959*)

(Although Robert Rossen's name follows Ivan's on the credits of this movie, Rossen's name is not included on the final screenplay. The

changes from final screenplay to release print were minor, apart from the
last scene, when Thorn [Gary Cooper] has become blind.)

EXT. MOUNTAIN CAMP — MEDIUM GROUP SHOT — NIGHT

The men are bedded down for the night. Only Thorn and
Adelaide [Rita Hayworth] are awake. She sits, serape
around her shoulders, near her fire, now and then taking
a drink from her bottle. Thorn drinks coffee by the light
of his own fire, and occasionally makes notes in his little book. He watches her. She is holding her bird [para-
keet] at her breast. She gets up unsteadily and as she
tries to tie the bird back to the saddle, her serape
falls to the ground. Drunkenly, she tries to pick it up,
then finds herself on the ground again. She laughs softly,
derisively, as she notices Thorn watching her. O.s, the
rumble of thunder.

> ADELAIDE
> (with mock politeness)
> Excuse me, Major Thorn. Not ladylike, I
> know . . . not ladylike.
> (again she laughs)
> And a senator's daughter should be ladylike.
> (suddenly)
> Ever hear of my father? United States Senator.
> Very important man. Very rich man.
> (chuckles)
> Convicted of selling Indian lands . . . Nine-
> teen hundred and eight. Big scandal . . . big
> man . . . big scandal . . .
> (suddenly reproving)
> You're not making notes in your book, Major. No
> citation for me?
> (laughs again)
> I've lived beyond the limits of human conduct.
> (to the bird)
> Haven't I, Palomito?
> (again the chuckle)

*Adelaide (Rita Hayworth) about
to help a distraught Major Thorn
(Gary Cooper) shave himself; Tab
Hunter in background*

Married three times.
(a pause)
Last husband I had—shot a man who was in
love with me. Happened in a hotel room in
Norfolk, Virginia. Big scandal. Big man's daughter . . . big scandal.
(a trace of bitterness)
They gave him custody of my two children.

She gets to her feet and strokes the bird.

ADELAIDE
Now the bird is my child.

THORN
And the bottle.

                         ADELAIDE
          (as she ties bird to saddle horn)
              And the bottle.

The bird screeches.

                         ADELAIDE
        Sssh, Palomito, sssh . . . wake <u>his</u> children.
        (looks at the sleeping men—her tone is acid)
              Heroes! Heroes! . . .

CLOSE SHOT — TRUBEE

He is awake. Next to him, Chawk is asleep. Trubee is listening. His eyes glitter.

BACK TO SCENE

Adelaide, the bird tied now, puts her head against the
saddle. Another rumble of thunder is heard. The bird
screeches again.

                         ADELAIDE
        Sssh, Palomito, sssh . . . you'll wake his
        children. His sleeping, snoring, dirty, sweaty,
        lecherous children.

She closes her drunken, sleepy eyes. The camp is silent
except for the rumble of thunder. It begins to rain.

EXT. MOUNTAIN CAMP — CLOSEUP — THORN'S FACE — DAWN

The rain has stopped. There comes the o.s. sound of a
woman's loud wailing. Thorn opens his eyes, sits up, sees
something.

CLOSEUP — ADELAIDE

Kneeling, she is crying in the sun, her face distorted
with anguish. CAMERA PULLS BACK to REVEAL the bird lying,
a wet-feathered lump, at her feet. The killing has obviously been savage.

MEDIUM SHOT — THORN

Half-dressed, he approaches Adelaide. As he sees the
bird, his face shows shock, disgust, anger.

CLOSE SHOT — ADELAIDE

In a high voice, she screams epithets in Spanish at the
men, accusing them of cowardice, every sort of vice.

MEDIUM SHOT — MEN

They are getting up, coming toward Adelaide in soaked
blankets, faces sullen as her curses rain down upon them.
Hetherington also approaches, already dressed from his
point of guard.

MEDIUM SHOT — WHOLE GROUP

As Thorn in a fury, and also bewildered, turns on the men.

                    THORN
          All right! Now who did this?

Silence.

                    THORN
              Speak up! Who?

Still silence.

                    THORN
     Of all the stupid senseless acts of pure sav-
          agery . . . Speak up! Who?

Still silence. Thorn stands there, anger and frustration
mounting.

                    THORN
                (to Fowler)
     Lieutenant, get these men ready to pull out.

                    FOWLER
     (obviously making a play in front of men)
         They haven't had their breakfast, sir.

                    THORN
           Let them go without it.
                (a pause)
     There will be no breaks today. Push them hard.

He turns and walk away. The men stare after him.

                              (They Came to Cordura)

Tender Is the Night (1962)

(Once, when David Selznick went to New York for just five days, I got a forty-five-page telegram from him about different aspects of the film. Delivered to the studio by Western Union. They didn't really do much good, those famous memoranda, only bits of them sometimes important. But everybody dreaded to receive them. [Director] Henry King didn't even bother to read them.)

Final Scene

INT. VILLA DIANA — DICK DIVER'S WORKROOM — DAY

Nicole [Jennifer Jones], Baby [Nicole's sister, Joan Fontaine] and Tommy [Tom Ewell] stand by the hall door-way and see Dick. He is just putting down two bags and his briefcase, and throws a trenchcoat and hat over them. He looks up at the three of them. There is silence.

                    DICK
    If you don't mind, I would like to say goodbye
                to Nicole. Alone.

                   TOMMY
                Of course.

He exits. So does Baby. Nicole and Dick stand looking at each other.

                  NICOLE
        Have you seen the children?

                        DICK
                     Not yet.

                       NICOLE
Dick, if you'd like for their sake—to stay on—
even keep up the marriage—

                        DICK
Be bad for the children. They'll be better off
with—with you.

                       NICOLE
They adore you . . . Things could never be the
same again—that's true—but we could still have a
marriage—of sorts, I suppose . . . It would be
no worse than with other people.

                        DICK
                     (quietly)
But we're not other people, Nicole. We're better
than that.

                       NICOLE
Are we? Are we, Dick? Maybe that's been our
trouble—thinking we're better than other people. I know now that I'm not. And I know that I
was unfair to you—I built you up in my mind as
some kind of a god . . .

                        DICK
               (slowly, with a wan smile)
                  Vanished, didn't he?
                 (looks away wistfully)
It's hard to say when. There were so many
moments. Each one chipping away at time—and
love.

There is a knock at the open doorway to the hall.

                        MAID
                    (in French)
I beg your pardon. The taxi is here. Shall I put
the luggage in it, monsieur?

                              DICK
                         (in French)
                  Yes, thank you, Jeanette.

The maid leaves.

                             NICOLE
                  (slight choke in her voice)
                          Oh, Dick . . .
                  (then controlling herself)
             Why are you taking a taxi? Take one of the
                              cars.

                              DICK
                         No thanks . . .
                      (looks at his watch)
          I'll say goodbye to the children. Can we just
          pretend to them I'm going away for a while?

                             NICOLE
             Of course. What time does your train leave?

                              DICK
                      Twelve-fifteen . . .
                          (smiles)
             By no means one of the worst times of the day.

He leaves. Nicole moves to the window, CAMERA WITH HER.
She sees Dick out on the terrace. Over her shoulder and
through the window, in the distance, we see the children
run to Dick. Nicole sees him get down on one knee and put
his arms around them.

                       LONGER ANGLE

Tommy and Baby reenter, close the door. Nicole continues
watching Dick, never taking her eyes off him during the
scene.

                    BABY
                (cheerfully)
                Has he gone?

                    NICOLE
        (still watching, very softly)
                He's gone.

                    TOMMY
                (casually)
        I wonder if Dick has any plans.

CAMERA MOVES SLOWLY in on Nicole as she looks out at
Dick.

                    BABY
        I asked him. He said no at first. Then I think he
        said something about a little place in upper New
        York State. I don't know if he meant trying to
        practice there, or getting some job, or what.
        Some little town, he said . . .

                    NICOLE
                (still gazing out)
        Glen Falls. He was born there.

                    BABY
                (casually, quietly)
        That's it. Near there, he said. Well, those lit-
        tle towns can be quite nice. I wouldn't be sur-
        prised if he ended up in that section of the
        country, in one town or another.

Nicole suddenly can't stand it, and as CAMERA REACHES A
CLOSE SHOT, she starts to leave.

                    BABY
                (firmly)
        Nicole, I suggest you let well enough alone!

CLOSEUP – NICOLE

As she arrives at the door, swings it open—Tommy moves
quickly into scene, turns her around, closes door and
leans against it. Then, holding her by both shoulders:

>   TOMMY
> Nicole, don't take advantage, <u>again.</u>

>   NICOLE
>   (indignant)
>   What do you mean?

>   TOMMY
> His weakness—his love for you. Don't you see
> that his last hope—his last chance—is to <u>get</u>
> <u>away from you?</u>

Nicole moves away and walks in a circle around the room.

EXT. VILLA DIANA – DAY

In the foreground Dick stands by the taxi. He surveys the
scene for the last time. He smiles wanly, makes a papal
cross over the scene, turns and gets into the taxi. It
starts, and CAMERA PANS as it drives away from us, to
reveal the blue Mediterranean and the strong sunlight
over Dick's Riviera. Then we hear a piercing scream.

ON VILLA STEPS – CLOSE – NICOLE

>   NICOLE
>   Dick!

She runs out of shot.

MEDIUM PAN SHOT — NICOLE

She runs to the spot where the taxi was. Now it's going
away up the road. She is frantic. She runs in a wide
circle.
FADE OUT

(Tender Is the Night)

The Grand Defiance

(*This unproduced 1996 screenplay, the last that Ivan wrote, is a World
War II story reminiscent of* The Great Escape *and* Colditz. *After being
captured by the Nazis in 1940, a famous French general conceives a daring plan of escape from the fortress of Koenigstein. Although its eventual
success is skillfully plotted, the elements are over-familiar; and the most
interesting scenes are the early ones between General de Forge and
Colonel Baron von Barnsdorf, the Kommandant of the fortress—a transparent homage to Pierre Fresnay and Erich von Stroheim in Renoir's* La
Grande Illusion.)

EXT. KOENIGSTEIN — BATTLEMENTS — NIGHT

De Forge, in sweater and muffler, is pacing up and down
for exercise. After a few moments von Barnsdorf appears
in the small doorway. He is resplendent in full-dress
uniform complete with two rows of ribbons, and the
Knight's Cross with diamonds hangs at his neck.

VON BARNSDORF
Good evening, General. I trust I am not
disturbing you.

DE FORGE
It takes more than you to disturb me, Colonel,
even when you're dressed up like that.

VON BARNSDORF
(laugh)
Had to attend a dinner for some local Party
bosses. Bunch of noisy bullies, mostly. But if
you put your Knight's Cross around your neck—all
of a sudden they're meek as mice.
(comes closer)
General de Forge, as long as you're here, you're
under the Army's protection, and the Nazis don't
dare lay their hands on you. But because in
French eyes you're already a hero, they would
love nothing better than to be able to announce
that you had been "shot while attempting to
escape." I admire you, General. I would hate to
have been a part of some tragedy which would
cost you your life.

DE FORGE
And possibly yours, too, I fear. Which I, too,
would equally regret. Or almost equally.

He looks at von Barnsdorf deadpan. The tiniest smile
crosses von Barnsdorf's face.

VON BARNSDORF
I have always appreciated the dry ironies of the
French, General de Forge.

DE FORGE
Then we have something in common, Baron.

Von Barnsdorf turns for a moment to stare out over the
battlements at the dark valley below.

                    VON BARNSDORF
We have something else in common, even if I say
it myself.

                      DE FORGE
                     Which is?

                    VON BARNSDORF
You are a famous general and I only an obscure
colonel, but we are both born of the same old
European order. All right, we're a vanishing
breed. All the more important, then, that
the values we hold dear should be kept alive—
somehow, somewhere—in this dark new world we see
around us.

                      DE FORGE
Colonel, obviously much that is happening in
Germany today, you resent, even hate. And yet I
see by your ribbons you fought in this war of
hers, and fought bravely.
                     (a pause)
                       Why?

Von Barnsdorf seems unable to formulate his answer.

                      DE FORGE
                   Why, Colonel?

                    VON BARNSDORF
General, with respect, I think only to a German
     could I answer such a question.
                     (a beat)
     And no German would need to ask it.

De Forge bows his head slightly in acknowledgment.

                    VON BARNSDORF
Honor is a strange thing to us. Sometimes a con-
tradictory thing. But there have been times in
our history when it was, literally, all we had
left.
              (silence for a moment)

General, please, I beg you, for the sake of <u>our</u> world, for the sake of all we have been through, and even more for what we will have to go through when this war is over, don't get yourself killed by trying to escape from Koenigstein!

AFTERWORD

London, June, 1998: the dining room of Marguerite and Mark Littman's house in Chester Square, Belgravia. Ivan is on a visit to London and Marguerite has invited him to lunch. Her other guest is Caroline Blackwood's youngest daughter, Ivana, who's visiting London from New York.

At the end of lunch, coffee is served. Then Marguerite suddenly gets up. "I'm sure you two have something to talk about," she says, and leaves the room. Although Ivan doesn't appear surprised, Ivana is extremely startled. But a moment later she realizes that "something" must refer to a rumor that she'd recently heard.

In 1966, the year Ivana was born, Caroline's marriage to Israel Citkowitz had been on the verge of dissolution. They separated later that year, and in 1970 she began an affair with Robert Lowell. In 1972, after flying to Santo Domingo for an instant divorce from their spouses, the couple got married there on the same day. In 1974 Citkowitz suffered a fatal stroke, and as Lowell had a fatal heart attack in a taxi only three years later, Ivana grew up without a father figure in her life.

At nineteen she decided (like Caroline in her youth) to become an actress, and acquired an agent who advised her to find a different last name. She changed it legally to Lowell, partly because she felt that her stepfather had been "wonderful" to her, and partly because her mother encouraged the idea. In 1987 Caroline decided to give up her London house and return to New York, taking both daughters with her. And a few months before she died of cervical cancer in February 1996, rumors had already begun to circulate that Israel Citkowitz might not have been Ivana's biological father—but rather Ivan or Robert Silvers, editor of the *New York Review of Books*.

In 1963, while still married to Citkowitz, Caroline had begun an affair with Silvers in New York. It lasted for the rest of the decade, during which Caroline also resumed her on-and-off affair with Ivan, when they were both living in London.

After Marguerite left the dining room, Ivan asked Ivana (whom he hadn't seen for some years) if she was aware of the rumors about himself and Bob Silvers. When she nodded, he said that they'd agreed to settle the matter by taking a DNA test. Personally, Ivan added, he believed himself to be Ivana's father, and took her hand "in a very paternal way." But she immediately pulled away. "Let's wait for the results of the test before we go any further," she said, and thought that if offered a choice, she would prefer Bob Silvers for a father, because she felt closer to him.

Ivan was someone she'd never known well. "He was around the house at Redcliffe Square from time to time, and when I was seven, he and Caroline took me to tea at Fortnum and Mason's." Then Ivan said, "I want to buy a present for this little girl," and took her to the toy department, where she chose the largest and most expensive teddy bear in the store. "Over the years he used to kid me about this, and it was really the extent of our personal contact, although I loved his imitations of people, and like everyone else I found him witty and charming."

Ivan had already made an appointment to take the DNA test on the last Friday in June, but on the preceding Wednesday he was hit by a car as he started to cross a London street. Rushed to hospital, where X-rays revealed multiple injuries to his ribs and legs, as well as a severe concussion, he was told by the doctors that an octogenarian must expect a slow recovery. But within two weeks, he was strong enough to recuperate at the country house of his cousin Virginia.

Before he left the hospital, the DNA specialist asked Ivan to set a new date for the test, and to send him a photograph. But Ivan declined to face the camera until every bruise on his face had disappeared. In fact he waited longer. After what Virginia described as "two months and two days of lovely times," he returned to California in mid-October without having taken the test. One reason was his reluctance for the truth to become official, especially in England where at least one tabloid had reported the "rumors." But the delay was also another example of the way Ivan could distance himself, "be there and not there," even when it involved a deeply personal matter.

He finally gave a sample for the DNA test in late autumn in the garden of a house above Sunset Strip, where Ivana's sister Evgenia (older by two years, and incontestably Citkowitz's daughter) lived with her husband, Julian Sands. By this time Evgenia had grown close to Ivan. From their first meeting in London when she was six, she recalled, "He seemed a wonderfully urbane figure, with a boyish grin, better clothes and manners than the people in Caroline's bohemian circle. He was genuinely fond of Israel and used to play chess with him. Once they finished their game in a taxi because Ivan was en route to some other, no doubt smarter engagement."

From the first, Evgenia had a strong intuition about the result of the test. "For me, the decisive clue was when Ivana changed her name to Lowell. Caroline didn't take it as a betrayal of Israel, but supported it. But I was still shocked when Ivan finally told me that he was Ivana's father. I started to cry, for Ivana, for my father, and then he got nervous. He started to cast doubts on what he'd just said, and begged me not to tell Caroline. He wanted me to know, but dreaded Caroline's outburst of rage when she learned he'd broken their understanding, whatever it was."

When Evgenia saw Caroline a month later, she asked for the truth, without mentioning her conversation with Ivan. "It was late at night, and my mother was sitting in a wing-backed chair, staring at me, her enormous eyes ringed with kohl. She paused—too long—while she processed the question, and before she denied the rumors, I could see her taking the decision to lie."

Although some people thought that Caroline had left an obvious clue in the name she gave her daughter, Evgenia found it too obvious. "Most likely it was designed to give the impression that if she really had something to hide, she'd never have chosen that name." At the time, in fact, she told several friends that she chose it as a gesture toward someone of whom she'd always been particularly fond.

But Ivana was deeply upset to learn the result of the test. "I didn't know whether to be angrier with Caroline or with Ivan for keeping the truth from me all those years," she recalled. "I suppose Caroline felt that Ivan would not be a very good parent, and it was better for me to think of Israel as my father." When her anger subsided, confusion took its place. "I'd always thought of myself as half British-aristocratic and half Polish-Jewish. Now what exactly was I? And what were the genetic implications?"

Perhaps coincidentally, perhaps not, Ivan had begun writing *Absolute Heaven* a few months after Caroline's death. In any case, he was finally prepared by then to examine his own life, although "how deeply," he once remarked, "I'm not sure." He put the book aside to complete a first draft of *The Grand Defiance,* and took it up again early in 1997. But he was soon diagnosed first with prostate cancer, then shortly afterward with cancer of the colon; and when he returned to *Absolute Heaven,* he

Caroline Blackwood, c. 1970, with her daughters Natalya, Ivana, and Evgenia, in the garden of her English country house known as the Owl House

found that he was slowing down. For an octogenarian who had survived two bouts of chemotherapy, this was not surprising. In fact, his friends were surprised that Ivan remained so tenaciously spry.

But as a writer Ivan never really recovered the focus that he first acquired from working with George Stevens; and even then, as George Stevens, Jr., remembered, it sometimes contended with his focus on social life, especially during his nine months on *Giant*. "That screenplay was a three-way collaboration, with Ivan writing some scenes, my father dictating others, and Fred Guiol, who did hardly any writing, but had a wonderful film sense, contributing some important visual ideas. However, Ivan was not at his best on mornings after a long dinner party."

Back in Los Angeles after the marriage to Kate ended, Ivan at fifty-five had been determined to resume the role of man-about-town that he'd played so successfully as a very young man in late-1930s and early-1940s London, and as a still youthful one during his first fifteen years in the "golden age." But during the 1970s, as that age receded into the past, his social circle narrowed. Preston Sturges had died in 1959; producer Jerry Wald in 1962; Aldous Huxley in 1963; David Selznick in 1965; producer William Goetz (with his wife Edie, Louis B. Mayer's daughter, a leading party-giver) in 1969; George Stevens in 1975; Chaplin (after living in Switzerland for twenty-five years) in 1977; Salka Viertel (after living there for almost as long) in 1978; Merle Oberon and Darryl Zanuck in 1979.

Although the movie industry admired survivors, it considered them professionally old guard. Not many offers came Ivan's way, and because he needed the money, he was grateful for those that did. The first was a rewrite job, without credit, to strengthen Laurence Olivier's scenes as a patriarchal tycoon in *The Betsy* (directed by Daniel Petrie). Judee Flick "heard Ivan's voice in some of Olivier's lines," but for his voice to be momentarily heard in an adaptation of Harold Robbins's hokey bestseller was a reminder of diminished possibilities. Two years later he accepted a more promising offer, but when Costa-Gavras was engaged as director of *Missing,* he threw out Ivan's screenplay and insisted on hiring a new writer.

Even Ivan's friend Billy Wilder was considered old guard after the commercial failure of one of his best films, *The Private Life of Sherlock*

Holmes; and he remained a master wisecracker who frequently directed his acerbic one-liners at the younger generation. Ivan was occasionally jealous of another writer's success, but his case of the Wilder bitters was milder. Another friend from the same era was Jerry's widow, Connie Wald, alkaline to Wilder's acid. She spoke of the past with affection rather than regret, and bore no grudge against the present. Ivan relied on her not only as the last Hollywood hostess who genuinely enjoyed entertaining, had no hidden agenda, and bridged the generational gap, but as a backgammon partner (against whom he could always be sure of winning), and as someone to call at the last moment when a blank social calendar made him feel lonely.

How greatly Ivan depended on Connie became clear to one of his new young friends, Holly Goldberg Sloan. "Ivan would sometimes ask me, on a night that Connie had told him she had an engagement, to drive past her house before we went out to dinner together. If she was really going out, he knew she'd leave her car outside. If she was staying home, it would be in the garage."

Writer-directors Holly Goldberg Sloan and her companion Gary

Ivan and Frank Capra, who had worked with George Stevens's company, Liberty Films, c. 1978

Rosen were part of a mostly female circle that formed around Ivan in his later years. But not all of them knew each other. He still compartmentalized his life, and according to Judee Flick, one reason was that "he realized his continuing success on the social scene was as a single man, and he never asked to bring a date when he was invited to a party."

The first member of Ivan's new circle was an English-born journalist, Caroline Graham. He met her at one of Connie Wald's parties in 1977, when she was working for David Frost, in California to tape a series of celebrity interviews. He found her extremely attractive, and according to Patrice Chaplin, "hoped to marry her. When she rejected him, he really took it to heart." Not true, according to Caroline: "Maybe he wanted to marry me, and never asked because he was afraid I'd say no. But we became good friends, and I once told him, 'If your life gets too lonely, you can live in the garage apartment of my house, as long as you give up smoking.' But he wouldn't do that, and in any case I think Ivan was basically a loner."

Next to join the circle was Victoria Looseleaf, who had started to write a novel when Ivan met her. Its title, *Stalking the Wild Orgasm,* immediately aroused his curiosity, and he was impressed when he read the first chapters. A close friendship developed, and although the novel was never published, Victoria became a dance critic for the *Los Angeles Times,* and host of a public access TV show, *The Looseleaf Report,* on which Ivan was a frequent guest.

Actress Candy Clark and filmmaker Pavla Ustinov, daughter of Sir Peter, completed the circle of first among equals, not all of whom met or liked each other (let alone considered themselves equals) when they did. In both cases the friendship survived an unsuccessful pass made to each by Ivan out of sense-memory rather than any serious intention. By then he was uncertain that he'd be able to follow through.

He also compartmentalized an outer circle of hopeful girls, described by Judee Flick as "just willing to be useful, driving Ivan around and running errands for him." Like the tourists who daydreamed as they stood in the footprints of the stars in the forecourt of Grauman's Chinese Theater, they were fascinated by "Old Hollywood." Ivan's stories made them feel part of it, and he naturally enjoyed being an object of fascination.

Connie Wald, who shared Caroline Graham's impression that Ivan was "basically a loner," believed that he was "a lonely person as well." This was almost certainly true of his last ten years. Ageism is not a problem for the writer of books or plays, only for the screenwriter, who's as vulnerable as a female star; and as a screenwriter who was also a great personality in a movie industry that appreciated (and created) personalities, Ivan in his way was a star. When the industry succumbed to conglomeration, which is impersonal by nature, it valued instant financial success to the exclusion of almost everything else, and Ivan responded by forming an inner circle of young people who appreciated his wit, the ease of his presence, and his pursuit of "the charm of life."

But above all they valued his values. In his later years Ivan often mentioned the Spanish proverb that Gerald Murphy once quoted to his friend Scott Fitzgerald: "Living well is the best revenge." For Murphy, "living well" was a declaration of personal independence, and a refusal to take the world at its own worth. "It's not what we do," he said, "but what we do with our minds that has any real meaning."

Although Ivan lived this way to the end of his life, he was unable to live "well" in another sense. He had earned a good deal of money in his time, but was improvident, and as offers of work dwindled, then stopped, he began to feel the pinch. For many years he had rented a comfortable inexpensive guesthouse in the Hollywood foothills, but in 1998 the original owners reclaimed it. Keeping up appearances had always been important, and he feared having to move to an unfashionable area. Then he heard of an apartment for rent at a very reasonable rate in Beverly Hills, and took it sight unseen.

But when Ivan saw it for the first time, he was totally unprepared for a shabbily furnished living room, a "bathroom" that was no more than a shower stall in the alcove of a narrow corridor leading to a kitchen with ugly tiled walls, ancient stove and refrigerator. He gazed around, thought he could never live in the place, then realized he had to come to terms with it.

After a while he even claimed to be happy at 249 S. Spalding Drive. At least he could work on *Absolute Heaven* at a desk in the living room, and replace the faded rug on the floor and the cracks in the walls with richly varied images from his past. But even if his health permitted, would he have finished the book? As Evgenia commented, "His past was so enthralling, the War experiences defined themselves, but the gallant, gentlemanly part of him would have balked at being indiscreet about many of his affairs." Equally important, the further he left the past behind, the nearer he came to a major piece of unfinished business in his own and Ivana's life.

In April 2002 Ivana invited her father to stay at the house in Sag Harbor that she'd inherited from Caroline. She thought of it as "a getting-to-know-you visit, because Ivan had once mentioned he wanted that." But it took Ivana four years to issue the invitation because her feelings were still unresolved; and meanwhile she had married, given birth to a daughter, then divorced her husband. She was also nervous about seeing her father again because "I'd heard he was very fussy about food." When she asked Marguerite Littman for advice, Marguerite told her, "Be sure and serve caviar. I did, and it pleased him, but then he complained about the butter."

From the start Ivana had resented Ivan for wanting the visit, and her resentment grew when he showed her photographs of Iris and Curtis Moffat, and his grandmother "Mameena," Lady Tree, now Ivana's great-grandmother. "The last thing I wanted was another grandparent," she recalled. "I'd already had a very powerful one [Maureen Dufferin] in my life, and in an angry moment I told Ivan that he'd never really done anything for me, and now it was all too little and too late."

The moment passed, "we had some good times together, and I asked a neighbor and friend, who was a professional photographer, to take pictures of Ivan in the garden." But on the last evening of her father's visit, they went to dinner with another neighbor, Jean Vanderbilt. She had also invited Jimmy Davidson, who knew Ivana and was a close friend of Marguerite. He remembered that "Ivana suddenly got very angry, and told Ivan the whole situation had shocked and disturbed her from the start, she wished he'd never told anyone about it, so she could always have thought that Israel was her father. Naturally Ivan was very shaken." Although father and daughter made a show of reconciliation before Ivan left, he knew that the visit had been a failure.

A month later the doctor who had treated his earlier cancers wanted to make further tests, but Ivan was unnerved. Instead of agreeing, he consulted Victoria Looseleaf, who advised him to get a second opinion. In the second doctor's office, when Ivan filled out the standard form about his medical history, he answered *no* to the question, "Have you ever been treated for any kind of cancer?" But after listening to an account of his symptoms, the doctor convinced him to agree to further tests; and a colonoscopy left no doubt that his cancer of the colon had not only recurred, but started to metastasize to the liver.

Ivan had just received the doctor's report when we had dinner on June 24, sitting at a sidewalk table of his favorite restaurant in Beverly Hills. Although it served only wine and beer, he was permitted as a regular customer to pour himself whiskey from a hip flask, and California law permitted him to smoke in the open air, heavy that night with fumes from passing traffic. He told me about the report in a totally dispassionate way, almost as if it concerned somebody else, then abruptly changed the subject, saying he really wanted to talk about *Absolute Heaven.*

He began with some vivid stories of World War II and the liberation of Paris, then explained the difficulties of writing about his life after Natasha's arrival in California as a war bride, as it involved so many people who were still alive. But instinct told me there was another problem. Ivan not only seemed more physically frail than at our last dinner two weeks earlier, but gave the impression that his inner light, always so steady, had started to dim. He must have known, I suspected, that his condition was inoperable and his time was running out.

Later I learned that a few hours before we met, Ivan had called Lorna in Monterey, told her the tests had revealed a small malignant tumor in his liver, but in a very early stage, and the doctor believed he had a strong chance of recovery. But on the evening after we met, he had dinner with Judee Flick, and "talked about dying." She asked if he believed in any kind of afterlife. "That's rubbish," he said firmly. "Dead is dead." Then she wondered if he had any regrets. After a moment he said: "I suppose one always has regrets." And after another moment: "I'm sorry it took so long for Ivana to find out."

Next day, June 26, he lunched with Holly at Le Dôme on the Sunset Strip. She told me that he seemed in good spirits, but as they left,

Ivan and Judee Flick at his
eighty-third birthday party

and walked out the door on their way to the parking lot, he said: "I don't feel well." Then he collapsed against her and lay unconscious on the sidewalk, facing the sky. Almost immediately a woman walked past, glanced at Ivan, took out her cell phone and dialed 911. "There's a man here who's had a stroke or a heart attack," she said, crisply matter-of-fact, gave the address, snapped her phone closed and walked on.

Holly followed the ambulance to Cedars-Sinai Hospital, where Ivan was admitted to Emergency on a gurney. The room was so crammed with stricken people that they had to wait in the corridor out-side. When Ivan recovered consciousness, he learned they'd been wait-ing for more than two hours. "Don't they know who I am?" he asked, half joking, half serious. Then Evgenia arrived, alerted by Holly, and took over. "He was lying crumpled on his side, facing the wall, and had to crane and twist his neck to look at me. Although clearly uncomfortable, he kept up a determinedly offhand front. 'Suppose I must look a fright,' he drawled, more slowly than usual because of the stroke."

Then he gave Evgenia an almost accusing stare and remarked that she looked well. "There isn't much competition here," she said. And with the boyish grin that often accompanied a remark he knew would entertain, Ivan came back with: "In the valley of the blind, the one-eyed man is king."

They had to wait another four hours, during which Ivan was "in turn warmly affectionate, frightened, crusty and impatient." But whatever the mood, his spirit was remarkable. When an orderly jolted him, lowering the bed so he could lie eye-level with Evgenia's chair, Ivan waited for the man to move on before fixing her with another accusing stare. "And you *thanked* him!" Then he surveyed the scene in the corridor. "In crowded places people feel the urge to make a noise and beat their breasts. But in the desert, no one speaks."

Finally Ivan was carried to the examination room, where tests revealed that he'd suffered a mini-stroke, followed by a major one; and twenty-four hours later, although he still couldn't walk, he remained in control. Because he seemed to be improving all the time, he told no one else in Los Angeles what had happened, and saw no one except Evgenia and Holly for the next two days. But he called Lorna in Monterey, told her that he'd been taken to hospital, and "not to worry, it's nothing serious, just a fainting spell, and I expect to be out very soon."

On the second day he asked Evgenia to collect the mail from his apartment, explained where to find everything, and what bills needed to be paid. Later, sitting up in bed, he paid his phone bill and balanced his checkbook. But although Ivan seemed to be recovering, the wait to take more tests, and hear the verdict on his liver, sometimes made him apprehensive. Appalled by the idea of a prolonged illness, he told Evgenia: "I don't know what to wish for." Then his mood changed, and "he reflected on the irony of his youth, when he'd imagined a movie death for himself, a glass of champagne, a pistol and a bullet to the head."

On the third day, Evgenia and Holly decided to clean Ivan's apartment, in case he was able to return there. While they were still at 249

S. Spalding, Victoria Looseleaf arrived at the hospital. Having heard from Lorna about Ivan's phone call, and anxious to see for herself, she found him in reassuringly good form. He confided that he'd hidden a pack of cigarettes in the drawer of his bedside table, and extorted a reluctant promise that "if I ever feel I must smoke, you'll help me."

Next morning she brought Ivan the *New York Times* crossword, which they often used to solve together. But he brushed it aside, announced that he craved nicotine, and reminded Victoria of her promise. When she tried to dissuade him, Ivan told her to stop arguing and keep her word. She kept it even more reluctantly than she'd given it, helped him out of bed, wheeled him to a nearby terrace, put a cigarette in his mouth and lighted it.

"Doctor says I can smoke!" Ivan said, took a triumphant puff and never spoke again. Almost at once his head slumped to his chest and he lapsed into terminal unconsciousness. But it's unlikely that the cigarette was responsible. The doctor had decided not to tell him that the cancer had spread to his lungs and there was no way he could survive for more than a few days.

As the news of Ivan's collapse spread, recent friends and former lovers began converging on the hospital: Candy Clark, Pavla Ustinov, Judee Flick, Linda and Lucy Lane. Later on the fourth day, Lorna returned from a trip to Big Sur and found a message from Victoria on her answering machine: "You'd better come right away, your father's not doing well." She drove down to Los Angeles, reached the hospital at three-thirty next morning, and a night nurse led her to Ivan's room. "He lay gray as death, breathing through a respirator. I knew at that moment he was going to die and wondered if I could bear it." When the nurse brought in a cot and set it beside Ivan's bed, Lorna lay down, held Ivan's hand, "and slept just like the old days, when we were father and daughter together."

Caroline Graham was out of town, but had arranged to lend Jonathan and Patrick her house. They flew in from England later on the fifth day, and during that afternoon Ivana flew in from New York. She saw her father lying very still, eyes closed, apparently unaware of her presence. "Then I told him I was here to see him, and he seemed to understand. 'Uh-uh-uh,' he said." But the doctor had assured everyone that Ivan was in a deep coma, and any sound he made or response he gave was unconscious, like the pressure returned when anyone took his hand, or the occasional tear that ran down his cheek.

Ivana didn't stay long, and neither did I, standing unnoticed in the doorway on the seventh day, when the monitors indicated that Ivan's breathing continued steady. The group keeping vigil was turned away from me, immersed in quiet conversation. Soon after I left, Lorna went to 249 S. Spalding and began sorting her father's papers, to see if he had any outstanding bills. She found, sadly, that Ivan's total funds were less than his total debts, mainly from overdue credit card payments. Around four o'clock, when she called Ivan's room at Cedars-Sinai, Jonathan answered the phone. "How is he?" Lorna asked. "You'd better come right away," he said.

Ivan's faint, calm breathing was the only sound in the room, and this time the group kept a very silent vigil. Most of the lines on his formerly ravaged face had been smoothed away, and Lorna broke a long silence by saying how peaceful he looked. A nurse entered. The monitors indicated that the patient had stopped breathing, she said, and Ivan's life had ended.

At first nobody spoke. Then, as the room filled with murmurs of "Goodbye, Ivan, goodbye," a woman appeared in the doorway, hurried to his bedside and whispered something in his ear. Yet another former lover, living in Tucson, Arizona, since she married a teacher there ten years ago, Audrey Steven was unknown to everyone except Lorna, who had phoned to tell her that Ivan was dying.

"No one will ever know what she said to him, but nothing revived Ivan like his lovers," Lorna said later. In a way she meant it literally. As Ivan's lover from the past hurried off to catch a plane back to Tucson, he unconsciously confounded medical science, and had the last, ghost-like word by exhaling one more faint, calm breath.

NOTES ON SOURCES

(Not acknowledged in the text)

INTRODUCTION

A Man of Diverse Parts: George Stevens, Jr., in *A Filmmaker's Journey,* a film by George Stevens, Jr., Creative Film Center Inc., 1984. Caroline Blackwood's talent: Ned Rorem in *Knowing When to Stop,* Simon and Schuster, New York, 1994.

The Genes: Beerbohm Family, Denys Parsons and Juliet Webster, editors, *Three Beerbohms,* privately printed, London, 1991; Madeleine Bingham, *The Great Lover, the Life and Art of Sir Herbert Beerbohm Tree,* Atheneum, New York, 1979; Nicholas Wapshott, *Carol Reed,* Knopf, New York, 1994. Walpole House: Daphne Fielding, *The Rainbow Picnic, a Portrait of Iris Tree,* Eyre Methuen, London, 1974. Holt Castle: Nancy Cunard in *G.M., Memories of George Moore,* Rupert Hart-Davis, London, 1956. Duke of Rutland's Mayfair town house: Diana Cooper, *The Light of Common Day,* Rupert Hart-Davis, London, 1959. Iris at Slade school: Gretchen Holbrook Gerzina, *Carrington,* Norton, New York, 1995. Iris in Hollywood: Constance Collier, *Harlequinade* John Lane/The Bodley Head, London, 1929.

Family Moffat/Tree: Penelope Smail, editor, *A Brief Outline of the Work of Curtis Moffat,* privately printed, London, 1993; Man Ray, *Self Portrait,* Little, Brown & Co, Boston, 1963; Cecil Beaton, *Self Portrait with Friends, Selected Diaries,* edited by Richard Buckle, Weidenfeld and Nicolson, London, 1979. Marriage and honeymoon of Iris and Curtis, and Iris's letters to Ivan: Daphne Fielding, op. cit. Curtis Moffat and Nancy Cunard affair: Penelope Smail to GL. Iris and Finch Hatton: Linda Donelson, *Out of Isak Dinesen in Africa,* Coulsong List, Iowa City, 1995. Iris and Max Reinhardt: Diana

Cooper, op. cit.; Gottfried Reinhardt, *The Genius, a Memoir of Max Reinhardt,* Knopf, New York, 1979.

The Son: von Mendelssohn and von Hofmannstal circles: Gottfried Reinhardt, op. cit. Dartington Hall: Michael Young, *The Elmhirsts of Dartington,* Routledge & Kegan Paul, London, 1982. Beatrice Straight and Uday Shankar: Michael Young, op. cit. Iris Tree on "private life": Daphne Fielding, op. cit.

The Young Man About Town: Michael Luke, *David Tennant and the Gargoyle Years,* Weidenfeld and Nicolson, London, 1991. Ivan and Communist Party: Mark Littman to GL. Communist cell at Cambridge: Michael Straight, *After Long Silence,* Collins, London, 1983. Rosa Lewis: Michael Luke, op. cit. Henrietta Law: Daniel Farson, *Never a Normal Man,* HarperCollins, London, 1997. Ivan and Dylan Thomas: Jonathan Moffat to GL; Paul Ferris, *Dylan Thomas, the Biography,* J.M. Dent, London, 1999. Iris and Friedrich Ledebur, Alan Harkness: Daphne Fielding, op. cit.

The Soldier: the George Stevens unit: George Stevens, Jr., writer-producer-narrator, *George Stevens: D-Day to Berlin,* New Liberty Productions, New Line Home Video, 1995.

The Husband: Ivan's marriage to Natasha: Lorna Moffat to GL. Natasha and Simone de Beauvoir, Oreste Pucciani, and Nelson Algren: Simone de Beauvoir, *Letters to Sartre,* edited and translated by Quintin Hoare, Radius, London, 1991. Ford Rainey: Daphne Fielding, op. cit. Ivan's love for Donna O'Neill and marriage to Katharine Smith: Lorna Moffat to GL. Ivan and Howard Hughes, financial problems and serial infidelity in London: Jonathan Moffat to GL. The Moffats and Maureen Dufferin in Sardinia: Leslie Caron to GL.

The Lover: Curtis Moffat lunch party: Daphne Fielding, op. cit. Schloss Kammer: Cecil Beaton, op. cit. Mercedes de Acosta, *Here Lies the Heart,* Reynal, New York, 1960. Casanova: Stefan Zweig, *Casanova,* translated by Eden and Cedar Paul, Pushkin Press, London, 1998. Ivan and Frances Heflin: Holly Goldberg Sloan to GL. Waitress at Paramount commissary: Patrice Chaplin to GL. Regency Hotel episode: Ivan Moffat to GL. Joan Elan (by implication, when Ivan discussed the abortion scene in *A Place in the Sun*): at AFI seminar. Patricia Cutts phone call: Lorna Moffat to GL. Ivan and screenwriter's wife in Rome: Holly Goldberg Sloan to GL. Caroline Blackwood: obituaries in *New York Times,* February 15, 1996 and *Guardian,* London, February 16, 1996. "Playing the Blackwood card": Ian Hamilton, *Robert Lowell,* Random House, New York, 1982. Paul Theroux to GL, Jonathan Raban in a letter to Evgenia Sands.

The Father: Curtis Moffat suicide: Penelope Smail and the late Lady Virginia Bath to GL. Lorna's childhood and Ivan's attitude to "spiritual talk": Lorna Moffat to GL. Iris's letter on "the charm of life": Daphne Fielding, op. cit.

The Writer: Faulkner and company in Hollywood: *West of Eden, Writers in Hollywood 1928–1940*, Richard Fine, Smithsonian Institution Press, Washington/London, 1993. *The Wayward Bus* and *Boy on a Dolphin:* Ivan Moffat to GL. *Bhowani Junction:* George Cukor Special Collection at Margaret Herrick Library, AMPAS; Ivan Moffat to GL. Cukor's later comments: Gavin Lambert, *On Cukor*, edited by Robert Trachtenberg, Rizzoli, New York, 2000. Nathanael West quote: Richard Fine, op. cit. *Tender Is the Night:* Ivan Moffat to GL, and Rudy Behlmer, editor, *Memo from David O. Selznick*, Samuel French, Hollywood, 1989. Ivan and Walter Wanger: Matthew Bernstein, *Walter Wanger, Hollywood Independent*, University of California, Berkeley, 1994. Ivan and the spoken word: Patrick Leigh Fermor, *Daily Telegraph*, London, July 10, 2002. Iris's memoir of Nancy Cunard: Hugh Ford, editor, *Nancy Cunard, Brave Poet, Indomitable Rebel 1896–1965*, Chilton Book Co., New York, 1968. Her lost memoirs: Daphne Fielding, op. cit.

ABSOLUTE HEAVEN

Raimund von Hofmannstal: Ivan Moffat, editor, *Raimund von Hofmannsthal, a Rosenkavalier*, Rowohlt Taschenbuch Verlag, Hamburg, 1975.

AFTERWORD

Lunch at Marguerite Littman's: Ivana Lowell to GL. Caroline and Robert Lowell: Ian Hamilton, op. cit. Ivan's DNA test: Evgenia Sands to GL. Ivan on starting his autobiography: Ivan to GL. Ivan and first cancer attacks: Connie Wald to GL. *Missing:* Judee Flick to GL. Pavla Ustinov and Ivan: Pavla to GL. "Living well" proverb: Ivan to GL. Gerald Murphy and Scott Fitzgerald conversation: Calvin Tomkins, *Living Well Is the Best Revenge*, Viking Press, New York, 1971. Ivan's reaction to 249 S. Spalding: Holly Goldberg Sloan to GL. Ivan's visit to second doctor: Judee Flick to GL. Ivan's phone calls to Lorna from hospital: Lorna Moffat to GL. Ivan's last cigarette: Victoria Looseleaf to GL. The visitor from Tucson and Ivan's last breath: Lorna Moffat to GL.

ACKNOWLEDGMENTS

The Ivan Moffat File originated with its editor at Pantheon Books, Shelley Wanger. She knew Ivan Moffat, encouraged him to write his autobiography, and even offered him an advance—which he gratefully refused, because he didn't want to feel under any kind of pressure.

After Ivan died, Shelley Wanger suggested that I read all the surviving pages he'd written, and any other important material among his papers. His daughter Lorna (Ivan's executor), and his sons Jonathan and Patrick, encouraged the idea, gave me unconditional access to their father's papers, and were wonderfully forthcoming with personal memories. Their cooperation, and my editor's belief in the book, made *The Ivan Moffat File* possible.

Equally invaluable was the cooperation of Caroline Blackwood's daughters, Evgenia Sands and Ivana Lowell; of Ivan's family in England, his cousin the late Lady Bath, his half-sister Penelope Smail, and his London friends, Marguerite and Mark Littman. George Stevens, Jr., supplied valuable insights into Ivan's work with his father, steered me to important material in the George Stevens Special Collection at the Margaret Herrick Library, and helped with permission to reprint copyrighted material.

I'm also deeply grateful to others who knew Ivan and talked freely about him: Colin Campbell; Patrice Chaplin; Judee Flick; Caroline Graham; Linda Lane; Lucy Lane; Victoria Looseleaf; Julian Sands; Holly Goldberg Sloan; Natasha Spender; Barbara Steele; Pavla Ustinov; Connie Wald. Also to Leslie Caron, Jimmy Davidson, Michael Luke, Lady Rumbold (Pauline Tennant), Georgia Tennant, Paul Theroux and Robert Wagner for incidental information and/or helpful suggestions.

Special and in some cases duplicate thanks to the following:

The late Lady Bath, for photographs of Ivan; Patrice Chaplin, for Ivan's tape about the English in Hollywood; Gary Conklin, for Ivan's tape about Hollywood personalities, and for Curtis Moffat's portrait of Diana Cooper; Michael and Randalyn Foster, for many photographs of Ivan, his taped memories of New York, and comments on Eisenhower vs. Stevenson; Victoria Looseleaf, for deciphering the often reader-unfriendly handwritten pages of Ivan's autobiography, transcribing tapes from *The Looseleaf Report,* and for photographs; Dottie McCarthy at George Stevens Productions for a transcript of Ivan's commentary for the DVD of *A Place in the Sun;* Jonathan and Lorna Moffat for family photographs; Jonathan Raban for permission to quote from his letter to Evgenia Sands; Holly Goldberg Sloan for a copy of *The Grand Defiance;* Penelope Smail for family photographs, and photographs by Curtis Moffat; Evgenia Sands for Ivan's tape about Caroline Blackwood, and for photographs of her.

More thanks: to Margarita Harder, Director of Film Clip Licensing at Columbia-TriStar; Deborah Marriot, Coordinator of Clip Licensing at 20th Century-Fox; Larry McCallister of Film Clip Licensing at Paramount Pictures; Judy Noack at Warner Bros.; Caroline Sisneros at the American Film Institute; the staff of the Margaret Herrick Library; and of UCLA Special Collections.

Finally, posthumous thanks to Ivan for a long friendship, and to Iris Tree for an all-too-short one, during her last visit to California in 1961.

INDEX

Page numbers in *italics* refer to illustrations.

PERMISSIONS ACKNOWLEDGMENTS

Grateful acknowledgment is made to the following for permission to reprint previously unpublished and published material:

The American Film Institute: "An Evening with Marion Davies" from the American Film Institute Seminar with Ivan Moffat, "Producing the Film" class held May 13, 1975. Copyright © 1975 by American Film Institute. Reprinted by permission of the American Film Institute.

Patrice Chaplin: "Hollywood and the English" from an 1982 interview. Reprinted by permission of Patrice Chaplin.

Evgenia Citkowitz: "Caroline Blackwood" from a taped interview with Ivan Moffat. Reprinted by permission of Evgenia Citkowitz.

Columbia Pictures: Excerpt from *They Came from Cordura.* Reprinted by permission of Columbia Pictures.

Gary Conklin: "George Stevens as Humorist," "Billy Wilder," and "An Evening with Marion Davies (1)," from a 1965 interview with Ivan Moffat. "Dylan Thomas in Hollywood," "Charlie Chaplin," "Preston Sturges," and "Aldous Huxley" from an interview with Ivan Moffat. All from the film *Remembering Paradise* by Gary Conklin Films. Reprinted by permission of Gary Conklin.

Michael S. and Randalyn Foster: "Eisenhower vs. Stevenson" and an excerpt from *New York Memories Interview* (May 20, 1965). Reprinted by permission of Michael S. and Randalyn Foster.

Lorna Moffat: Excerpts from *A Place in the Sun, The Grand Defiance,* a memo to George Stevens (May 11, 1949), and Ivan's Notebook #3. Copyright © by Lorna Moffat. Reprinted by permission of Lorna Moffat.

George Stevens, Jr.: "Bick Benedict: A Profile," "Leslie: A Profile," and "Jeff Rink: A Profile" (George Stevens Special Collection, Margaret Herrick). Excerpt from the interview with Susan Winslow from *The Greatest Story Ever Told* (George Stevens Special Collection). "The Liberation of Paris," "Meeting on the Elbe," "Geroge Stevens and

World War II," and "George Stevens as Director" from an interview with Ivan Moffat (June 15, 1982) for *George Stevens: A Filmmaker's Journey*. Reprinted by permission of George Stevens, Jr.

Twentieth Century-Fox: Excerpts from *Tender Is the Night*. Copyright © 1962 by Twentieth Century-Fox. All rights reserved. Reprinted by permission of Twentieth Century-Fox.

ILLUSTRATION CREDITS

191   Courtesy of Michael Luke
192   Private collection
203   Private collection
215   Copyright © Richard Hoar, courtesy of George Stevens, Jr.
218   Copyright © Richard Hoar, courtesy of George Stevens, Jr.
224   Courtesy of the Academy of Motion Picture Arts and Sciences
229   Courtesy of the Academy of Motion Picture Arts and Sciences
232   Courtesy of the Academy of Motion Picture Arts and Sciences
245   Private collection
251   Private collection
259   Courtesy of the Academy of Motion Picture Arts and Sciences
261   Courtesy of the Academy of Motion Picture Arts and Sciences
267   Courtesy of the Academy of Motion Picture Arts and Sciences
273   Courtesy of the Academy of Motion Picture Arts and Sciences
275   Courtesy of the Academy of Motion Picture Arts and Sciences
284   Courtesy of the Academy of Motion Picture Arts and Sciences
302   Private collection
304   LPI/Long Photography Inc.
309   Courtesy of Victoria Looseleaf